WITH
REFERENCE
TO
REFERENCE

WITH
REFERENCE
TO
REFERENCE

CATHERINE Z. ELGIN

with a Foreword
by Nelson Goodman

HACKETT PUBLISHING COMPANY
Indianapolis • Cambridge

For further information, please address
Hackett Publishing Company,
Box 44937, Indianapolis, Indiana 46204

Library of Congress Cataloging in Publication Data

Elgin, Catherine Z., 1948–
With reference to reference.

Includes bibliographical references and index.
1. Reference (Philosophy) 2. Goodman, Nelson.
I. Title.
B105.R25E43 1982   160   82–15488
ISBN 0–915145–52–9
ISBN 0–915145–53–7 (pbk.)

For Jim

TABLE OF CONTENTS

FOREWORD

For some philosophers, the recognition that everything is relative and nothing certain is the end of the road. Philosophy becomes idle conversation, with truth replaced by whim or fashion. For others, such as Catherine Elgin, skepticism and relativism function rather as climate and stimulus not for seeking certified or exclusive truth or absolute reality but for constructing nonexclusive maps or versions or visions to be judged—fallibly indeed—by the insight and understanding they provide, quite apart from any question of agreement with a unique and inaccessible World.

This book is a study of how such maps and versions and visions, how texts and pictures and scores and samples and diagrams, function as symbols. Concerned rather with geography than with genesis, it offers a systematic analysis, a taxonomy, a vocabulary, of basic species of reference. On the one hand, it bypasses such currently popular topics as the speech act, intention, and so-called 'causal' and other theories of the roots of reference, and focusses on relations of reference, and relations between these relations, however they may be established. On the other hand, it covers important and often neglected topics, transcending the too-frequent limitation of reference to literal verbal denotation by including in its scope reference both literal and figurative, linguistic and nonlinguistic, denotational and nondenotational, direct and mediated. What matters here, of course, is not that all these types of relationship between symbols and symbolized be called "reference" but that all be considered together so that their common and their distinctive features can be discerned.

Many ideas scattered through my own work have been incorporated here, but these have been supplemented, often rephrased and extended, and organized into a systematic whole. Since some of this development has resulted from continuing discussions between us, detailed attribution of credit is difficult, and Catherine Elgin has been overgenerous to me in this.

Advances in science or philosophy often depend upon or consist in the fashioning of new and apt conceptual apparatus. The wide-ranging and novel taxonomy of reference set forth here makes possible the raising or reframing and the pointed investigation of many a significant and stubborn question. Through recognition of the almost universally overlooked referential relation of exemplification and its interconnection with denotation and expression, along with the study of referential chains comprised of links of these three kinds, this book provides sensitive and illuminating ways of tracing the various modes of simple and complex symbolization, from literal description to allusion of several kinds, in literary and other works. How statements, questions, commands, exclamations may refer is the subject of a novel and fascinating discussion. The book also makes sense of, and

1

proposes an answer to, the urgent question, curiously avoided by linguists, what features distinguish language as a special type of symbol
system. And by providing a classification of types of symbol system
and function, it can make for more significant experimental inquiry in
psychology into interaction among certain skills and between behavior and physiology. Even beyond this, it contributes to the badly
needed clarification of the much misunderstood kinships and contrasts
between the sciences and the arts.

Yet even so consequential a book, since it ignores the faded Great
Issues of philosophy, since it is less concerned with deciding any
familiar philosophical dispute than with constructing an effective conceptual apparatus, since it does not even claim that this apparatus is
exclusively right, and since it seems to treat more of symbols than of
worlds, may put the reader off guard. The subversive power of a radical reorganization of categories should not be underestimated.
Readers must be warned that the prescription offered here may have
severe side-effects, including drastic disorientation.

June 18, 1982   Nelson Goodman

PREFACE

Reference is a popular subject in contemporary philosophy. Hence, in setting out to write about it one confronts a vast array of material on a wide range of related (often very distantly related) topics. Disagreements abound—not only over which theory is ultimately correct, but also over what problems a theory of reference should be expected to solve, what methods of analysis it can legitimately employ, and what criteria of adequacy it should satisfy. It would be instructive, perhaps, to investigate the various extant theories and evaluate their relative strengths and weaknesses. I have not done so. Instead, I have chosen to articulate and extend a single account—one that can be found scattered through the works of Nelson Goodman. What results seems to me to be a powerful system that answers important questions and satisfies reasonable constraints.

In writing this book I have accumulated the usual debts of gratitude. These should be acknowledged even if they cannot be repaid. My intellectual debt to Nelson Goodman is evident on every page. Equally great, if not equally obvious, is my personal debt to him. His kindness and encouragement made the task less daunting; his rigorous standards and acute criticism made the result less flawed. Manifestly, any errors that remain should be attributed to him.

I also want to thank Jonathan Adler who read the entire manuscript and argued with me about most of it. As usual, my work is better for the critical attention he accords it.

Ann Lear has my gratitude for her careful preparation of the manuscript, and for giving me unexpected and valuable editorial assistance besides.

The manuscript was completed during the 1981–1982 academic year when I held an Andrew W. Mellon Faculty Fellowship at Harvard. I am grateful to the Andrew W. Mellon Foundation for its support and to the Harvard University philosophy department for its hospitality.

Finally, I want to thank my husband, Jim Elgin, to whom the book is dedicated. I do not know enough about symbols to know how to express all that I owe to him.

3

NOTE

The following abbreviations are used throughout the text to refer to Goodman's various works:

[FFF]   *Fact, Fiction and Forecast*, second edition, Harvard University Press, 1983.

[LA]   *Languages of Art*, second edition, Hackett Publishing Company, 1976.

[MM]   "Metaphor as Moonlighting," *Critical Inquiry* 6 (1979), pp. 125–130.

[PP]   *Problems and Projects*, Hackett Publishing Company, 1972.

[RR]   "Routes of Reference," *Critical Inquiry* 8 (1981), pp. 121–132.

[TAJ]   "Truth About Jones," (with Joseph Ullian), *The Journal of Philosophy* 74 (1977), pp. 317–338.

[WOW]   *Ways of Worldmaking*, Hackett Publishing Company, 1978.

I PROBLEM AND PROJECT

1. THE SUBJECT

A theory of reference should identify and characterize the relations between a language (or, more broadly, a symbol system) and its objects, and explain the ways the language functions in or contributes to our understanding of those objects. Literature and the fine arts, as well as science and "common sense" contribute to our understanding of the world and our place in it. To account for our understanding then, a theory of reference should comprehend the metaphorical as well as the literal, the fictive as well as the factual, the expressive as well as the descriptive. And it should relate linguistic symbols to such nonlinguistic symbols as diagrams, pictures, and musical scores.

In what follows, I set forth a theory that does just that. My account has its source in the works of Nelson Goodman. I follow him in taking denotation and exemplification to be basic modes of reference, and in taking much of semantics—including the interpretation of fictive, figurative, and expressive language—to involve reference by some symbols to others. Indeed, my project is largely a matter of integrating, systematizing, and extending Goodman's various remarks about reference. I show that they can serve as the basis for a comprehensive general theory that avoids many of the pitfalls of currently popular accounts. Although the explications of the basic devices will be familiar to those acquainted with Goodman's work, much of what I have to say about their application is new. My discussions of the interpretation of metaphors and allusions, of fictions and counterfactuals, of mathematical theorems, scientific theories, and ethical treatises reveal something of the scope and power of this constellation of semantic devices. Many of Goodman's remarks about reference occur in the context of discussions of aesthetics. He contends, however, that his semantic categories have important applications beyond the aesthetic realm. I show this contention to be correct. One of the results of my study is that we cannot hope to draw sharp disciplinary boundaries along semantic lines. Contrary to popular opinion, the vocabulary of the sciences is not exclusively literal, factual, and descriptive; nor is that of the arts exclusively metaphorical, fictional, and expressive.

But it is not my purpose here to anticipate the results of my investigation. Instead, I want to say something about the nature of the problems I seek to solve and the constraints on an adequate solution. Reference is a popular subject in the philosophy of language. But there is little agreement about what its important problems are and perhaps even less agreement about how they are to be solved. Thus, it seems advisable to identify the ones with which I am concerned and to locate my account in the context of other contemporary discussions of reference.

A context is extensional if and only if any substitution of coreferential expressions for its terms preserves the truth values of the original sentences. Predicative, truth-functional and quantificational contexts are extensional, for what matters in an extensional context is (roughly) what you say, not how you say it. Other contexts—such as modal, mental, metaphorical, and fictional contexts—are frequently held to be intensional. For, it is maintained, in these contexts what matters is not what objects are referred to, but how they are referred to, identified, or described. Accordingly, in such contexts intersubstitutability *salva veritate* does not normally obtain. Coreferential terms that differ in intensionally relevant respects cannot be freely substituted for one another.

The truth value of a sentence depends on what its objects are. Thus, if we are to construe certain contexts as intensional, we require a way of individuating objects that is more restrictive than intersubstitutability *salva veritate*. In *The Merchant of Venice* Bassanio believes that Portia is his wife. But he does not believe that Balthasar is his wife, for he does not realize that Balthasar is Portia. The problem is to develop a semantic account according to which 'Portia' and 'Balthasar' are not intersubstitutable here, but which nevertheless relates the use of 'Portia' and 'Balthasar' in the statement of Bassanio's belief to the character Portia. The semantical issue is further complicated by the fact that *The Merchant of Venice* is a work of fiction. Thus, none of its principals exists. What constitutes our attribution of these beliefs to *Bassanio* rather than to the Easter Bunny, the decimal equivalent of π, or the null set? The nature of the intensional objects—of Portia and Bassanio in Shakespeare's play, and of Portia and Balthasar in Bassanio's belief—and of their relations to each other and to their extensional counterparts must be explained if the intensionalist enterprise is to succeed. It must be determinate whether two expressions (or two uses of a single expression) in an intensional context have the same object.

In point of fact no adequate intensional semantics has been developed. This may simply be a consequence of the unfortunate state of current formal semantics. If so, it is reasonable to expect that with sufficient cleverness, insight, and luck the problem will eventually be solved. This, after all, is the view one takes of other tricky problems, such as that of providing a semantics for adverbs.

I believe, however, that the problem of developing an intensional semantics for a natural language is hopeless from its inception. For under an intensional semantics, the distinction between what you say and how you say it requires such notions as meaning, sense, content, and/or essence to back it up. Because of the seemingly irreducible unclarity of this entire constellation of notions, a theory of reference that appeals to intensions is not explanatory. I conclude that the attempt to ground semantics on a distinction between intensional and extensional contexts, each with its appropriate realm of objects, is doomed.

This leads me to attempt to construct a theory of reference that is fully extensional. The success of this endeavor depends on the extension of 'reference' itself. I follow Goodman in believing that it is wider than is ordinarily recognized, and that many of the functions attributed to such notions as meaning, essence, and synonomy are functions of different modes of reference or of coreferentiality.

It might be thought that by broadening the extension of 'reference' I am weakening it, that by recognizing different modes of reference I am simply reintroducing the suspect intensional entities under a different label. But this is not the case. Intensional idioms are to be rejected because no criterion has been provided for the individuation of their objects. Since I admit only individuals and sets[1] into my ontology, it is straightforward to provide for each mode of reference a standard for the individuation of the entities referred to. Note, however, that I am claiming only that under this theory of reference the individuation of objects will be determinate. I neither expect nor require an epistemically accessible general decision procedure for telling whether any two expressions are coreferential. Indeed, for semantically dense symbol systems,[2] there typically is none. But the lack of a decision procedure no more impugns the claim of a theory of reference to be extensional than it does that of quantificational logic. Accordingly, if exception is taken to my approach it can be only because extensional premises are too weak to yield a sufficiently comprehensive theory of reference, or because there are specific objections to the expressions I take to refer or to the relations I take to be referential. I attempt to answer objections of the latter sort as I develop my position. The former cannot be answered in advance, for it constitutes an evaluation of the program as a whole. It is therefore left as an exercise for the reader.

An extensional theory might be developed in either of two ways: we might decide to recognize as language only those contexts that are unproblematically extensional. This amounts to excising from our language—as e.g., meaningless, merely emotive, or ill-formed—all of the difficult cases. But then there will be no way, within the language, to perform the functions that the intensional idioms were introduced

1. Goodman, as a nominalist, is committed to recasting all talk of sets in terms of talk of individuals. Here, however, I am concerned only to give an extensional theory of reference, not a nominalist one.

2. A system is semantically dense if and only if it provides for infinitely many compliance classes so ordered that between any two there is a third, and dense throughout if no insertion of additional compliance classes in normal position will destroy density [LA, 153]. Density of symbol systems is discussed in Chapter VI.

to perform. We render the language extensional by restricting its scope. Or we might extend the scope of 'reference' in a way that shows the difficult cases to be extensional as well. Which alternative to choose depends on the importance one attributes to those functions. If they are genuinely "idle wheels" the first alternative is attractive, for economy can be achieved by fiat. If they are not, then the success of the extensionalist enterprise depends on our doing the second.

The difference between the two alternatives parallels the difference between eliminative materialism and other forms of materialism in the philosophy of mind. The eliminative materialist maintains (roughly) that both mental talk and its ostensible objects are to be eliminated from the philosophy of mind—that a comprehensive, true theory of the world makes no mention of mental or psychological states and accordingly there is no philosophical merit in retaining the vocabulary of the mental. Other materialists agree that peculiarly mental *objects* are to be eliminated from our ontology, but maintain that (in one way or another) mental discourse is to be reinterpreted so that it refers to, or is about, physiological states, processes, or events. I do not intend to enter into this debate. I mention it only because it is an area of philosophy in which the sort of distinction I want to draw has become familiar.

The attempt to develop an extensional theory of reference by restricting the scope of the language sacrifices too much. It is difficult to maintain that a theory which is forced to discount as deviant both literature and our accounts of our mental lives is a satisfactory general theory of language. Even Quine, who is inclined to eliminative extensionalism, opts for a double standard in the end. Although he thinks they have no role in limning the true and ultimate structure of reality, he concludes that the idioms of propositional attitude cannot be expunged from our language.[3] But we needn't enter into debates concerning how much nonscientific discourse we ought to be willing to sacrifice to gain an austere, extensional, scientific language. For science itself cannot but employ the linguistic devices in question. Dispositional terms are regularly used in science long before the underlying structure of their objects is known. Fictive language is used in the idealization of laws and experimental situations. And metaphorical language is used to project the knowledge gained in one domain onto another (as, e.g., when human cognitive processes are described in terms taken from computer science). Thus, even if we expect that in the end of science these will be replaced by literal statements in Quine's canonical notation, the claims of current and foreseeable future science are not of this form.

The failure to secure distinctions between meaning and belief, essence and accident, analytic and synthetic, suggests that the attempt to separate the language of science from expressive language, literary

---

3. W. V. Quine, *Word and Object* (Cambridge: M.I.T. Press, 1960), p. 221.

language, and everyday language is doomed to fail. Language is interconnected. The differences between literal and metaphorical, descriptive and expressive, factual and fictive are not marks of a difference between separate or separable languages. They are categories of a system for classifying the terms or sentences belonging to a single language.

One might argue that at best the foregoing discussion shows that an adequate philosophy of language must somehow comprehend our mental, metaphorical, fictive, and dispositional discourse. But is there any reason to believe that this is a task for the theory of reference rather than say, a theory of syntax, or a theory of rhetoric? To answer this requires that I say something about the character of theories. A theory is an economical system which exhibits a network of relationships among the entities in its domain. Theories are more *ad hoc,* and so less attractive, the fewer and weaker the interconnections among their parts. Accordingly, an integrated theory that explains literal, metaphorical, fictive, and dispositional claims in terms of a single metalinguistic category is to be preferred to a loosely related coalition of theories in which, e.g., literal discourse is explained in terms of reference, metaphorical and fictive discourse in terms of rhetoric, and dispositional claims in terms of their logical or syntactical form.

Economy, however, speaks only to the form of a theory. To justify my choice of reference as the central metalinguistic concept, I must speak also of the content. The choice of a theoretical vocabulary determines which among the relations of entities in a domain we can exhibit. I take reference rather than some other metalinguistic category to be central because of the sort of knowledge I want my theory to provide. Since language contributes to, indeed is crucial to, our understanding of its objects, the explanation of that understanding should be in terms of its relation to those objects. The nonliteral as well as the literal devices I have mentioned, and others besides, contribute to that understanding. Thus, a theory of reference that comprehends the literal and the nonliteral is required for a knowledge of language that explains the role of language in knowledge.

Since the theory is developed to serve a certain purpose, it is not undermined by theories of language serving other purposes. And if other theories serve this purpose equally well, they have equal claims on our intellectual allegiance. In putting forth my theory, then, I make no claim to uniqueness or to epistemic priority.

Interconnectedness affects not only the scope of a theory of reference, but its character as well. The reference of a term depends not on its use in a single sentence, or on its use in a sentence in a context, but rather on its role in a language. It is important that this be construed as a metaphysical claim, not an epistemological one. It is not merely that we do not know the reference of a term unless we consider its place in a linguistic system; it is rather that what the reference of a term is depends on the structure of the language. The traditional metaphysical problems of the one and the many, permanence and change, and the identity and diversity of individuals and of kinds are solved by a complex constellation of linguistic devices which integrate terms into the language. A theory of reference is primarily a theory of reference for a language. The semantic structure of a language is not the result of the independently fixed reference of each of its primitive terms. It is rather the structure of the language that confers on the expressions the reference they have. And it is only from the perspective of a theory of the referential structure of a language that any of its expressions can be construed as primitive.

2. ROADS NOT TAKEN

Frequently when philosophical questions concerning reference are raised, they take the following form: given an uninterpreted calculus and the linguistic behavior of native speakers, can we discover the correct interpretation of their language? Problems with doing so abound, for it is not clear what standard to invoke to decide which interpretation is correct. Quine has argued that the full specification of the syntactical structure of the language and the detailed description of the environments in which its speakers use, or are disposed to use, its various locutions are inadequate to fix the reference of its terms.[4] Others, including Lewis,[5] Field,[6] and Katz,[7] reply that this shows only that Quine has failed to include enough factors in his data. The problem then is to specify the additional factors that should be recognized.

It is sometimes suggested that the speaker's account of his own utterances should, in general, be decisive. But once we deny the epistemological doctrine of privileged access, it is not clear why this should be the case. The problem is not just one of epistemic privilege, however. For Quine argues that the problem of radical translation applies to our own idiolects. Thus, nothing in the speaker's epistemic relation to his own sentences is sufficient to decide their interpretation.

A second suggestion, sometimes made independently and sometimes in conjunction with an emphasis on the speaker, is that we need to use a more powerful logic to delineate the syntactical structure of the language and/or a better psychological account of the speaker than

4. *Word and Object*, pp. 26–79.

5. David Lewis, *Counterfactuals* (Cambridge: Harvard University Press, 1973), pp. 84–91.

6. Hartry Field, "Tarski's Theory of Truth", *Journal of Philosophy* LXIX (1972), pp. 347–375.

7. Jerrold Katz, "Analyticity and Contradiction in Natural Language", *The Structure of Language* ed. Jerry A. Fodor and Jerrold J. Katz (Englewood Cliffs: Prentice-Hall, 1964), pp. 519–543.

Quine's behaviorism provides. Plainly, the richer our syntactical and psychological theories, the more constraints they impose on the interpretation of the language, and the fewer alternatives they leave open. The question is whether psychology and the theory of syntax will prove able to specify sufficiently powerful, independently warranted constraints to determine the interpretation of the language uniquely. Quine contends that they will not. He argues that it will always be possible to generate an alternative interpretation of the language—however gerrymandered and implausible from the point of view of the speakers—that satisfies the theoretical constraints.

It is not my purpose to enter into this debate. I mention it only to differentiate the problem I am concerned with from what has become a popular problem in the philosophy of language. Instead of starting with an uninterpreted system and asking whether we can discover its proper interpretation, as Quine, his defenders, and his opponents do, I begin with an interpreted system. Granting that expressions in such systems refer, I am concerned to explain how they do so.

I present a scheme in terms of which the relations between language and its objects are to be classified. When the language is organized according to such a scheme, it exemplifies a certain structure. A theory of reference of this type is then a conceptual geography: its system of classification calls attention to various features of and relations in the conceptual, or linguistic terrain.

This project is to be distinguished from two others that are somewhat similar. One is a project of conceptual history that seeks to explain how a language came to have a structure that it has; the other is a theory of language use that seeks to explain the language user's knowledge of the structure or structures of his language. I discuss these briefly. By showing why each is inadequate for my purpose, I hope to clarify what that purpose is.

Kripke[8] and Putnam[9] propose theories of reference according to which the reference of some terms, at least, is a function of their history. When we use a proper name like 'Moses' or a natural kind predicate like 'water', what we refer to depends on our historical relation to the agent who introduced the term into our language, and on his intention in introducing it.[10] The value of this account lies in its

---

8. Saul Kripke, "Naming and Necessity", *Semantics of Natural Language* ed. Donald Davidson and Gilbert Harman (Dordrecht: D. Reidel, 1972), pp. 253–355, and 763–769.

9. Hilary Putnam, "The Meaning of 'Meaning'", *Mind, Language, and Reality* (Cambridge: Cambridge University Press, 1975), pp. 215–271. Since this was written, Putnam's views have changed substantially.

10. Although I disparage intensions for the reasons mentioned above, I have no quarrel with intentions as such. These are aspects of the individual's psychological state, intimately related to his plans, expectations, and actions. What I deny is that such psychological states play any special role in the theory of reference. I am, of course, committed to the thesis that statements of intention, expectation, action, and the like are to be analysed extensionally.

recognition that language is a social matter. To use a term referentially, the individual speaker need not be able to identify its referent uniquely. In so using the term, he intends to refer to whatever the term is supposed to refer to. And 'what the term is supposed to refer to' is explicated noncircularly by the fact that he belongs to a community into whose language the term was introduced to denote a specific individual or kind. On this account it is a historical relationship rather than an epistemic one that grounds reference.

It is precisely its reliance on a matter of historical fact that raises problems for this account of reference. Since these problems can be seen most vividly in the case of natural kind predicates, I focus my discussion on these. Typically, we do not know the intentions of the speakers who introduced these predicates into our language. Assuming that the story Putnam and Kripke tell is approximately correct, a term like 'cow' was introduced to refer to things like a specific ostended example. But as soon as we talk about 'things like this' (for any 'this'), we have a problem of projection. Granting that a given individual is to be included in the extension of 'cow', what else is to be included? How is the term 'cow' to be projected to cover new instances?

One might maintain that the dimensions along which we are required to project are likewise determined by the speaker's intention. In that case, however, what we now refer to is determined by a historical fact. And if that fact is unknown, then so is the extension of 'cow'. Moreover, if the introducer intended 'cow' to refer to all herbivores, all mammals, or all brown things in a particular field, then *that* is what fixes the extension of 'cow' and not anything in our current usage of the term.

But it is not plausible that the discovery of what that individual intended would amount to a discovery that we are right or wrong about the referent of 'cow'. Our language might, of course, develop in such a way as to change the reference of the term 'cow'. But we could not *discover* that although the animals that current usage classifies as cows exist, the term 'cow' does not really refer to them, but to some other entities. Were we to discover that the introducer did not intend 'cow' to refer (even approximately) to the animals we now call cows, we would find out something about the etymology of the word, but nothing (or at least nothing particularly important) about its reference.

The history of conceptualization is a reflective history. We modify our categories (or concepts, or systems of kinds) in light of our knowledge in order to better suit our linguistic purposes. Accordingly, we cannot assume that the speaker's intention in introducing an expression into the language is authoritative in determining the extension of that expression.

Kripke and Putnam, of course, do not maintain that the extensions of our natural kind predicates are determined by the unknown intentions of unknown agents. Once an expression is introduced into the language, it becomes to some extent independent of any particular occasion of its use. To understand the role of a term's origin in their accounts, it is crucial to recognize that they want a theory of reference to answer two different questions:

1. To what do we refer when we use a natural kind term t?

2. Do we and our ancestors (or we and members of some other linguistic community) refer to the same things when we use t in the context of different belief systems or theories?

Current scientific theories both tell us (sometimes obscurely, sometimes inconsistently, sometimes ambiguously) what there is, and repudiate prior theories. The problem that the second question addresses is determining what form this repudiation takes. We might maintain that prior theories referred to nothing—that current science demonstrates that there simply are no such things as masses as characterized by Newton, or genes as characterized by Mendel. Or we might maintain that prior theories referred to the same things as current theories but, by and large, made false statements about them.[11]

Kripke and Putnam want to say the latter. The difficulty is that typically there is no core of beliefs that a science retains throughout theory change. As it develops, it rejects even the most central claims of earlier theories. They conclude that it is historical continuity that preserves reference across such changes. If the term t as used in theory T_n was acquired through a historical/causal chain that includes t as used in theory T_m, then the two tokens of t have the same referent. And however remote from one another T_m and T_n may be, if the use of t in each is a historical/causal consequence of the same introducing event, in the context of both theories t refers to the same thing.

They may be correct in holding that the question of the continuity or discontinuity of reference across theory change is an historical question. But the emphasis on a common origin seems misplaced. Whether the referents of terms appearing in our current theories are the same as those appearing in prior theories, or whether our current theories demonstrate that the terms appearing in their predecessors failed to refer appears to be the sort of question that requires a detailed examination of the relations between the theories under discussion. Probably some cases are better understood one way, some the other. Because science is a critical, self-reflective discipline, the fact that terms appearing in two theories have a common etymological origin is inadequate to show that they have a common referent.

Unlike Kripke and Putnam, however, I do not take the second question to pose a central problem for the theory of reference. I am concerned with delineating a structure that the language has, not with

11. Cf. [WOW, 116–120], and *passim*.

explaining how it came to have that structure. Accordingly, it is relatively unimportant whether a term's current reference displays continuity or discontinuity with its previous applications. An expression becomes a referring term by being so used, and its use depends to some extent on its history. Nevertheless, the characteristics and functions of such terms can be studied quite apart from the acts or beliefs that brought their referential relationships about.

It remains to consider the way in which Kripke and Putnam answer the first question—a question that is plainly central to a theory of reference.

As I mentioned above, they contend that science provides the answer to this question, for it is the business of a science to discover the essence, or the nature, or the character of its natural kinds. Thus the problem of how to project a natural kind predicate is solved when the predicate is incorporated into a mature science. By determining the 'essence' of the kind, the science determines the respects in which new instances must resemble old ones to belong to that kind.

The role of the introducing event in answering this question is to give us a way of individuating the predicate t, the essence of whose objects the relevant science is to discover. All uses of tokens of t that are appropriately related to the same introducing event are tokens of the same term. The relation to the introducing event that classifies tokens as tokens of a single term thus determines a natural kind. The introducing event then serves as a device for disambiguation.

The role of the introducing event in answering the first question is then quite minimal. It serves merely to identify the subject matter of a science. Nevertheless, this account is unsatisfactory. If we do not know the history of an expression, as we normally do not, then we do not know whether two tokens are appropriately related to the same introducing event. In that case, we do not know whether the term is ambiguous. Another problem is that it is extremely difficult to characterize the "appropriate relation" between the introducing event and later uses of the term. Since I want to reject the thesis that the coreferentiality of two tokens depends on any relation between them and the introduction of the term into the language, I will not stop to develop this point.

The reason for my rejection is this: it is simply not the case that the sole source of ambiguity in a language is the introduction of homonyms on separate occasions. Accordingly, tracing the history of a term back to its origin is not what is required to discover ambiguity. A term that was originally unambiguous can become ambiguous as the language develops. An example of this is the stale metaphor. In using a term metaphorically, we invite comparison between its literal referent and its metaphorical referent. When its application to the latter ceases to invite comparison with the former, the term can become ambiguous. The question of ambiguity then is not whether two tokens are appropriately related to some third (the introducing event), but whether they are appropriately related to each other.

Kripke and Putnam restrict their attention to predicates that are of concern to science. They characterize the role of science in telling us how to apply these predicates as discovering the essences of the corresponding kinds. They are surely correct in saying that we defer to scientists to decide the application of the predicates in question. But it is equally true that we defer to experts in other fields to settle the application of their terms. We look to musicians to determine the extension of 'cadenza', to lawyers to determine that of 'contract', and to polo players to determine that of 'chukker'. There appears to be nothing that differentiates the relation of science to its vocabulary from the relation of these other fields to theirs. The suggestion that science is metaphysically or semantically more fundamental is unfounded. There is thus no basis for saying that science discovers essences, but other fields do not. Nor is there any point in saying that each field discovers its appropriate essences. For once we grant that a particular group of specialists is authoritative in deciding the application of a term, nothing is added by saying that they do so by discovering the essence of its objects.

These considerations might seem to force us to conclude that the use of a term in a language determines its reference. Unfortunately, the story is not so simple. Use is undeniably central to the philosophy of language, for it is use that identifies its subject matter. Thus, a referential or semantic system should be reasonably faithful to the actual usage of terms in the language. But such fidelity is not sufficient to determine the system. It is a basic feature of language that we can apply old words in new situations. Although there is widespread disagreement as to how the reference of a term like 'asparagus' is fixed, no one thinks that it applies to all and only those things to which it has been (successfully) applied in the past. Whatever a semantic system is, it is not just a summary of past uses of terms.

A system of reference is required to solve problems of projection: given the way a term has been applied in the past, to what other things does it also apply? The answer to this question is, to be sure, guided by the actual uses of the term as well as by dispositions to use or withhold it in hypothetical situations (the "intuitions" of native speakers). But the competence of native speakers to use a term does not amount to a decision procedure for applying or withholding it in every imaginable, or even in every actual, case. In some situations intuitions of different native speakers conflict. In others a single speaker may be unsure whether to apply or withhold a term. And in many situations, although we are sure that a term applies, we do not know how to characterize its application.

A couple of examples may help to illustrate the problems. Presumably, most of us are competent in the use of the term 'dog'. Let us agree with Kripke and Putnam that it is the province of biologists to decide the extension of this term. Currently two independent criteria are employed. Biochemists maintain (roughly) that all living organisms with the appropriate sort of DNA are dogs. Evolutionary biologists maintain that all living organisms with the appropriate evolutionary history are dogs. So far as is known, these two criteria mark out the same sort of animals. But suppose we discover animals on a remote planet that have the same biochemical makeup as our dogs but that evolved independently. Should they be included in the extension of 'dog'? There appears to be no basis in our competence to use the word 'dog' for deciding. If we have any intuitions about this case, they are reasonably weak, and we could probably find equally competent speakers with opposing intuitions. Moreover, deferring to the experts is of no help, for the biochemists would presumably give one decision and the evolutionary biologists the other. Nothing in our use of the term 'dog' tells us how to project the term should the two criteria diverge. How to project 'dog' in that situation is a matter for stipulation. One stipulation may be better than another for reasons of simplicity, fit with other systems of classification, or the like. But insofar as our competence or linguistic habits betray no strong preference one way or the other, there is no question of right or wrong.

A different sort of case arises when we know how to apply a term but not how to classify its application. Consider, for example, the assertion made in the 1960s that the military draft is a form of slavery. It might be construed as a metaphor to point up similarities between the condition of a conscripted soldier and that of a slave. Or it might be taken literally. In that case, if it is true, it shows that the literal extension of 'slavery' is wider than people had previously realized. It is not obvious that there is anything in the statement or in the intentions of the people who made it that determines whether it is literal or metaphorical. To be sure, its utterers intended to say something true. But since metaphorical as well as literal claims can be true,[12] the intention to speak truly does not amount to or entail an intention to speak literally. The role of a system here is to legislate. If the system takes 'slavery' to have the narrower scope, the claim is metaphorical. If it takes 'slavery' to have the broader scope, it is literal.

One final account of reference that deserves mention is that of speech act theorists. They contend that referring is primarily something that speakers do, not something that expressions do. Accordingly, a theory of reference should be part of a theory of linguistic activity. To evaluate their claims about reference, we must first sketch the theory of linguistic activity.

Communication is held to be the core of language, and the basic unit of linguistic communication is the speech act—the production of a linguistic token by an individual speaker and its effect on an individual hearer. What differentiates a speech act from other noises is

---

12. Of course, metaphorical statements are normally literally false. But the distinction between true and false for metaphorical sentences closely parallels that between true and false for literal sentences. Accordingly, I follow Goodman in thinking it appropriate to classify both literally true sentences and metaphorically true sentences as instances of true sentences. I argue for this in chapter IV.

that it is produced with the intention "to communicate things to my hearer by means of getting him to recognize my intention to communicate just those things".[13] But not every such attempt counts as a speech act. Some birds, upon sighting a predator, utter distinctive warning cries to alert others of their kind to approaching danger. Barring cavils about the nature of intention, such cries seem to satisfy the foregoing condition. But is is not obvious that they should be classified as speech acts. Searle contends that for my utterance to be a speech act, I must also "intend this recognition to be achieved in virtue of the fact that the rules for using the expressions [I] utter associate the expressions with the production of the effect".[14] A speech act then is a product of intention and convention. The sorts of speech acts I can perform using a given expression are a function of the role of the expression in the language.

Reference on this analysis is a speech act that is a component of a larger speech act—questioning, asserting, commanding, or whatever. In evaluating this account of reference, two points need to be made—one concerning the role of intention in reference, the other concerning the role of convention. First, intending to produce an effect by getting one's audience to recognize one's intention to produce that effect is not, or at least is not always, required for reference. Someone talking in his sleep or under the influence of anesthesia or, for that matter, someone who is unconsciously 'thinking out loud' may have no such intention. Whether to say that such a person refers depends on how his words are interpreted. If we can make no sense of his utterances we put them down to inchoate ramblings. If their interpretation is straightforward, we take his utterances to be sentences, and the terms in them to refer. It is the availability of a reasonable interpretation rather than the intention with which they were produced that is crucial in deciding whether his words refer.

Second, if the role of a term in a language determines the sorts of acts of referring in which it can be used, then an account of the semantic or referential structure of the sort I seek to provide appears to be a prerequisite for any theory of the speech act of referring. We cannot say how speakers refer without first understanding how their language refers. And whether we shall require an additional account of speaker's reference once we have a theory of reference for the language remains to be seen.

The individuation of terms is a matter of grouping together tokens as replicas of one another, or as tokens of the same type. The projection of a term is a matter of going beyond present applications to classify new instances. A referential system determines both by legis-

13. John Searle, "What is a Speech Act?", *Readings in the Philosophy of Language* ed. Jay F. Rosenberg and Charles Travis (Englewood Cliffs, N.J.: Prentice-Hall, 1971), p. 620.

14. "What is a Speech Act?", p. 622. This applies only to the literal use of language. With metaphor things become even more complicated.

lation. But there is no suggestion that there is a unique, or even a best system of legislation. So long as our linguistic practices are adequately reflected, the choice of a system is a matter for decision, not discovery. A system's solutions to the problems of the individuation and projection of terms are neither true nor false. For to the extent that they go beyond use, there is nothing for them to be true or false about. They are, rather, authoritative.

It may appear surprising that it is not a criterion of adequacy for a referential system that it be recognized as correct by native speakers. But by taking the metaphor of conceptual geography seriously we can see why this is the case. Natives of a region do not normally require maps to get around in their homelands. Nor do they typically learn their way around by consulting maps. Correspondingly, they do not need conceptual maps to get around, or to learn to get around, in their home languages. The role of a map in both the literal and the metaphorical case is to mark out and exhibit relations that are important in their practices of getting around—whether the "routes" in question be from home to market or from instance to kind. And the criterion of adequacy of a map is that it accurately represent those features of the terrain that are geographically important. It is the role of the geographer, knowing why the map is wanted, to decide what these are.

I do not then take intentions, whether individual or social, to be authoritative for a system of reference. Although the intentions of its speakers undeniably influence the course of its development, the resulting language has a character that is independent of the intentions of the agents who produced it. Accordingly, accounts of the referential structure of the language need not be framed in terms of those intentions. As a result, we can distinguish between what a speaker intends to refer to and what he actually refers to. We can divorce the question of whether computers use symbols referentially from the question of whether they have intentions. And we can explain how it is possible to discover more in a literary work than its author intended, or even recognized in it.

II ON DENOTING

1. DENOTATION

(1) Scott is the author of *Waverley*.

A student of reference need not be a student of literature to know that. Since our interest is semantic rather than literary, we are concerned to determine what is denoted here. The answer is straightforward: 'Scott' denotes Scott; 'author' denotes each author; '*Waverley*' denotes the collection of books that constitute the *Waverley* series; and 'the author of *Waverley*' denotes the author of *Waverley*, viz., Scott. According to Russell,[1] (1) is equivalent to

(2) $(\exists x)$ $((x$ wrote *Waverley*) & (y) $(y$ wrote *Waverley* $\equiv$ $y = x)$ & $(x = $ Scott$))$

In that case x and y denote Scott as well. Despite the triviality of this account, certain features of denotation begin to emerge.

Denotation is a two-place semantic relation between a symbol and the objects to which it applies. A symbol denotes whatever complies with, or satisfies, or is an instance of it. Thus, a name denotes its bearer; a variable, its values; and a portrait, its subject. A predicate denotes severally the objects in its extension. It does not denote the class that is its extension, but rather each of the members of that class. If the class itself is denoted at all—a matter of dispute between nominalists and platonists—it is denoted by the abstract singular term associated with the predicate. 'Human' then denotes each human being, and if anything denotes the class of those individuals, 'humanity' does.

Some expressions—most proper names and definite descriptions, as well as predicates that are uniquely satisfied—denote singly. Others, including the majority of predicates, denote generally. Still others—those that lack compliants—have null denotation. Consider

(3) Leprechauns are mischievous.

Here 'mischievous' denotes each mischievous individual. But the denotation of 'leprechauns' is null, for there are no leprechauns.

There is some temptation to introduce "possible objects" to serve

---

1. Bertrand Russell, "On Denoting", *Logic and Knowledge* ed. Robert C. Marsh (New York: Capricorn Books, 1956), p. 51.

as the referents of terms like 'leprechauns'. Such a move, it is argued, will clarify (among other things) fictive discourse and negative existential sentences. This temptation should be resisted, and the clarification, if required, sought elsewhere. For there is no basis for saying unequivocally when two expressions denote the same "possible object". Because of the unclarity as to the individuation of "possible objects" then, it is best to take denotation to be an extensional relation between expressions and actual objects. Since all and only expressions alike in denotation are coextensive, all expressions whose denotation is null have the same extension.

Although I follow Goodman in countenancing no "possible objects", I also follow him in recognizing as individuals things that are not normally taken to be such [SA, 47]. An individual need not be compact or continuous. Quine has suggested that we treat a mass term in subject position as a singular term and take the scattered stuff in its compliance class as a single sprawling object.[2] In that case 'water', as the subject of a sentence, denotes the scattered individual composed of all the stuff in ponds, pools, puddles, and the like, to which the predicate 'is water' applies. Granted the aforementioned individual is not in one place, but many individuals are not. The British Empire was at one time spread throughout the world, and a spicy rumor may be all over town.

Quine's scattered individuals are homogeneous, but as Goodman notes [SA, 47] other scattered individuals are not. Buying a new car involves picking a standard model and choosing among a variety of options. Presumably, many combinations of options are instantiated in one or another vehicle, but suppose some combination is not. We need not introduce "possible cars" to interpret the salesman's claims about this combination. Even though no single car ever built will have precisely that combination of features, still some car or other has each of them. Let us then consider the package in question to be a scattered individual consisting of the chassis of car s, the engine of car p, the brakes of car q, the transmission of car r, and so on. This individual is, to be sure, not a car, for its components are not appropriately combined. But there is no logical or semantic ground for denying that it is an individual. 'A package of options' never to be instantiated in any single automobile then denotes such a scattered individual.

Instead of introducing "possible objects" to make sense of contexts like this, like Goodman I recognize more and different objects as actual. The objection that the individuation of "possible objects" is unclear does not apply to scattered individuals. If we can identify the chassis of car s, the engine of car p, etc., the individuation of the object made up of them is unproblematic.

Some expressions denote nonlinguistic objects, others denote linguistic ones. Thus 'poodle' denotes poodles, and 'book' denotes books. Yet others denote both sorts of object. 'Expensive' denotes

---

2. *Word and Object*, p. 98.

expensive things, including pedigreed poodles and rare books. I will argue below that much of what has been taken to involve reference to "possible (nonlinguistic) objects"—unicorns, frictionless planes—in fact involves reference to actual linguistic or pictorial objects. This will serve as the basis for an account of fictive language that requires reference to nothing but the actual.

'Denote' is to be understood tenselessly. The compliance class of a term (that is, the class of things it denotes) includes everything past, present, and future to which the term applies. The extension of 'person' does not vary with changes in the population, but comprehends every individual throughout history to whom the term applies. Nor is the extension of 'dinosaur' null because dinosaurs are extinct. It includes, rather, every dinosaur who ever lived. Indeed, today's utterance of 'the sea fight tomorrow' denotes tomorrow's naval battle, if there is one, even though it has yet to take place. If the morrow is free of naval engagements, the denotation of today's utterance is null. Terms appearing in sentences in the past or future tenses do not denote nonexistent objects. Either they denote actual objects or their denotation is null.

Epistemic problems, of course, remain, for it is not always easy to discover the extension of a term. We may have to wait until tomorrow to find out whether today's utterance of 'the sea fight tomorrow' is satisfied, and we may never know whether 'warm-blooded dinosaur' is. But such epistemic difficulties should no more force us to restrict denotation to objects in our immediate temporal neighborhood than similar difficulties force us to restrict it to objects in our immediate spatial neighborhood.

We are not required to settle the extension of a term prior to employing it. In investigative enterprises from scientific inquiries to criminal investigations we establish criteria for the satisfaction of a term without knowing whether anything actually satisfies it. 'Quark' is satisfied just in case there are quarks. 'The murderer's accomplice' is satisfied just in case the murderer had help. Should it turn out that there are no quarks, and that the murderer acted alone, the extensions of these terms are empty. Scientific theories no more denote "hypothetical entities" than police conjectures denote "possible accomplices". But both may contain terms whose denotations are not settled by anything we know so far.

Some philosophers, following Frege, maintain that declarative sentences, as well as their component expressions, denote. According to Frege, all true sentences denote The True, and all false ones The False.[3] Such an account is objectionable for a number of reasons [RR, 122]. Not only does the reification of truth values violate Occam's razor, but there is a good deal of unclarity as to what sorts of entities The True and The False are supposed to be. Moreover, since all

---

3. Gottlob Frege, "On Sense and Reference", *Translations from the Writings of Gottlob Frege* ed. Peter Geach and Max Black (Oxford: Basil Blackwell, 1970), p. 63.

sentences alike in truth value have the same denotation, the denotation of a sentence depends hardly at all on the denotations of its component expressions.

> Scott is the author of *Waverley*

and

> Snow is white

are alike in denotation despite the fact that

> Scott's being the author of *Waverley*

and

> Snow's being white

are not. One final worry is this: Such an account supplies denotations only for assertions. It says nothing about the denotations, if any, of commands, questions, exclamations, and the like. But once we admit that

> Scott is the author of *Waverley*

has a denotation, there seems little reason to deny that

> Let Scott be the author of *Waverley*!

> Is Scott the author of *Waverley*?

and

> Is Scott ever the author of *Waverley*!

have denotations as well.

Accordingly, it seems preferable to deny that sentences denote. The closest thing to the denotation of a sentence is that of a corresponding phrase—e.g.,

> Scott's being the author of *Waverley*.

The same phrase corresponds to commands, questions, and exclamations with a single subject matter, while phrases differing in denotation correspond to sentences whose subject matters differ. This is not to say that statements, commands, questions, and the like lack reference altogether. We shall see that they may refer by means of exemplification. But it seems best to deny that they have denotational reference. The denial that sentences denote does not sacrifice anything required for logic or the theory of truth. For we can class some declarative sentences together under the predicate 'true' without ontological commitment to truth, just as we can class some animals together under the predicate 'human' without ontological commitment to humanity. Nor does it sacrifice anything required to determine what a sentence is about. For neither a sentence nor any of its component terms need denote the objects that the sentence is about. Just how a sentence is related to the things it is about is a surprisingly complicated matter—one which I consider in detail in chapter IX.

2. COMPLICATIONS

Most of this account is familiar enough and may even appear trivial. But complications set in almost immediately. A term denotes whatever it applies to. This information is helpful only if we have a way to identify terms and their ranges of application. Neither is straightforward.

To recognize an expression as a term is to recognize that it functions referentially. But there are serious disagreements as to which expressions do so. The dispute between nominalists and platonists concerning the status of abstract singular nouns is a case in point. A singular term is, or is replaceable by, a quantifiable variable. A general term is true or false of the objects denoted by such a variable. Since nominalists admit nothing but individuals into their ontologies, a problem arises regarding the interpretation of abstract singular nouns. Some follow Goodman in taking such terms to denote scattered individuals. Others construe them nonreferentially, holding them to be syncategorematic, or to belong to an unperspicuous shorthand. When the shorthand is appropriately transcribed, the resulting sentences will contain expressions that refer only to individuals. Platonists admit classes as well as individuals into their ontology. Thus, they hold abstract singular nouns to be genuine terms, immediately replaceable by quantifiable variables. Some nominalists then disagree with platonists over the sorts of expressions that can legitimately be supplanted by variables. Other disagree with them over the range of values of individual variables.

It should not, however, be supposed that the problem of deciding the semantic parsing of a sentence arises only in the context of recondite metaphysical disputes like the one between nominalists and platonists. It arises whenever we are concerned with the logical form of a sentence. Consider the expression 'bigger than a breadbox'. Should we interpret it as an unbreakable one-place predicate true of some things and false of others? Or should we interpret 'bigger than' as a two-place relational predicate? Deciding between these alternatives amounts to deciding whether, in the context in question, 'breadbox' can be replaced by a variable.

Our problems are not over yet. Suppose we choose to treat 'bigger than' as a two-place relational predicate. We must then ask what ontological resources are available for its interpretation. Can we take it to be satisfied by ordered pairs of objects, or should we eschew pairs and admit only individuals into our ontology?

The important thing to notice is that the answers to these questions cannot be "read off" the language we seek to interpret. They are supplied by our referential system—the framework of commitments we bring to the task of interpretation. Given such a framework of commitments, the identification of terms and the resources for their interpretation are fixed. But they are fixed by a system that we supply, not by one that is waiting to be discovered in our subject matter. The referential structure of a sentence varies with the system in terms of which it is interpreted.

The problem of identifying diverse utterances and inscriptions as instances of a single term has both a syntactic and a semantic component. The syntactic component involves setting conditions for identifying utterances and inscriptions as instances of a single character. The semantic component involves setting conditions for taking utterances and inscriptions of the same character to have the same referent(s).

Let us consider the syntactic component first. For two marks to belong to the same character, each must be freely replaceable by the other without syntactic effect. All instances of a single character are then syntactically equivalent [LA, 131–2]. Whether this is the case cannot be decided on the basis of perceptual similarity. Utterances that sound very much alike, and inscriptions that look very much alike may belong to different characters. A native Bostonian's utterances of 'park' and 'pack' may be phonetically indistinguishable. And, if his handwriting is sufficiently illegible, his inscriptions of them may be indistinguishable as well. Nevertheless, even in his idiolect, the two do not belong to the same character.

Moreover, utterances and inscriptions quite different in appearance may belong to the same character. Contrast British and American pronunciations of 'schedule', or its shape when printed in different type fonts. An even better example is this: Printed and spoken tokens of the same word are syntactically equivalent. But if utterances and inscriptions alike are instances of a single character, then the attempt to establish character membership on the basis of perceptual similarity is doomed. For surely one noise is perceptually more akin to another noise than it is to a configuration of ink on paper. Perceptual similarity among marks is then neither necessary nor sufficient for membership in a common character.

Regardless of differences in sound, shape, or medium, linguistic marks belong to the same character, or are character-indifferent, if they are spelled alike—if, that is, there is an exact correspondence between them as sequences of letters, spaces, and punctuation marks [LA, 115]. Any other mark whose spelling precisely agrees with that of a given mark is syntactically equivalent to it.

Character-indifference depends on sameness of spelling. But the question of sameness or difference of spelling arises only for a symbol system that has an alphabet. An alphabet is a finite string of marks out of which all of the characters in the system are to be constructed. The identity of a mark as an instance of a character in that system depends entirely on its construction out of the system's alphabetic elements.

An alphabetic system then is authoritative regarding matters of spelling. Correspondingly, what counts as a difference in spelling depends on what marks belong to the alphabet. Suppose two overlapping alphabets differ only in that according to one the accent mark belongs to the alphabet, and according to the other it is a pragmatic cue to pronunciation, but not a part of the alphabet itself. An accented and an unaccented sequence of the same letters belong to different characters according to the first alphabet, but to the same character according to the second. Relativity to a system of classification is inescapable even at the syntactic level.

Any symbol system with an alphabet provides a basis for distinguishing between constitutive and contingent features of a mark [LA, 116]. Those features that affect its spelling are constitutive; all others are contingent. And once we identify the features of a mark that are constitutive of its identity as a character of the system, we can rule that any other marks with those features belong to the same character, however much they may differ in other respects.

For systems without alphabets (such as pictorial systems), the distinction between constitutive and contingent features cannot be drawn. In these systems we cannot take any mark to be character-indifferent with any other, for no matter how alike they are, we have no basis for ruling that their differences do not matter [LA, 116].

In seeking to fix the identity of a word, it has been common since Peirce to distinguish between types and tokens. A type is a linguistic universal among whose tokens are its inscriptions and utterances. For followers of Peirce, what is important is not the actual tokens that are uttered or inscribed, but the universals that they instantiate. Words then are identified with linguistic universals. And since a theory of reference is supposed to explain how words refer to their objects, when words are identified with types, the focus of the theory is on types rather than tokens.

A Peircean account commits us to platonism, for types are abstract entities. In addition to the obvious nominalist scruples, however, there is another reason for dissatisfaction with this sort of account. It is not unusual for character-indifferent tokens to have different referents. This is the case not only for ambiguous expressions, but also for metaphorical expressions and indexicals, or indicator words— words whose reference varies systematically with context.

In these cases it is clear that the tokens themselves refer. We might treat such cases as deviant, recognizing them as cases of token-reference, but insisting that type reference is the rule. Although simple ambiguity may be sufficiently rare to be discounted as deviant, metaphorical and indexical expressions are pervasive. It is perhaps better, therefore, to unify our account by taking the focus of the theory of reference to be individual utterances and inscriptions throughout. In that case we can satisfy our nominalist scruples by eschewing linguistic types altogether. Instead of asking whether utterances and inscriptions are tokens of same type, we ask directly whether they are replicas of one another.[4] Utterances and inscriptions are not treated as mere samples or instances, but as the real thing— letters, words, sentences in their own right.

If we take this route, we can, of course, continue to classify locutions as we have in the past. Classification requires only that we have an appropriate stock of predicates, not that we recognize abstract entities corresponding to them. Just as we need not recognize humanity to classify individuals under the predicate 'is human', we need not recognize the linguistic type 'human' to classify individual marks under the predicate 'is "human"'.

Utterances and inscriptions are syntactically equivalent, and thus replicas of one another, if they are spelled alike. Replicas are semantically equivalent if they are instances of the same term. But if diverse replicas have different compliance classes, or if an individual mark has more than one compliance class, the character is ambiguous. Syntactic equivalence then does not guarantee semantic equivalence.

A character is ambiguous if it admits of a variety of separate interpretations. If these are independent of one another, it is *simply ambiguous*.[5] Sometimes simple ambiguity arises because diverse replicas differ in extention. Thus, e.g., there are replicas of 'cape' that denote land masses but no cloaks, and replicas that denote cloaks but no land masses. In other cases a single utterance or inscription admits of distinct interpretations. Thus 'My lawyer lost her case' is ambiguous as between her having been bested in a legal battle and her having mislaid her briefcase. Where contextual cues are inadequate to decide among rival interpretations, explicit stipulation is required to fix the reference of ambiguous expressions. Otherwise their interpretation is indeterminate.

That a single character picks out independent compliance classes is, as it were, an accident of the symbol system. The very same classes might be picked out and the very same relations among them exemplified by a language with separate labels for the members of each class. Since the alternative interpretations of a simply ambiguous expression are semantically independent of one another, the descriptive and expressive powers of the language are unaffected if distinct labels

---

4. Israel Scheffler, *Beyond the Letter* (London: Routledge & Kegan Paul, 1979), p. 13. Notice that this definition of 'replica' does not require that the letters of the alphabet be construed as syntactic types. Since any alphabet is finitely long, its elements can be given as a list of predicates. Thus, two atomic inscriptions are replicas if both are instances of 'is an *a*', or 'is a *b*' or . . . see Goodman and Quine, "Steps Toward a Constructive Nominalism" [pp. 173–198].

5. For a discussion of the semantic features of different types of ambiguous expressions, see *Beyond the Letter*, pp. 11–36.

are introduced to denote the members of each of their compliance classes. Simple ambiguity is then in principle eliminable without loss to the language.

A character that has a metaphorical interpretation, like one that is simply ambiguous, has distinct ranges of application. In the case of simple ambiguity, the alternative applications are independent of one another. But the metaphorical application of a character is guided by its antecedent literal application [LA, 74; MM, 129]. A metaphor is interpreted against a background of literal usage. It functions to instigate an implicit comparison of the objects in the literal and the metaphorical extensions of a character. I will argue below that because metaphor both depends on and violates previous usage, it is a vehicle for effecting novel classifications that extend the descriptive and expressive powers of the language. Because I discuss metaphor extensively in what follows, I mention it here only briefly, as a kind of ambiguity in which one interpretation of an ambiguous character depends on another.

Indicator words, or indexicals, are systematically ambiguous in that their role in the language requires replicas produced in different circumstances to have different referents [SA, 359–71]. That role is to locate what is denoted by an utterance or inscription on the basis of its relation to the conditions of production (or the ostensible conditions of production) of that utterance or inscription. Personal pronouns, verb tenses, spatial and temporal indicators—such as 'here' and 'now'—frequently function indexically as do such common expressions as 'home', 'mother', and 'father'.

A personal indicator indicates the relation between its producer (or ostensible producer) and the individual(s) it denotes. Each replica of 'I' denotes its own producer; each one of 'we', its producer and some contextually specified others, etc.

Although we rarely have difficulty identifying the referents of such terms, the distinction between actual and ostensible producers should be noted. The replica of 'I' appearing in a manuscript is produced by the author; the one in the typescript, by the typist. If we insist that the referent of each replica of 'I' is its actual producer, we should take the replica in the typescript to refer to the typist, not the author. In practice we ignore the typist and look to the author of the manuscript to fix the denotations of the personal indicators therein. The actual producer of the manuscript is the ostensible producer of the typescript, and in this case it is the relation to the ostensible producer that determines denotation.

We cannot, however, conclude that whenever a person copies what someone else has written, the reference of indicators is to be determined by relations to the original author. A politician commits himself, not his speech writer, when he says, "If elected, I will lower taxes". Different linguistic conventions determine whether the denotation of personal indicators depends on their actual or on their ostensible producer. Given the variety of ways we can speak for each other, it is not surprising that these are easier to recognize than to classify. In any case, no attempt at classification will be made here.

Spatial indicators indicate the relation between the place of their actual or ostensible production and that of their denotation. What context determines in this case is how much space is included in the extension of the indicator. Does 'here' comprehend this room, this city, this country? How far must one travel to comply with the advice 'Go west, young man.'?

Temporal indicators indicate the relation between the time of their actual or ostensible production and the time at which the denoted events take place. There are two sorts of temporal indicators: words like 'now' and 'henceforth', and effectively tensed verbs. The former function in much the way that spatial indicators do. The latter have a dual role; they function as both indicators and predicates. As indicators they specify the relation between the production of a mark and the events it denotes. As predicates they give a general classification of those events. 'Finagled' indicates events occurring prior to its production, and classes together events that are instances of finagling. It thus denotes instances of finagling that occurred prior to its production.

There are a number of indicators that fall under no neat classification. Some, such as 'this' and 'that' are quite general. Their various replicas denote places, things, events, and actions. Others are fairly specific. The various replicas of 'home', interpreted literally, all denote homes. The indexical element here serves only to shift the denotation from one home to another.

Expressions I have characterized as indicators do not always function as such. Personal pronouns sometimes serve as variables rather than indicators: 'If anyone wants to volunteer, he should raise his hand.' 'To get to the park, you go down Maple Street.' Distributive singular terms also raise problems, as they are singular in grammatical form, but general in denotation. And nouns which function indexically when used as genuine singular terms do not do so when used as distributive singular terms. 'The home is the center of civil society.' 'The mother is the most important influence on her infant.' Moreover, although every sentence contains a tensed verb, in some sentences (including this one), the verbs function tenselessly. 'Variables denote their values.' 'Chickens lay eggs.' Care must be taken in the interpretation of such expressions, for not every instance functions indexically. Context thus plays a dual role in the interpretation of indicator words: We appeal to the linguistic context to decide whether a mark functions as an indicator, and to both the linguistic and the extralinguistic contexts to discover what is indicated.

The reference of indicator words is not indeterminate even though replicas differ in denotation and appeal to context is required to decide each case. Although it might be desirable for some purposes to replace sentences containing indicator words with eternal sentences—that is, sentences which are freely repeatable without change of truth value—the original sentence is not defective as it stands, or in any way parasitic on its eternal counterpart.

It might be maintained that such sentences are defective, not because they are context dependent, but because their context dependence results in vagueness. It is unclear how much of the surrounding territory is comprehended in a given 'here', or how much time included in a given 'now'. But this is no worse than the problem of vagueness in general. Some sentences are quite precise as to the extensions of their indicators; others are quite vague. Contrast the precision of an utterance like this:

> 'We must neither speak of tonight's events outside of this room, nor to anyone but each other.'

with one like this:

> 'It was the best of times; it was the worst of times.'

The former is quite precise; the latter quite vague. Vagueness and ambiguity are distinct features of language, and neither is especially symptomatic of the presence of the other. A decision to eschew vagueness then does not carry with it any objection to indicator words or to other ambiguous expressions in principle, but only to those expressions, ambiguous or not, that are deemed unacceptably vague.

Let me summarize the foregoing discussion of ambiguity. The existence of ambiguous expressions in a language demonstrates that syntactic equivalence is not sufficient for semantic equivalence. If syntactically equivalent marks differ in interpretation, or if a single mark has more than one interpretation, the character to which the marks belong is ambiguous. In that case, we must appeal to features of the context in which the mark appears to decide among rival interpretations. And if these prove inadequate, we must settle its interpretation by decree. Cases of simple ambiguity are contingent features of our symbol systems, and can be eliminated to increase clarity. Indicator words and metaphorical words are cases in which ambiguity is constitutive of the functioning of the symbols. To the extent that the functions are worth performing, to the extent that indicator words and metaphors contribute to the efficiency, system, or descriptive and expressive powers of the language, devices for varying reference with change of context should be counted an advantage rather than a defect in the language.

3. PREDICATION

A predicate denotes generally the objects in its extension. It associates together under a common label the things to which it applies. The role of a predicate is thus twofold: to denote and to classify the objects in its extension. Language is not, as the early Wittgenstein thought, a Doppelgänger of the world.[6] It is rather a system that orders, classifies, and describes the objects in the world.

There are two central problems for a theory of predication: roughly, identifying predicates, and identifying the objects that fall under them. Somewhat less roughly: the first problem is how to decide which sets[7] are to be recognized as the extensions of predicates, and correlatively, how to decide which among the coextensive labels that pick out those sets are to be recognized as predicates of the language. The second problem is this: given a sample, how to determine what else is included in the extension of a predicate.

Let us begin with the problem of identifying the extensions of our predicates. One solution that is frequently proposed is this: objects are to be classed under a single predicate just in case they are similar to one another. This solution is tenable only if backed by a nontrivial, noncircular account of similarity. Such an account is not easy to come by. If classification under a single predicate requires only that objects somehow resemble one another, then every set is the extension of some predicate. For any two objects belong to indefinitely many of the same sets and can be classified as similar to one another on the basis of their common membership in any of them. A head of cabbage is then similar to a head of state in that both belong to the set of shoes and ships and sealing wax and cabbages and kings.

If we attempt to construe 'similarity' more narrowly, so that two objects are similar just in case they belong to all or most of the same sets, we will find little, if any, similarity among objects. For any two objects are such that each belongs to indefinitely many sets from which the other is excluded.

Moreover, similarity cannot determine the extensions of even our most familiar predicates, regardless of the criterion we employ for counting two objects as similar. For similarity is not a transitive relation. A yellow square resembles a red square in shape, and a yellow circle in color. But it resembles a red circle in neither shape nor color. When A is similar to B, and B is similar to C, we are typically willing to conclude that A is similar to C only if A and B are similar to one another *in the same respect* as B and C. It is not similarity then, but similarity in a single respect, that is required to determine the extension of a predicate.

The problem then is to identify the respects in which objects must resemble one another to be classed under various predicates. But this is just the problem with which we began: Objects are alike in respect of color just in case they are the same color. Identifying the respects in which things must be alike to be classed under a given predicate is identifying the conditions for the satisfaction of the predicate.

6. The phrase is Putnam's.

7. I speak of sets as the extensions of predicates in this section as a matter of convenience. Nominalist reconstruals of my claims are not difficult to formulate.

Similarity by itself cannot serve as the basis for distinguishing between sets that count as the extensions of predicates and those that are but arbitrary assemblages of objects. And similarity in a single respect simply raises the original question in another form. For to identify the extensions of predicates is to identify the respect in which their instances resemble each other. And to distinguish between extensions of predicates and arbitrary assemblages is to distinguish between respects that matter and respects that don't.

To be instances of a common predicate, or to belong to the same kind, two things must be similar to one another in *important* respects. Or, if we want to abandon talk of similarity and respects of similarity as useless in developing a theory of predication, we can simply say that it is *the important sets that are the extensions of our predicates.* The problem then is to discover what makes a set important.

Some philosophers have maintained that the difference between important and trivial sets is an ontological one. They argue that a theory of language must distinguish between 'natural' and 'artificial' kinds, and between 'properties' and mere collections, for the former member of each pair is ontologically basic, while the latter is somehow contrived. Two sorts of argument have been advanced for this view. According to one, the distinction is grounded in "the dictates of language". According to the other, it is grounded in "the dictates of science".

The "dictates of language" argument is familiar enough. It maintains that certain modes of organization are built into our language. It is these that serve as the fundamental categories in terms of which we organize our experience and that sustain our counterfactual, hypothetical, and projective claims.

The failure to sustain the analytic/synthetic distinction (of which more will be said later) makes this position difficult to justify or even to state with much precision. Nevertheless, some philosophers and linguists feel that there must be something to it, because in testing "linguistic intuitions" investigators frequently find widespread agreement across a population. By appealing to a variety of real and hypothetical circumstances, the investigator seeks to discover what a speaker takes himself to be committed to in using a particular locution. General agreement across a linguistic community as to the real and hypothetical circumstances in which an expression applies constitutes evidence that the expression is a genuine predicate of the language rather than an arbitrary or contrived classification.

If we take such agreement as evidence for an ontological thesis, we revert to a Doppelgänger theory. Our linguistic intuitions are treated as evidence for "real properties" or "natural kinds"—as evidence, that is, for a metaphysical taxonomy that is independent of any classifications we may make. According to this account, language mirrors reality—a platonist reality composed of universals as well as particulars. Instantiation is an ontological relation, not a semantic or conventional one.

But if we ask what answers to the field linguist's questions really provide, we find them to be surprisingly lacking in metaphysical implications. To the extent that the method works, it yields information about the linguistic habits of native speakers. Suppose a linguist asks about the following scenario:

> Suppose . . . there have never been cats. . . . Every movement, every twitch of a muscle, every meow, every flicker of an eyelid is thought out by a man in a control center on Mars and is then executed by the cat's body as the result of signals that emanate not from the cat's 'brain' but from a highly miniaturized radio receiver located, let us say, in the cat's pineal gland.[8]

We might reply that in that case there are no cats, only robots; or that cats are actually robots, not animals; or we might be too dumbfounded by this hypothesis to reply at all. Our response, whatever it is, tells the linguist something about the way we are prepared to project 'cat' in unusual situations.

If native responses to the field linguist's queries are supposed to mark out the distinction between natural and unnatural kinds, between the extensions of predicates and mere collections of unrelated objects, then the distinction comes to this: Predicates are just those modes of classification for which we have linguistic habits to guide their applications in new situations.[9] The difference between 'cat' and 'shoes and ships and sealing wax and cabbages and kings' then is that our competence with respect to the former gives us some guidance as to what to say about the case that Putnam describes, whereas our competence with respect to the latter gives no hint as to whether, say, the glue on an envelope (a latterday descendant of sealing wax) is to be classed under it or not.

There are two problems with taking this distinction to be a metaphysical one: first, it seems to be a matter of degree. Although 'cat' is as legitimate a predicate as we could hope to find, it is not at all clear that our "intuitions" concerning it are sufficient to yield an unequivocal answer to the question Putnam's linguist poses. On other hand, our "intuitions" concerning 'shoes and ships and sealing wax and cabbages and kings' do yield the decision that a new hybrid cabbage, like other cabbages, belongs to its extension. There is neither reason to believe that "intuitions" concerning predicates are so strong as to decide every new case, nor that those concerning contrived classifications are so weak as to decide none. The strength of our convictions regarding the classification of new instances is sufficiently variable that we cannot reasonably hope to draw a sharp distinction between the extensions of predicates and other sets on the basis of it.

8. Hilary Putnam, "It Ain't Necessarily So", *Mathematics, Matter and Method* (Cambridge: Cambridge University Press, 1975), p. 238.

9. Cf. [FFF, 98–99] on the role of habit in projection.

Second, as we modify our habits of speech, contrived classifications are elevated to the status of predicates, and predicates demoted to that of contrived classifications. This seems to me to be precisely what happens as language evolves, but it is difficult to square with the thesis that our linguistic habits reflect ontologically fundamental kinds.

The test of "linguistic intuitions" asks how we expect to apply certain labels. If it is our guide, then what makes some sets important is that they are associated with particular labels—labels that we are accustomed to use. But as we have seen, the test reveals habit, not ontology. And we should not hope that an improved test will do better. For it is hard to see how the availability of certain labels can be expected to reveal anything more ontologically fundamental than the constitution of the language or symbol system of which they are a part. Perhaps then, we should seek to discover the locus of their importance in the sets themselves rather than in the labels associated with them.

It is here that the "dictates of science" argument is brought into play. This is the thesis that the sets which are important, and which serve as the basis for a system of predication are those which are required by our scientific theories (or, more precisely, by the true successor theories to which current theories are approximations). Our chemistry requires that we distinguish between organic and inorganic compounds; our biology, that we distinguish between vertebrates and invertebrates. And the success of such theories attests to the correctness of the scientific systems of classification. Quite so. Given certain interests, purposes, and values—simplicity, comprehensiveness, predictive power, elegance of formulation, ease of calculation, etc.— these sets, or some quite close to them in extension, are important. If you want to do science like this, you need systems of predicates very much like these. But it does not follow from their being important relative to these aims, that they are important *tout court*. For relative to another set of aims—even another set of scientific aims, for science is not a monolith—they may be quite inappropriate. It has been argued that the predicates needed for, e.g., action theory,[10] aesthetics [WOW, 111], and law[11] do not map at all well onto those needed for physics or biology. And given the diverse interests that these enterprises serve, there is no reason to believe that even ideal theories 'in the limit' will do so. Accordingly, the success of science provides small support for the thesis that the predicates needed for the natural sciences are more fundamental than those needed for other human activities.

To the question, "What makes the labels we use and the sets to

10. Donald Davidson, "Mental Events", *Essays on Actions and Events* (Oxford: The Clarendon Press, 1980), pp. 207–225.

11. H. L. A. Hart and A. M. Honoré, *Causation in the Law* (Oxford: The Clarendon Press, 1959), pp. 24–57.

which they correspond important?'' the answer is simply that we take them to be important. We do not choose them because they are antecedently important. Rather, they become important *by being chosen.* The validity or authority of a "linguistic intuition" is just that of a habit.

The language then provides a system of labels for classifying together those things that it is committed to recognizing as alike. 'Similarity' falls out: A and B are similar, relative to a given language, just in case the language contains some predicate ϕ of which A and B are instances. Once a predicate is introduced into the language, it applies to everything past, present, and future that complies with it. Accordingly, it does not follow from the fact that a predicate is introduced in, say, 1850, that the things that fall under it are alike after 1850, but before 1850 they were not. Prior to 1850 the language lacked a vehicle for associating them under a common label. The label is indeed new. But since similarity is a direct consequence of predication, and predication, as a form of denotation, is tenseless, the similarity is neither new nor old.

We have found no *a priori* method for saying what the principles of classification should be. As we progress, we come to recognize the fruitfulness of new ways of organizing our domains. "Linguistic intuitions" or the force of habit competes with the need for innovation and accommodation. Linguistic habits do not, for example, prepare us to classify caterpillars and butterflies as members of the same biological kinds, or to identify a particular caterpillar and a particular butterfly as time slices of the same individual. It is the biological theory of the life cycle of Lepidopterae that serves as the basis for these identifications. Because languages are developed, used, and modified in various ways to suit our varying purposes, there appears to be no way to specify in advance the sets that will remain arbitrary groupings and those that are or will come to be extensions of predicates.

It is therefore preferable to admit the full range of sets as candidates for labeling through predication. Which sets actually come to be correlated with labels depends on the interests of the language users and on the vicissitudes of linguistic development. Predicates describe what they denote, and the descriptive resources of the language—the labels available for describing—depend in large measure on the sort of description we want to produce, and on the efforts we are willing to make to develop symbol systems capable of producing them.

This is not to say that with enough effort we can so design a language as to be able to describe things in any terms we like. It is commonplace that our goals may not be mutually satisfiable. Where they are not, trade-offs must be made, or some goals abandoned. For example, one of the problems of twentieth-century physics might be described as the incompatibility of the goal of a deterministic system with the goal of describing that system in terms of its most elementary particles. Where we talk of individual protons and electrons, we must settle for statistical generalizations. Where we speak deterministically, no mention of individual particles can be made. That these goals are incompatible cannot be discovered by consulting our linguistic intuitions or our goals in theory construction. To discover this required the development of quantum mechanics.

The dependence of our systems of kinds on our theories, and the dependence of these in turn on our interests, values, technology, and the like, make questionable at best the thesis that our predicates pick out real properties or natural kinds whose existence, extension, and metaphysical status are independent of any contribution of ours. And the claim that just these kinds or properties are required to answer scientific questions or provide scientific explanations supports that thesis only if backed by an account of why these questions or forms of explanation have priority—an account that does not in turn appeal to the practices or institutions of which they are a part, else all questions are begged.

4. PROJECTION

The foregoing discussion was based on the premise that the extensions of the various sets are given. The problem was to select those with which predicates of the language are to be correlated. A separate question, and one that is more apt to be encountered in actual language use (since we seldom wonder why the language contains no simple label for members of the class consisting of $\sqrt{2}$, my mother-in-law, and the state of New Jersey), is this: given a used predicate, how do we determine its extension? And correlatively, given a pair of predicates, how do we determine that they are coextensive? Formally, of course, the answers are easy: the extension of a predicate comprises whatever the predicate applies to; and two predicates are coextensive if they apply to exactly the same things.

The problem is that what a term applies to and whether two terms apply to the same things cannot be read off the language. Even a comprehensive history of the language can reveal only how its terms have been used to date. But a complete listing of past uses does not, as Wittgenstein recognizes, afford a unique basis for saying, "Now I can go on,"[12] or for criticizing or applauding the ways in which others go on to use a term. The problem is a problem of projection [LA, 201–2]. Given the way a term has been applied and occasionally misapplied, to date, to what else does it apply?

Usage does not supply the answer, for given any sample applications of a term, there are indefinitely many ways of rounding out the class in question. This is true even if we include linguistic intuitions or dispositions to apply a term as well as actual applications. For these, as I argued above, are just habits of speech—ways in which we are

12. Ludwig Wittgenstein, *Philosophical Investigations* (Oxford: Basil Blackwell & Mott, 1958), #151.

accustomed, through training and practice, to employ our expressions. But our habits of speech are developed to deal with clear cases. And as we get further away from the clear cases that our terms were designed to accommodate, the force of habit weakens. Should it turn out that those things we have always taken to be cats are in fact robots controlled by Martians, competent speakers, without betraying any linguistic idiosyncracy, may well differ as to whether the predicate 'cat' applies. The case is sufficiently extreme that the decision to apply or to withhold the term is bound to appear somewhat arbitrary.

To fix the extension of a term it must be determinate for each object whether or not the term applies to it. The identification of our linguistic habits concerning a term can serve to articulate our implicit knowledge of the term's extension. But the force of habit is not sufficient to decide every case. Precisely because our terms are developed, learned, and used for more or less specific purposes, in more or less restricted contexts, there are bound to be some cases that habit does not decide. Habits, linguistic or otherwise, do not provide the requisite guidance as to how to behave in remote or unusual environments.

Cases that previous usage augmented by habit do not decide fall within a term's penumbra of vagueness. These must be decided somehow, for if we give in to the temptation to say that in these cases the term "both does and does not apply", we sanction contradiction. It may not matter whether we say that the term applies or that it does not, but it is crucial that we cannot, without equivocation, say both. The problem which gives rise to this temptation is that once we have exhausted actual usage and the linguistic intuitions of native speakers, there is nothing more to appeal to. Accordingly, where the facts of language use do not decide, it is a matter for decree. We close out the extension of a term by stipulating which among the objects in its penumbra of vagueness are to be taken to satisfy it.

Since it is a matter for stipulation or decree, there is no question of truth or falsity. Since we legislate that the automata Putnam describes are, or are not, to be included in the extension of 'cat', no sense can be given to the question, "But what if they *really aren't* cats, and we mistakenly stipulate that they are?"

Nevertheless, there may be good reasons for preferring one decree to another—reasons grounded in our aims and interests in employing a predicate, and in the sort of system of predicates we hope to produce. To see this, let us turn to another of Putnam's science-fiction examples.

> We shall suppose that somewhere in the galaxy there is a planet we shall call Twin Earth . . . [A]part from the differences we shall specify in our science fiction examples, the reader may suppose that Twin Earth is *exactly* like Earth. . . . One of the peculiarities of Twin Earth is that the liquid called 'water' is not H_2O but a different liquid whose formula is very long and complicated. I

shall abbreviate this chemical formula simply as XYZ. I shall suppose that XYZ is indistinguishable from water at normal temperatures and pressures. In particular, it tastes like water, and it quenches thirst like water. Also, I shall suppose that the oceans, lakes, and seas of Twin Earth contain XYZ and not water, that it rains XYZ on Twin Earth and not water, etc.[13]

In deciding whether to include a particular sample of liquid in the extension of 'water', what is important to a chemist is its chemical composition; to a biologist, its ability to sustain life; and to a bartender, its potability when mixed with Scotch. So the question "Is XYZ to be included in the extension of 'water'?" might well be answered with another question: "Who wants to know?"

The role of legislation is not limited to deciding as yet undecided cases, however. Decrees serve to correct past practice as well. The reclassification of whales as mammals rather than fish is a case in point. The "intuitive" classification was sacrificed for an elegant taxonomy. But although our linguistic practices are not immune to revision in the interest of theory, there is some tendency to prefer decrees that bring theory into accord with practice to those that modify practice to suit theory. For habits, even bad ones, are difficult to break.

5. SYSTEM

Taken in isolation, a predicate is simply a device for grouping together the objects that comply with it. Predicates, however, are rarely taken in isolation. They typically function as members of families of alternatives—families which sort the objects in a given domain. Let us, following Goodman, call such a family a *scheme*, and the objects it sorts its *realm*. The realm associated with a given scheme consists of the objects to which any of the scheme's predicates apply. Thus the scheme consisting of the characters 'odd' and 'even' is assigned to the realm of integers; and the scheme consisting of 'animal', 'vegetable', and 'mineral', to that of physical objects, etc. A *system* is a scheme applied to a realm [LA, 72].

The alternatives of which a scheme consists need not be mutually exclusive. Thus, e.g., a scheme might include a formula such as

$$(x) \, (Sx \, \ddot{R}x)$$

which is interpreted according to a color system as

Everything scarlet is red.

Moreover, a single term may be incorporated into several different systems. Thus, e.g., we might take the extention of 'turquois' to be

13. "The Meaning of 'Meaning'", p. 223.

included in that of 'green', in that of 'blue', in neither, or in both. So
any of the following might be used to schematize the term:

a. $(x)(Tx \supset (Gx \ \& \ \sim Bx))$

b. $(x)(Tx \supset (Bx \ \& \ \sim Gx))$

c. $(x)(Tx \supset (Bx \ \& \ Gx))$

d. $(x)(Tx \supset (\sim Bx \ \& \ \sim Gx))$

These need not disagree about the extension of the term 'turquois'.
What they disagree about is the way that extension is related to the
extensions of other color terms.

There are, however, cases in which the extension assigned to a
term depends on the system we employ. For whether something is to
be classified under a particular label often depends on what alternative labels are available. Within the animal/vegetable/mineral system
we readily classify poison ivy as a vegetable. Still, we would hesitate
to include it in a salad whose recipe calls for mixed vegetables—even
if the recipe encourages us to "be creative". In a system appropriate
for interpreting the recipe 'vegetable' is restricted in its application to
plants used as human food.

I have been speaking as though the objects in a realm are determined independently of any scheme that organizes them. This is an
oversimplification. For among the expressions whose interpretation is
fixed by a system are 'is identical to', 'is the same thing as', and the
like. And by fixing the interpretation of these expressions, a system
sets the conditions for the individuation of the objects in its realm
[WOW, 8].

Quine maintains that individuation is determined by "a cluster of
related grammatical particles and constructions: plural endings, pronouns, the 'is' of identity and its adaptations 'same' and 'other'."[14]
This is fine, as far as it goes. But the interpretation of these is not to
be settled without considering the sort of thing they are individuating.
This requires that they be interpreted as part of a broader system.
And their interpretation varies as they are incorporated into different
systems.

Consider 'sunset'. How we are to interpret the 'is' of identity,
'same', and 'other', how we are to decide if we are seeing the very
same thing we saw last night, depends on whether we are concerned
to identify suns or settings. The same sun sets day after day, but
every dusk brings a new setting. What counts as being the same thing
varies from one sort of object to another [WOW, 8]. It is the relation
of the cluster of particles and constructions that Quine identifies to

---

14. W. V. Quine, "Ontological Relativity", *Ontological Relativity and Other Essays*
(New York: Columbia University Press, 1969), p. 32.

the various denoting phrases of a system that determines the conditions on the individuation of the objects in its realm. And under different interpretations, the realm consists of quite different elements.

This is not, of course, to say that we can specify the kinds of things we are individuating prior to the interpretation of the devices in question. Clearly, neither kinds nor things can be characterized without employing such devices. It is only to say that the interpretation of these devices cannot be settled in advance. It is the system as a whole that settles the conditions on the individuation of the objects in its realm, and not any separable cluster of especially 'logical' or individuating particles.

If a realm does not consist of antecedently individuated entities, one might wonder how it contributes to a system. Is it no more than Locke's substance—"something we know not what", introduced to satisfy ancient prejudice, but contributing nothing to the system? Actually it is not. The same scheme can organize different realms, yielding different but related systems. I shall argue below that this is central to the explanation of metaphor. Moreover, different schemes may organize the same realm. Here too, the result is different, but related, systems.

The problem in making out this last point is clearly that of explaining what justifies us in identifying the realms of two systems with one another. On what basis can we say that it is the same realm that the two carve up? We cannot identify with one another all and only realms consisting of exactly the same objects, for objects may be individuated differently under the different systems. The solution is to leave it to the systems themselves to decide. If there is a general identifying description of the realm on which the systems agree, then the systems share a common realm. Thus Aristotelian and Darwinian biological systems sort the realm of living things; Newtonian and quantum systems, the realm of physical objects and events; diatonic and twelve-tone systems, the realm of musical tones. Their joint characterization of the realm is not neutral in any absolute sense (whatever that might mean). It is neutral only insofar as it is shared by the systems under discussion. It is, of course, itself part of a broader system.

It must not be supposed that what I have labelled 'a system' is identical to a language or that the appropriate system for interpreting a particular language, discourse, or document can be directly read off it. 'System', 'scheme', and 'realm', like 'reference', 'denotation', and 'extension' are technical terms of semantic theory. And just as the untutored observation of a collection of objects does not determine how its elements are to be identified and classified for the purposes of chemical theory, simple observation of a collection of discourses and documents does not determine how its elements are to be identified and classified for the purposes of semantic theory.

Often we have no difficulty deciding what system is required to correctly interpret a given discussion. Its presuppositions, context, and purpose make the selection of a system reasonably straightforward. A particular colored light might readily be classified as 'orange' according to a color system that includes that label. This information is not, however, likely to move a traffic cop who has just charged you with entering an intersection after the light turned yellow. For the appropriate system for classifying traffic lights has as its only alternatives 'red', 'yellow', and 'green'. And a light that is correctly labelled 'orange' when that label is available, is labelled 'yellow' when it is not.

In other cases, however, appeal to context and the presuppositions of a discussion may not be sufficient to decide among rival systems. This is one way of understanding disagreements as to the limits of a vague term. The disagreement over whether a woman 5'7'' in height is tall will be resolved only by deciding among systems for classifying women according to height. But there may be nothing in the case on the basis of which to decide whether, e.g., a system that simply distinguishes between 'tall' and 'short' is appropriate, or one that introduces such refinements as 'average', 'above average', 'well above average', and the like, nor to decide among systems that draw the boundaries of their predicates in different places. Nevertheless, without a decision as to which system to invoke, we will be unable to decide whether 'She is tall' is true.

More interestingly perhaps, the failure to appreciate the way semantic systems function seems to be the source of philosophical debate over "conceptual change" in science. Kuhn and Feyerabend contend that major theory changes bring with them changes in the reference of key theoretical terms. Putnam and Boyd contend, on the contrary, that such terms typically retain their reference across theory change.[15] Thus Putnam and Boyd maintain while Kuhn and Feyerabend deny, that, e.g., 'electron' has the same reference in the Bohr-Rutherford theory of the early part of the century as it does after the development of quantum mechanics. Each faction supports its position by pointing to features of the way the expression is used in scientific discourse.

If we employ the semantic devices introduced above, we see that appeals to scientific discourse are inadequate to decide the issue, and indeed, that there does not seem to be any substantive issue to decide. Kuhn and Feyerabend interpret the claims of pre-quantum theories to be true under an old, inappropriate system, but false under the new, more appropriate one. They maintain that the introduction of a revolutionary theory involves a redrawing of the boundaries between predicates. Putnam and Boyd take it that a single system is employed throughout. The introduction of quantum theory does not bring about a change in the extension of 'electron', but the discovery that many of the claims we once accepted about the objects in that extension are false.

15. Cf. Hilary Putnam, *Meaning and the Moral Sciences* (London: Routledge & Kegan Paul, 1978), pp. 22–24.

But there is nothing in the scientific literature itself that determines what features belong to a system as criteria for applying 'electron', and what are true and false sentences within a system that makes reference to electrons. The scientific literature then does not tell us whether to interpret sentences of outdated theories as true under an inappropriate scheme or false under an appropriate one. And this should not surprise us. The people using the word 'electron' are doing physics, not philosophy. So long as they have the resources to say that the Bohr-Rutherford theory is wrong, and current theory is right (or, at any rate, comes closer to being right), it doesn't matter for their purposes whether the Bohr-Rutherford theory contained false statements about the very same things we now label 'electrons', or that as physics developed 'electron' and assocated signs changed their extension.

Scientific theories can, as Kuhn has argued, be so schematized that the extensions of important predicates change from one theory to the next. But Kuhn's account of this is wrong, and it is important to see why it is wrong, since it established the framework for an ongoing, apparently fruitless debate in recent philosophy of science.

Languages cannot be identified with theories. A sentence and its negation belong to the same language. But it is only in inconsistent theories that both a sentence and its negation occur. Nor can languages be identified by reference to theories. For a theory does not determine what system should be employed to explicate its referential structure. Any body of discourse can be systematized in a variety of ways, and for different purposes different systems may be appropriate. An account of scientific development that seeks to emphasize continuity might do well to interpret the claims of successive theories in terms of a single system, while one that seeks to emphasize change might exemplify differences between successive theories by casting each theory in a different system. There may be sound historiographical reasons for preferring one way of characterizing theory change to another. But no appeal to the "facts of language use" will decide the case.

In summary: we can, by fiat, let almost anything denote anything else. Thus, the Monday morning quarterback, using his breakfast dishes to demonstrate how a key play should have been run, lets his coffee mug denote the quarterback. And we can, by fiat, class almost any group of objects under a single label, as when for the purposes of illustration he classifies the salt shaker, the sugar bowl, and his wife's soft-boiled egg as 'the defensive line'.

Such stipulations are arbitrary, however, unless they are part of a system. A system involves a term in a network of labels that organizes, sorts, or classifies the items in a domain in terms of the types of diversity that the system is prepared to recognize. And a system sustains continuity of reference from one use of a sign to another by determining criteria for the reidentification of individuals and for the classification of diverse individuals as instances of the same kind.

A system for the interpretation of a used language should, as far as is plausible, be faithful to prior usage, but beyond that it is authoritative. It is a feature of language that old terms are applied in new situations, so prior usage is never sufficient to determine the limits of a term's application. (To so restrict its application, we must stipulate that it is not to be projected beyond previous uses.) The caveat "as far as is plausible" is required because systems do not merely reflect linguistic practices. They refine and extend those practices as well. They disambiguate ambiguous expressions, and sharpen the boundaries of vague ones. And, as the classification of whales as mammals shows, they occasionally correct linguistic practice in order to simplify theory.

Fidelity to prior usage requires only that a system's verdicts as to whether expressions are applicable generally agree with the verdicts of competent speakers of the language. The system need not reflect any psychological process by which speakers come to their verdicts. Nor need it employ criteria that they antecedently recognize or implicitly employ. Thus, a system that labels all and only samples of H_2O 'pure water' is not undermined by the fact that members of the linguistic community make no chemical tests before applying the term, or by the fact that the term belonged to the language prior to the development of chemistry. If the system applies the label to the same things as competent speakers do, its application is faithful. All that is required of a faithful system then is that distinctions be properly marked.

III LABELING LABELS

1. FICTIVE LABELS

Any comprehensive theory of language must include an account of the interpretation of fictive terms. This poses a particular problem for extensionalists, as we are unwilling to introduce 'possible individuals' as referents of fictive terms, or 'possible worlds' about which fictive sentences are true. Instead, we want to insist that the denotation of fictive terms is null. Nevertheless, we acknowledge that 'the melancholy Dane' is a description of Hamlet. But how can it be both a description of Hamlet and, Hamlet failing to exist, a description of nothing? Indeed Peter Pan doesn't exist either. But we are not prepared to admit that 'the melancholy Dane' describes Peter Pan, despite the fact that 'Hamlet' and 'Peter Pan' are alike in denotation. Do we violate a law of logic by insisting that fictive contexts are extensional, yet refusing to substitute fictive terms freely for one another?

We do not. In any context in which their denotation is at issue, fictive terms are indeed intersubstitutable *salva veritate*. But our interest in fictive terms is typically *not* in their denotation. It is rather in the terms themselves and in the works in which those terms appear. Discussions of *Hamlet,* for example, concern not what the work denotes or describes, but what it is. The world contains pictures and descriptions as well as cabbages and kings. And just as we develop systems to classify the world's flora and fauna, we develop systems to classify the world's pictures and descriptions. We are not primarily interested in determining what fictive symbols—verbal or pictorial —denote, but rather in determining what expressions denote them.

That our interest is in the fictive symbol itself may be overlooked, and a desperate, if futile, search for its referent undertaken, if we fail to recognize that 'picture of P' and 'description of P' are ambiguous [LA, 22]. On one interpretation each is the schema for a two-place semantic predicate that links a symbol and the objects it denotes. According to this interpretation, a picture of the Eiffel Tower depicts, and a description of the Eiffel Tower describes, the Eiffel Tower. And a picture of Peter Pan depicts, and a description of Hamlet describes, nothing. On the other interpretation, 'picture of P' and 'description of P' are schemata of one-place predicates that classify symbols according to kind. 'Description of Peter Pan' groups together some representations; 'description of Hamlet', others; and 'description of the Eiffel Tower', yet others. Replacements for 'picture of P' and 'description of P' are predicates of symbols themselves according to this interpretation, and make no commitment as to what, if anything, those symbols denote. Let us follow Goodman's suggestion [LA, 22] and disambiguate by restricting 'picture of P' and 'description of P' to their two-place semantic interpretation, and introduce 'P-picture' and 'P-description' as one-place predicate schemata whose replacements classify representations themselves.

Since fictive symbols all have, and are known to have, the same (null) denotation, differentiation among them is on the basis of their kind. Although 'description of Hamlet' and 'description of Peter Pan' are indeed coextensive, 'Hamlet-description' and 'Peter-Pan-description' are not. The former denotes portions of Shakespeare's work but none of Barrie's, while the latter denotes portions of Barrie's work but none of Shakespeare's.

Our interest in factual terms normally focuses on what they denote. But a term need not be empty to fall under a replacement for 'P-description'. There are Napoleon-descriptions as well as Hamlet-descriptions, and horse-pictures as well as unicorn-pictures. The system for classifying fictive terms serves to classify factual ones as well. Indeed, an expression like 'Napoleon-description' comprehends both factual descriptions (such as those appearing in histories), and fictional ones (such as those appearing in *War and Peace*). To say that a real person appears in a work of fiction then is to say that the expression that results when we substitute his name for *P* in the schema has both factual and fictive descriptions in its extension. Nor is it the case that we are always more interested in what a factual representation denotes than in how it is to be classified. If a number of artists paint pictures of Saint Jerome, the common classification of them as Saint-Jerome-pictures may be of greater interest to art historians and critics than the fact that they depict a particular historical figure. And if a group of assertions appears to be particularly self-serving or biased (or, in an extreme case, a pack of lies), we may classify them together as, e.g., what-Daddy-did-in-the-war-descriptions without ruling on, or even taking much of an interest in, their denotation.

The ability to identify and classify representations does not depend on any prior ability to identify and classify their objects. We need not already know how to classify individuals as unicorns in order to learn to classify tapestries as unicorn-pictures and stories of virgin capture and water conning as unicorn-descriptions. Nor need we already know how to identify kangaroos in order to learn to identify kangaroo-descriptions and kangaroo-pictures. Indeed, the ability to identify such descriptions and pictures may enable us to recognize a kangaroo when we first encounter one. We acquire a good deal of knowledge from books. Learning from books requires the ability to identify and classify the verbal and pictorial representations they contain. So if we ask, with Aristotle, what is first in the order of knowing, we find that frequently it is a knowledge of P-descriptions and P-pictures that precedes and informs our knowledge of their objects.

Even though acquaintance with their objects is not a prerequisite for learning how to classify representations, seekers after the possible might still want to maintain that the classification of representations must reflect an antecedent classification of their objects. In that case, objects—real and fictional—are first in the order of being even if not always first in the order of knowing. As a general thesis, this is untenable. For there is a variety of ways of classifying representations that do not depend on any classification of their objects. We classify representations on the basis of medium, genre, technique, and style. And even when we employ a system whose predicates apply to objects as well as to their representations, the classification of a representation need not reflect that of its objects. There are biased reports of unbiased decisions, and angry accounts of complacent politicians. Accordingly, we cannot in general conclude that the classification of a picture or description depends on the classification of its objects. Labeling a symbol a 'Hamlet-description' is like labeling a symbol 'baroque'. Although the principles of classification differ, in each case we classify symbols directly, without consulting their referents.

Although it is a predicate of symbols that does not depend on their denotation, 'Hamlet-description' is not a syntactical predicate. Specifically, its extension is not the set of descriptions in which replicas of 'Hamlet' appear. Expressions that include no replica, such as 'the melancholy Dane', are Hamlet-descriptions. And expressions that include a replica, such as 'Hamlet, the kennel club champion,' are not.

Just how we decide what falls under 'Hamlet-description' is perhaps as difficult to say as how we decide what falls under 'desk' or 'granite' or 'novel'. Indeed, the problems are one and the same, whether our domain consists of representations or rocks. I am concerned here with finished systems, not with what possessed us to construct them in the first place. So I shall engage in no psychohistorical speculations about their origins. Nevertheless, it is important to notice that as we learn to read books and pictures we develop the facility to identify representations as P-pictures and P-descriptions with varying degrees of ease and confidence in our judgments. The explanation of the process by which we do so is perhaps best left to learning theorists.

How then does such a system hang together? Relations of inclusion, equivalence, and exclusion are established among descriptions. All and only Hamlet-descriptions are melancholy-Dane-descriptions, all Hamlet-descriptions are tragic-hero-descriptions, no Hamlet-descriptions are Ophelia-descriptions, and so on. A system fixes Hamlet's fictive identity by determining that various replicas of 'Hamlet', 'sire', 'my son', and so on, as well as selected pronouns are Hamlet-descriptions. The identity of Hamlet as a fictional character is determined by a collection of the descriptions that are Hamlet-descriptions. The extension of 'Hamlet-description' is not, of course, limited to portions of Shakespeare's play. Undoubtedly, more Hamlet-descriptions occur outside of the play, in words of literary criticism and the like, than occur in it. Nevertheless, it is Shake-

speare's Hamlet-descriptions that determine the identity of the fictional character. To qualify as Hamlet-descriptions, remarks by critics
must be reasonably faithful to Shakespeare's characterization. But
fictive identity is not always determined by the P-descriptions occurring in a single work. The extension of 'Mephistopheles-description',
for example, is determined by portions of several stories, plays, and
operas. The same fictional character appears in different works when
members of the collection of descriptions that determine the fictive
identity in question belong to different works.

Since we cannot determine the extension of replacements for 'P-
description' on purely syntactical grounds, the problem of ambiguity
arises. A replacement is ambiguous if diverse replicas differ in extension. There is no decisive test for fictive ambiguity. Replicas that denote portions of different works are not *ipso facto* ambiguous for, as
we saw above, the same fictional character—a Falstaff or a
Faust—may appear in several works. Accordingly, we cannot me-
chanically disambiguate by restricting the application of a replacement of the schema to portions of a single work and works of criticism about it. In any case, the problem of fictive ambiguity is not just
to decide how such character-indifferent replicas apply to different
works. For a replacement of the schema may apply ambiguously to a
single work. 'Henry-description' denotes portions of Shakespeare's
Henry IV plays that concern King Henry, and portions that concern
Prince Hal. The problem of deciding whether a replacement for 'P-
description' is ambiguous then is the same as that of deciding whether
any other predicate is. The criterion for ambiguity is that one of a pair
of syntactically equivalent replicas denotes something that the other
does not. And determining whether this criterion is satisfied is no
more automatic in the case of fictive labels than it is in the case of
factual ones.

Moreover, disagreements may arise as to whether a replacement for
'P-description' is actually ambiguous. An example is the disagreement
among Shakespearian scholars as to whether the Falstaff of *The
Merry Wives of Windsor* is the same as the Falstaff who appears in
Henry IV. The disagreement is to be resolved by deciding what limits
a system for describing the plays places on the application of
'Falstaff-description'. Under a system that imposes relatively weak
constraints, the term will apply generally but unambiguously to portions of both. Under a system that imposes strong constraints, it will
be ambiguous. And here, as elsewhere, there may be reasons favoring
the choice of either sort of system.

It is important to notice, however, that the ambiguity of a replacement of 'P-description' does not derive from any ambiguity of its
components. Consider two tokens of 'Antonio-description': one denoting portions of *The Merchant of Venice,* the other denoting
portions of *The Tempest.* Tokens of 'Antonio' in the former are coextensive with tokens of 'Antonio' in the latter, for in each play 'Antonio' is a fictive term whose denotation is null. And Antonio-

descriptions that denote portions of *The Merchant of Venice* as well as those that denote portions of *The Tempest* are genuine descriptions. 'Description' then is a general term that comprehends both sets of Antonio-descriptions. The ambiguity of 'Antonio-description' thus does not result from an ambiguity in either 'Antonio' or 'description'. For neither is ambiguous. Scheffler calls this type of ambiguity compound-ambiguity.[1] One reason for maintaining that replacements for 'P-description' are semantically simple one-place predicates is that they are liable to compound ambiguity. They may be ambiguous even though their components are not.

Although they are semantically simple, replacements for 'P-description' are perspicuous in a way that other symbols typically are not. The extension of 'Hamlet-description', for example, is the intersection of the set of Hamlet-representations (which contains pictures as well as descriptions) and the set of descriptions. This information can be read off the sign itself. Certain relations are thus more clearly displayed in systems that classify representations than in systems that classify tables and chairs.

Fictive labels do not, however, function only as parts of such compounds as 'Hamlet-description' and 'unicorn-picture', or as alternative labels for the null set. They function mention-selectively as well.[2] In a mention-selective application, a term is applied not to what it denotes, but to what it mentions. Thus a term *t* applies mention-selectively to whatever '*t*-representation' applies denotively. The term 'unicorn', for example, applies mention-selectively to unicorn-mentions—that is, to unicorn-pictures and unicorn-descriptions.

Mention-selection helps to explain how we recognize competence with fictive terms. How to demonstrate competence with such terms is problematic, since they apply to nothing. One symptom of having mastered a fictive term is correctly refraining from applying it to anything. This symptom, however, is equivocal, for we also refrain from applying terms that we don't know. Should we conclude that a child who calls nothing a centaur has mastered 'centaur', or that the term is not part of his vocabulary? A further difficulty with treating the failure to apply such terms as symptomatic of competence is that all fictive terms have null denotation. But we cannot take the child's failure to apply 'unicorn' and 'centaur' to anything to be evidence that he can, or that he cannot, distinguish between them.

With the recognition of the mention-selective application of such terms, these problems are overcome. Although all and only unicorns are centaurs, it is not the case that all and only unicorn-pictures are centaur-pictures. If a child correctly applies 'unicorn' mention-selectively to unicorn-pictures, and refrains from applying it to any animal he encounters, we have strong evidence that he has mastered the term. Indeed, in teaching children language we often speak

1. *Beyond the Letter*, p. 31.

2. *Beyond the Letter*, pp. 31–36.

mention-selectively, asking them to point to the unicorn in the book when, of course, what we want them to do is point to the unicorn-picture in the book. Nor is teaching by means of mention-selection restricted to fictive language. We can as easily ask the child to point to the horse in a picture as to point to the unicorn. By means of mention-selection the child may acquire many of the terms (such as 'dinosaur') that denote things remote from his experience. And as he learns to distinguish those among the terms so acquired that have a non-null denotive application from those that do not, he learns to distinguish factual from fictive language.

Mention-selection is not, however, restricted to learning contexts. Paintings and poems are often labeled mention-selectively. Instead of calling a picture 'Woman-with-a-Jug-Picture', we give it the short mention-selective title 'Woman with a Jug'. And instead of calling a poem 'Poem Describing Dawn', we simply call it 'Dawn'. Literary critics apply terms mention-selectively when they say things like "Hamlet was a man who couldn't make up his mind" rather than "Hamlet-descriptions are man-who-couldn't-make-up-his-mind-descriptions". A more prosaic use of mention-selection occurs when a victim, pointing to a mug shot, or hearing a description of a *modus operandi,* says, "That's the man who robbed me". If the victim's claim were denotive, then most of the police work on the case would be done. For once a victim identifies the robber, it is easy enough to take him into custody. But since the victim's claim is mention-selective, a good deal of police work is likely to remain. For the claim identifies only a representation of the assailant. The police still have to go out and find him.

Occasionally someone suggests that although 'horse' denotes horses, 'unicorn' denotes portions of unicorn-stories. This thesis is untenable, for it rests on a confusion of use and mention. When 'unicorn' is applied to such stories, it is applied mention-selectively. It singles out the words and phrases in the story that are unicorn-mentions. When applied denotively (hence, used), it denotes nothing. For among the world's fauna no unicorns are to be found. Indeed, were the thesis correct, a sentence like 'There are no such things as unicorns' would be not only false, but self-defeating. For the sentence itself contains a unicorn-mention which, according to the proposal, is what the term 'unicorn' denotes.

Fictive terms do not, of course, appear exclusively in works of fiction. It was noted above that fictive terms whose origin is in works of fiction also appear in works about fiction. This use of fictive terms is parasitic on their original use, for the ways they are originally used in fiction constrain the ways their replicas may be used in works about fiction. In addition, fictive terms are applied metaphorically in a number of contexts. Discussion of this use of fictive terms must, however, be postponed until an account of metaphor has been presented. There is yet another use of fictive terms. They are employed in factual works whose subject matter, unlike that of literary history or criticism, is not fiction. In particular, I am concerned here with the use of fictive terms in the sciences. Scientists use such terms as 'a perfect vacuum', 'an ideal gas', 'a free market', despite the widespread recognition that there are, properly speaking, no perfect vacuums, ideal gases, or free markets.

These expressions function not denotively, but mention-selectively. In introducing such a term, we introduce a label that mention-selects an idealization obtained by, e.g., letting the values of certain variables go to zero. Since the values in question do not in fact, or at any rate, do not all at once, go to zero, the idealization does not describe any actual situation. Thus, in giving an account of the semantics of a theory, we are not concerned to ask, 'What is an ideal gas?' for the answer to that is straightforward: nothing. We are concerned, rather, to ask, 'What is an ideal-gas-description?' The answer to this is provided by one or another formulation of the ideal gas law. The point of introducing such fictive terms into scientific discourse is to effect a simplification by highlighting features that the theory takes to be significant or central and overshadowing those that appear unimportant. And the scientific ground for criticizing a theory's employment of such terms is not that their denotation is null, for that was known from the beginning, but that the theory oversimplifies, or introduces inappropriate simplifications by, e.g., treating as negligible some magnitude that is, in fact, important in the systematic characterization of the behavior of actual gases.

The systems that determine the application of fictive terms in science are different from those that determine their application in fiction. The criteria of application for fictive terms in science are refined and articulated by different writers as the theories to which they belong are developed. This does not occur in systems whose realm is fiction.

A work of fiction (or a body of works of fiction) delimits the descriptions that are mention-selected by its fictive terms. We are not prepared to conclude that Shakespeare's Hamlet-descriptions are wrong, and those of a commentator right, no matter how interesting and provocative the latter's claims. We might, of course, decide that Shakespeare's Hamlet-descriptions are psychologically implausible, or politically naïve. But the system for describing fiction is such that it is not open to us to conclude that they are false. For it is Shakespeare's Hamlet-descriptions that serve as the touchstone against which the Hamlet-descriptions of the critics are to be tested. If the Hamlet-descriptions of some later writer, Schultz, are incompatible with those of Shakespeare, then unless Schultz's descriptions are simply incorrect, he has introduced a new term. In that case, 'Hamlet-description' is ambiguous. Some of its replicas denote portions of Shakespeare's work; others denote portions of Schultz's. Under a system suitable for describing fiction, a correct application of a fictive term must be relatively faithful to its applications in the work in which it originally appeared. If Schultz's *Hamlet* is sufficiently close to the original, the extension of 'Hamlet-description' may come to be delimited by portions of more than one work, as the extension of 'Faust-description' is. Otherwise, if his application is correct, Schultz's work constitutes a new original, and 'Hamlet-description' is ambiguous. There is no way according to the system to say that Schultz corrects mistakes in Shakespeare's characterization—that Schultz's Hamlet-descriptions show where Shakespeare's went wrong.

But what if some of Shakespeare's Hamlet-descriptions are incompatible with others? In that case we construct a system according to which only some of his descriptions fix Hamlet's fictive identity. (I leave it to critics to decide which ones.) Because of the role of Shakespeare's descriptions in fixing Hamlet's fictive identity, we are likely to conclude that he went wrong only if they are mutually inconsistent, not if they are inconsistent with the Hamlet-descriptions of others. The same reasoning applies if there is an inconsistency in the Faust-descriptions in the various works that are taken to fix Faust's fictive identity. If the problematic descriptions appear in different works, we may resolve the inconsistency by taking 'Faust-description' to be ambiguous, or by taking some of the Faust-descriptions appearing in them to be wrong. Which course is wiser is again left to critics to decide.

In the case of scientific discourse, such fidelity to the works in which a fictive term originates is not required. Subsequent works may challenge, correct, or refine the claims of the original without introducing ambiguity. Disagreements among economists as to which descriptions are free-market-descriptions serve as an excellent case in point. Free-market-descriptions are conditions-of-unrestricted-buying-and-selling-descriptions. But economic theorists disagree about what happens "in the limit" as restrictions on buying and selling are successively removed. Hence, they differ as to which descriptions are free-market-descriptions. A fictive term that belongs primarily to scientific discourse is autonomous from the context in which it is introduced in a way in which a fictive term whose primary occurrence is in fiction is not.

A system whose realm is scientific theories is developed to describe what are generally works in progress—and works of many hands, at that. It accords autonomy to fictive terms because the theories in its realm are developed through processes of criticism and reformulation, and are in principle always open to correction on the basis of new evidence. A system suitable for describing science then should permit revision of the mention-selective applications of fictive terms as well as of the denotive applications of factual ones as science progresses.

2. COUNTERFACTUALS

This account of fictive language provides the basis for an analysis of counterfactual sentences. Briefly, the proposal is this: counterfactual sentences are fictional sentences. Accordingly, we are concerned not with what their expressions denote, but rather with what expressions denote or mention-select them. Counterfactual sentences set forth relations held to obtain among their component expressions. Thus, 'If kangaroos had no tails, they would fall down' is correct or incorrect depending on whether kangaroo-lacking-tail-descriptions are kangaroo-falling-down-descriptions. This account has the advantage of requiring reference only to actual entities—descriptions (and, if extended in the obvious way, pictures). Nor is failure of reference a worry. Although there may be no kangaroos lacking tails, there is certainly at least one kangaroo-lacking-tail-description, for the counterfactual sentence itself includes one. Counterfactual sentences then contain replicas of expressions whose semantic classification they concern.

The problem, of course, is how to determine what those semantic relations are. When we seek to construct systems to classify fictive terms occurring in fiction or in science, our domain at least is easily identified. It is reasonably clear against what body of discourse we are to test our Hamlet-descriptions and our ideal-gas-descriptions. But against what class of descriptions are the P-descriptions of counterfactual sentences to be tested? The answer varies with context and with the presuppositions of the discourse in which a counterfactual sentence occurs. For it is these that determine what background beliefs are to be carried over into the fiction, and what beliefs are to be suspended in the fictive context.

Contrast

> If Julius Caesar were alive, he would use a catapult.

with

> If Julius Caesar were alive, he would use the atom bomb.

There seems to be no basis for saying absolutely that one is correct and the other incorrect. For whether the Caesar-descriptions we incorporate into fictions of modern warfare should be Caesar-using-catapult-descriptions, or Caesar-using-atom-bomb-descriptions depends crucially on the story we are telling or on the point we hope to make by the use of those fictions. If our point is that it is not great generals, but superior weapons that win wars, the first sentence might be appropriate. If our point is rather that a great general uses the most powerful weapons at his disposal, the second might be appropriate.

The question we are concerned with then is this: given the denoting expressions and, perhaps, some already accepted fictive expressions that are classed together under a replacement for 'P-description', to what other expressions does that replacement unambiguously apply? In attempting to discover the "essence" of water, Putnam asks, in effect, whether 'XYZ' and 'H₂O' are both water-descriptions. And in attempting to establish conditions on the reference of proper names, Kripke asks, in effect, whether an account according to which Moses never left Egypt falls under the same 'Moses-description' as the Biblical account.[3] The efforts of philosophers to determine identity across possible worlds are reconstrued according to this deflationary metaphysics as efforts to construct systems to fix the extensions of certain replacements of P-description. That is, to construct systems to determine what accounts, fictive as well as factual, are mention-selected by, e.g., proper names and natural kind terms.

Theories of counterfactuals of the sort David Lewis, Saul Kripke, and Hilary Putnam propose might be construed alternatively as theories about how we do, or as theories about how we should, classify our descriptions and pictures.[4]

If construed as descriptive theories, then empirical methods are appropriate to discover which provides the best reflection of our linguistic habits. Given the descriptions of actual cats to which 'cat-description' applies, to what fictive descriptions does it also apply? The investigation seeks to deepen our understanding of competence with respect to 'cat' by determining the things to which it applies mention-selectively as well as the things to which it applies denotively. And just as a term may be vague as to the limits of its denotive application, it may be vague as to the limits of its mention-selective application. We may be uncertain whether 'cat' applies denotively to a civet and whether it applies mention-selectively to a Martian-controlled-automaton-description.

If construed as normative, theories of counterfactuals are recommendations as to which fictive descriptions should be classed with factual descriptions under various replacements for 'P-description'. To choose among them, we must consider why descriptions of descriptions are wanted. The interests served by these descriptions are varied, so there is no more reason to expect that a single system for labeling labels will suit every purpose than there is to expect that a single system for labeling persons will do so.

The foregoing discussion has focussed on those counterfactual sentences for which evidence about our linguistic habits is particularly germane. There are others whose acceptance or rejection seems to depend on background knowledge of a somewhat different sort. Consider, for example, the sentence

If the glass were dropped, it would break.

We are still concerned with the semantic relations between a description of the antecedent and a description of the consequent. Specifically, is a the-glass-is-dropped-description a the-glass-breaks-

---

3. "Naming and Necessity", p. 277.

4. Cf. *Counterfactuals*, "Naming and Necessity", and "The Meaning of 'Meaning'".

description? But the evidence we use to decide comes largely from a physical theory which says something about crystal structure and the force of an impact. Nor is it the case that the background information to which we appeal is always an established scientific theory. Consider

> If you were to marry him, you wouldn't be happy.

Here we appeal to "common sensical" beliefs about the personalities of the protagonists and the circumstances of their relationship to decide whether a you-are-married-to-him-description is a you-are-unhappy-description. It is quite clear that with variations in the background beliefs against which we decide, we will get different answers. For the correctness of a fictive sentence varies with the story we are telling. Whether a the-glass-is-dropped-description is a the-glass-breaks-description may depend on whether the descriptions in our fiction are Earth-descriptions or moon-descriptions, for the force of gravity is crucial. And whether a you-are-married-to-him-description is a you-are-unhappy-description may depend on whether it is part of a you-go-to-live-in-rural-Wyoming-story.

This analysis of fictive language appeals only to what exists, but it recognizes that there exist pictures and descriptions as well as tables and chairs. The problem to be resolved in interpreting fictive language is how descriptions (and, by extension, pictures) are to be classified. It is resolved, as is any problem of classification, by the construction of a semantic system. There is some degree of freedom in the construction of such a system, for there is typically a good deal that is left undecided by the utterances and inscriptions it is the business of such a system to interpret. But there are constraints on the construction of such systems as well. For we are not at liberty to say anything we like in a fiction. In a fictive account as in a factual one we are typically forbidden to make statements that are logically inconsistent with one another. Other constraints, of varying force, apply to some types of fiction but not others. Although fictive accounts are normally expected to comply with natural laws, science fiction stories need not do so. In historical fiction a certain measure of historical accuracy is normally required, and so on. Similar combinations of liberties and constraints apply to systems designed for the interpretation of counterfactual sentences. Claims about what could have happened at time t are constrained by some of the historical conditions that obtained at t. Claims about what is possible are normally constrained by natural law. Yet others are constrained not by the actual facts or laws, but by what are believed to be the facts or laws. All are constrained by logic. These liberties and constraints are no less real for being tacit and varying with context.

The liberties and constraints amount to parameters on systems of descriptions of descriptions. The question 'What is possible for X?' amounts to 'What factual and fictive descriptions are X-descriptions?'—a question that will be decided differently under different systems.

According to my account of fictive reference, there is not a whole lot more than meets the eye. There is nothing but the fictive sentences themselves and the ways in which they are appropriately classified and described. The required descriptive categories need not be mentioned in the work itself. So, for example, a fictive character may be correctly labeled a Christ-figure even though no mention of Christ is to be found in the text. Accordingly, it is not always easy to determine how the work is to be appropriately described. But, however difficult it is, once we have accomplished this, our task is complete. We needn't worry about what is going on in another part of the forest while the action of *Winnie the Pooh* takes place in the Hundred Acre Wood. If the correct descriptions of the fictive claims make no commitment as to what is happening elsewhere, not only is there, as Quine says, no fact of the matter, there is no fiction of the matter either.

3. LIKENESS OF MEANING

Terms are coextensive just in case they apply to exactly the same objects. Sometimes it seems that although two terms are in fact coextensive, this is something of an accident. It could equally well have turned out that their extensions diverge. This is perhaps the case with 'creature with a heart' and 'creature with kidneys', with 'human being' and 'featherless biped' and with 'unicorn' and 'centaur'. In other cases we may be more reluctant to maintain that things could have turned out otherwise. Perhaps 'bachelor' and 'unmarried man', and 'human being' and 'rational animal' are cases of this sort.

The problem is to say how the distinction between the two sorts of case (if there really is one) is to be drawn. Plainly, we do not want to claim that pairs of the latter sort, but not of the former, have the same intension, sense, connotation, or meaning. For it remains to be explained how intensions, senses, connotations, and meanings are to be individuated. And without a criterion for their individuation, they are useless to explicate the difference in question. Accordingly, we seek to draw a finer distinction than that between sameness and difference in extension, but to restrict ourselves to the resources of an extensional language. Goodman[5] has developed a criterion to do just that.

Terms function not only as simple subjects or predicates of sentences, but also as parts of compounds. Following Goodman, let us call the denotation of a term its *primary extension,* and the denotation of any of its compounds a *secondary extension.* The extensions of some compounds depend on the extensions of their components.

    5. Cf. "On Likeness of Meaning" [PP, 221–230]; "On Some Difference About Meaning" [PP, 231–238]; and [LA, 204–205].

'Father of P' varies with different replacements for P. If P is replaced by a term whose denotation is null, such as 'a unicorn', the denotation of the resulting compound, 'father of a unicorn', is also null. A term with a null primary extension has some null secondary extensions—those that result from compounding it with expressions like 'father of'. Other compounds, however, function differently. We noted above that the extensions of 'P-description' and 'P-picture' vary independently of the extensions of the terms that replace P. There are unicorn-pictures and centaur-descriptions despite the fact that there are neither unicorns nor centaurs. Terms whose primary extensions are null then have some non-null secondary extensions. Again, terms that are alike in primary extension may differ in some secondary extensions. Although 'creature with a heart' has the same primary extension as 'creature with kidneys', it does not have all the same secondary extensions. For not every creature-with-a-heart-description is a creature-with-kidneys-description. Terms with the same primary extension may differ in fiction if not in fact.

Presumably terms that are synonymous are alike in both fictive and factual applications. This, perhaps, is what we are getting at when we distinguish between coextensive terms that could have turned out differently, and coextensive terms that could not. We are prepared to supply fictive bachelor-descriptions that are not unmarried-man-descriptions. Coextensive terms then seem to differ in meaning to the extent that they differ in their mention-selective applications.
supply fictive bachelor-descriptions that are not unmarried-man descriptions. Coextensive terms then seem to differ in meaning to the extent that they differ in their mention-selective applications.

Goodman's proposal is this: two coextensive terms are synonymous just in case every compound obtained by combining some words with one of the terms is coextensive with the compound obtained by combining exactly the same words with the other [PP, 232]. Let us call the compounds so obtained *parallel compounds*. Coextensive terms each pair of whose parallel compounds are likewise coextensive are synonymous.[6]

The requirement that parallel compounds be coextensive is quite strong. It is much stronger, for example, than the requirement that each compound of one term be coextensive with some compound of the other. Synonymy requires more than that there be some mapping of secondary extensions onto one another. It requires that there be a point-by-point agreement in both primary and secondary extensions. But the price of this agreement is high. Synonymy, so construed, is strictly intralinguistic. The definition gives no standard for interlinguistic translation, for the various replacements in compound con-

6. Let us exclude from consideration the so-called "intensional" compounds like 'meaning of P', and 'thought of P'. Since we do not know how to determine their extensions, we cannot tell whether parallel compounds are coextensive. Since we can tell what is included in the extensions of 'P-picture' and 'P-description', these compounds do not fall under the interdict.

structions must belong to the same language. The compounds that result from replacing

> dog

with

> Hund

or

> chien

by and large belong to no language.

Indeed, one might wonder whether the standard is so high as to preclude intralinguistic synonymy as well. Goodman thinks that it does. There are expressions whose form is 'P that is not Q'. These are P-descriptions, but typically are not Q-descriptions. 'Unicorn that is not a centaur' is a unicorn-description but not a centaur-description. This shows that 'unicorn-description' and 'centaur-description' differ in primary extension and thus that 'unicorn' and 'centaur' differ in meaning. This, of course, is the result we hoped to achieve. But the schema yields 'bachelor that is not an unmarried man' which demonstrates, contrary to our expectation, that 'bachelor' and 'unmarried man' differ in meaning. Indeed, it even yields 'triangle that is not a trilateral', demonstrating that 'triangle' and 'trilateral' differ in meaning [PP, 228]. We cannot burke this result by claiming that nontrilateral triangles and married bachelors are impossible, for we have found no standard of impossibility that does not depend on the extension of a term and its compounds. In any case, what we are directly concerned with here is descriptions and not their objects. And since a triangle-description that is not a trilateral-description and a bachelor-description that is not an unmarried-man-description occur in the compounds under discussion, it will be difficult to maintain that the descriptions themselves are impossible.

The schema does not, however, yield the anomalous result that replicas differ in meaning. Although 'triangle that is not a triangle' is both a triangle-description and a not-a-triangle-description, it does not follow that it both is and is not a triangle-description. For being a not-a-triangle-description is not the same as and does not entail not being a triangle-description.

> One basic principle is: *any phrase such as "_____ that is a . . ."* *is a _____ -description and a . . . -description.* Thus "_____ that is not a . . ." is both a _____ -description and a not-a- . . . -description. By a second principle, however, a not-a- . . . -description is not a . . . -description unless the first principle (or some other) makes it so [PP, 228].

It follows then that no two terms are precisely synonymous. If this result is implausible, we may want to weaken the standard for synonymy. To do so, let us exclude from consideration constructions like 'P that is not a Q' from which differences in meaning automatically result regardless of what terms we substitute for P and Q. These constructions function like a universal solvent—dissolving pretensions to synonymy of any pair of terms. But just as we may not want to conclude that all solids are soluble simply because they will dissolve in a universal solvent, perhaps we should not conclude that all terms differ in meaning just because under such a schema their secondary extensions diverge. It may be preferable then to ignore any schema from which it follows that parallel compounds of every pair of terms diverge. In that case it is not clear whether we will get the result that no two terms are exactly synonymous. Nevertheless, pairs of synonymous terms will be hard to come by. If all that is prohibited in constructing fictive descriptions is explicit logical contradiction, we should expect that the parallel compounds formed according to the schema 'P-description', which denote fictive as well as factual locutions, will differ in extension.

The consequence that exact synonymies are rare or even nonexistent is not particularly untoward. Often what appears at first blush to be exact equivalence in some magnitude turns out on examination to be merely a close approximation. We are not troubled to learn that containers that we took to be equal in volume are only approximately so. Nor should we be troubled to discover that terms we took to be synonymous are only very similar in meaning. One of the benefits of Goodman's proposal is that it gives us a way to recognize likenesses of meaning that fall sort of synonymy. By considering which parallel compounds of coextensive terms are themselves coextensive, and in what contexts other parallel compounds are so, we can distinguish kinds and degrees of likeness of meaning. It is perhaps not so important to demonstrate that 'bachelor' and 'unmarried man' are exactly synonymous if we can show that they are, in any case, very much alike in meaning.

An example of the way we can talk about likeness of meaning in a limited context may be helpful. Suppose we are interested in whether in its political application 'freedom' means (approximately) the same as 'liberty'. We will then ignore freedom-descriptions that appear in metaphysical debates concerning determinism and the denotation of 'freedom' in such metaphysical claims. We will focus on the question of whether 'freedom' and 'liberty' apply to the same political situations, and whether 'freedom-description' and 'liberty-description' apply to the same political statements. If so, and if other relevant parallel compounds line up, we should conclude that in the context with which we are concerned, 'freedom' and 'liberty' are alike in meaning.

Goodman's account avoids a misinterpretation that has plagued Quine. Both Goodman and Quine deny the analytic/synthetic distinction. But what critics of Quine (at least) often seem to miss is that it is the distinction itself that is gainsaid. Neither Goodman nor Quine maintains that there is a genuine distinction, but since every sentence falls on the synthetic side, the distinction is a useless one. According to Quine, our claims have a double dependence on language and the world, but we cannot separate out the contribution of each. Because the world contributes something, no sentence is purely analytic. But because language contributes something, no sentence is purely synthetic. A change in either language or the world suffices to turn a true sentence into a false one. It is the distinction between analytic and synthetic that is untenable. Goodman's account, by explicitly recognizing degrees of likeness of meaning, reflects this at the same time as it captures something of what the old distinction was supposed to do. With it we can mark more refined distinctions among coextensive terms and establish conditions on the interchangeability of terms that are binding on their fictive as well as their factual uses.

Secondary extensions are important for another reason as well. We saw that expressions formed by compounding a term with '-description' or '-picture' yield secondary extensions that do not depend on the term's primary extension. Thus, e.g., the extension of 'bear-description' (and, hence, a secondary extension of 'bear') is not determined by the primary extension of 'bear'. For there are fictive as well as factual bear-descriptions. And even those that are known to be fictive are partially determinative of the "meaning" of the term 'bear'.

Moreover, it is reasonable to assume that the meaning of a term influences the way we decide its application in borderline cases. So whether to call a panda 'a bear' depends not only on what animals have previously been included in the primary extension of the term, but also on what pictures and descriptions have been included in its secondary extensions. That is to say, the bear-stories that have been told and the bear-pictures that have been drawn influence the range of animals we are prepared to call 'bears'. Our fictions thus pervade our facts by influencing the construction of systems by which we fix those facts.

IV METAPHOR

1. METAPHORICAL DENOTATION

In the literal use of language, our application of old words to newly encountered objects is guided by habit and stipulation. By force of habit we will readily apply the term 'car' to most of the vehicles produced by the Ford Motor Company during the next model year, whatever their appearance or power source. And by stipulation, nothing is to be labeled 'hamburger' unless it is composed entirely of beef. Where its reference is determined by antecedently established habit or stipulation then, there is no reason to withhold a term from an object. By stipulation newly encountered ground beef patties are appropriately classified as hamburgers, and by habit newly encountered Fords are appropriately classified as cars.

In the case of metaphor, however, the application of a term to a new object is not so straightforward. For the metaphorical application of a term is both suggested and precluded by the habits and stipulations that guide its literal application [LA, 69]. Typically, a term does not have its metaphorical object in its literal extension. Consider the following passage:

> The weeds which his broad spreading leaves did shelter,
> That seemed in eating him to hold him up,
> Are plucked up root and all by Bolingbroke [*Richard II*, III, 4].

People do not belong to the literal extensions of botanical predicates. Accordingly, Richard has no sheltering leaves, nor have his flatterers roots. Nevertheless, the way weeds weaken the plants that shelter them, and disfigure the garden they infest, suggests the way Bushy and Green while under Richard's protection and apparently supporting him, undermined his reign and damaged his realm. Bolingbroke, like a gardener, had them destroyed to avoid the further damage they would do if left unchecked. We see here how the metaphorical interpretation of a term depends on its prior literal interpretation. It is because we know how to characterize plants as weeds that we know how to employ the term in the characterization of people.

In saying that the literal application of a term is semantically prior to the metaphorical, I am not just making an historical or etymological claim. It is not only because the application of 'weed' to plants antedates its application to people that the latter is deemed metaphorical. Rather, the claim to semantic priority concerns the current applica-

59

tion of the term to the objects in the two extensions. It is because the term has a particular literal extension that it is appropriate to apply it metaphorically to a given range of objects. The application of 'weed' to uncultivated plants that weaken the soil, deprive other plants of nutrients, and eventually take over a garden is what justifies the metaphorical application of 'weed' to Richard's flatterers. If neither interpretation recalls and depends on the other, then regardless of their etymology, there is in current usage no metaphor.

Ordinarily, the sorting of objects effected by a term's literal application is reflected in the sorting effected by its metaphorical application. This does not account for the metaphorical application of fictive terms, however, for they sort nothing. Whatever I am getting at when I say that Smith is a Don Juan, I am not (even metaphorically) consigning him to the null set. The metaphorical application of a fictive term reflects rather the way the term itself is sorted [WOW, 104]. Some predicates that apply mention-selectively to Don-Juan-descriptions—e.g., 'rake', 'seducer'—apply denotively to Smith. But as in other cases of metaphor, there may be no single literal predicate that serves as the basis for metaphorical transfer. Applying 'Don Juan' metaphorically to Smith may bring about a likening of Don-Juan-descriptions and Smith-descriptions that no literal predicate captures. Moreover, a fictive term may be used metaphorically in a fictional characterization, as it is when we say that Rhett Butler is a Don Juan. Since neither 'Rhett Butler' nor 'Don Juan' denotes, the metaphor brings about no reclassification of denoted objects. But a reclassification of secondary extensions is brought about. 'Don-Juan-description' applies metaphorically to what 'Rhett-Butler-description' applies literally.

A slightly different case concerns the metaphorical application of a non-null term in a fictive context. Consider 'Don Juan is a wolf'. The predicate 'wolf' literally denotes wolves and metaphorically denotes obsessively amorous men. Accordingly, it metaphorically mention-selects obsessively-amorous-man-descriptions, including Don-Juan-descriptions. To say that Don Juan is a wolf is then to effect a metaphorical classification of Don-Juan-descriptions. The metaphorical application of a term thus brings about a new classification not only of the objects it denotes, but also of the pictures, descriptions, and the like that it mention-selects.

Literal application is guided by habit, and where habit leaves off, decided by fiat. We might fix the literal extension of 'weed' by deciding to include (or to exclude) clover. The function of our decision is to render determinate, or at least more determinate, the extension of a predicate that is vague in its ordinary usage as to its applicability to the plants in question. The important thing to notice is that there is nothing in that usage to prohibit the application of 'weed' to clover.

A term like 'weed' that applies to many things is a general term. If all of its replicas apply to the same things, the term is unambiguous. But if one of a pair of syntactic replicas has in its extension something that is not in the extension of another, the term is ambiguous. Since some replicas of 'weed' denote unwanted plants but no clothes, and others denote mourning clothes but no plants, 'weed' is ambiguous.

If an expression is simply ambiguous, separate rules and habits determine its application to the objects in each extension. Simply ambiguous replicas are semantically independent of one another. Knowing that 'weed' denotes undesirable plants is of no help in identifying the articles of clothing that are called 'weeds'.

To apply a term metaphorically is not, however, to introduce a simple ambiguity into the language. Metaphor resembles simple ambiguity in that a term that applies metaphorically to an object does not typically apply to it literally. But while the several interpretations of a simply ambiguous expression are semantically independent of one another, the metaphorical application of a term depends on its literal application. It is because some tokens of 'weed' apply literally to unwanted plants that others apply metaphorically to Richard's flatterers. The role of 'weed' in classifying people then recalls and is guided by its role in classifying plants.

A metaphor, according to Goodman, is "an affair between a predicate with a past and an object that yields while protesting" [LA, 69]. Metaphor depends on both attraction and resistance. A term resists its metaphorical application, for typically the objects to which it applies metaphorically do not belong to its literal extension. But it attracts that application as well, for it likens the objects in its metaphorical extension to those in its literal extension.

Both attraction and resistance can fade with overfamiliarity. When this happens, the metaphor dies. If it is the attraction between literal and metaphorical applications that is lost, the term becomes simply ambiguous. Perhaps calling a mind 'sharp' no longer invites comparison with knives, blades, needles, and the like. In that case 'sharp' no longer applies metaphorically to minds. It is simply ambiguous. Some replicas denote knives but no minds; others denote minds but no knives. If it is the resistance between literal and metaphorical applications that is lost, the literal application of the term is expanded. The term 'calculator' used to be applied to machines metaphorically; now it is applied literally. For we no longer resist saying that both people and machines do arithmetic. As resistance died, the literal extension of the term was broadened to comprehend both the people and the machines who do sums.

2. METAPHORICAL SYSTEMS

The metaphorical application of a term is rarely a semantically isolated occurrence. Whether explicitly or tacitly, an entire scheme is typically employed metaphorically to sort the objects in a new realm. The assignment of predicates of the scheme to the new realm reflects their prior assignments to the objects in their literal extensions.

In some cases the metaphor may consist simply in providing new labels for classes already recognized by predicates that apply literally to the objects in question. Then there are literal expressions with which the metaphorical expressions are coextensive. Labeling alternatives in a binary system 'pass' and 'fail' is an example of this. In these cases the function of the metaphor is to point up or exemplify features which are shared by the metaphorical and the literal extensions of the term.

But such cases are comparatively rare. Typically there is no literal scheme that sorts the objects in a realm into the same classes as the metaphorical scheme. So typically the metaphorical scheme effects a novel sorting of the objects in the realm as well as exemplifying features they share with the objects to which the terms apply literally. The entire scheme need not, of course, be explicitly mapped onto the new realm. In the metaphorical as well as the literal case semantic systems are systems of implicit alternatives. If we label a new social program a 'war on poverty' we introduce a novel network of terms for characterizing our responses to social conditions. With some we are at peace. Among these are allies in the current war (e.g., public education), as well as potential foes (perhaps industrial pollution) with which we are not yet ready to do battle. Our various attempts to alleviate poverty can be described in terms of campaigns, battles, skirmishes, and be evaluated as victories or defeats. These need not be made explicit. By the simple fact of calling our program a war, we have made the descriptive resources of the system to which 'war' belongs available for describing the social realm of which poverty is a part.

Metaphor does not require that the realm to which a scheme is newly applied be an alien one. In some cases the scheme is applied to its home realm in such way as to effect a novel sorting. If we label someone 'an intellectual midget', we employ a scheme that literally classifies people on the basis of stature to classify them on the basis of learning. A new sorting of the realm results, for physical size is no measure of learning.

A consequence of metaphorical resorting of the home realm is that the same term may apply literally and metaphorically to a single object. A man of impressive size and achievement is both literally and metaphorically a man of weight. A problem of interpretation may result. It is clear that when the expression is applied to someone great in bulk but modest in achievement, it is to be construed literally. When applied to someone modest in bulk but great in achievement, it is to be construed metaphorically. But when it is applied to someone of significant size and accomplishments, its interpretation may not be obvious.

The problem is resolved when we discover what semantic system is in effect—when we discover how the scheme is applied to the realm. We do this by seeing how other individuals in the realm are sorted by the scheme. In calling someone a man of weight, is he being compared (implicitly or explicitly) with others lesser in size or lesser in achievement? When contextual cues are too meager, there may be no basis for deciding a particular case. The case then is one of interpretive indecision. "Either interpretation will enable us to understand what attribution is accomplished in [the context] by the presence of [the term]. Yet we cannot find sufficient reason to choose between them; the alternative interpretations are equally reasonable."[1] The matter must be decided by stipulation.

But suppose the problem is even more general. Suppose literal and metaphorical replicas of a term are coextensive. If all and only those who are literally men of weight are also metaphorically men of weight, can we still distinguish between the literal and the metaphorical construals without appealing to 'senses'? We can. As in the previous case we interpret replicas of 'a man of weight' now literally, now metaphorically according as a literal or a metaphorical scheme is in effect in the context in which a particular replica appears. We can then sort replicas of 'man of weight' into literal-man-of-weight-descriptions and metaphorical-man-of-weight-descriptions. Although all and only persons who are literally men of weight are metaphorically men of weight, it is not the case that all and only descriptions as literally a man of weight are descriptions as metaphorically a man of weight. Coextensive literal and metaphorical replicas thus differ in mention-selection.

Metaphor then is a displacement of the original application of a term or a scheme under the influence of the rules and habits that determine its original application. There are metaphorical displacements that involve neither a shift of a scheme to a new realm nor a reorganization of the home realm by a novel application of the scheme. These apply a scheme metaphorically to a realm to which it applies literally without altering the organization of the realm that its literal application effects. The objects that are classed together under a single metaphorical predicate are just those that are classed together under a single literal predicate. What the metaphorical devices do is relabel the objects so classified [LA, 81–5].

In irony the scheme is simply inverted, as when we call an archenemy an old friend. The same sortings are effected by the ironical scheme as by the literal, but the opposite predicates are applied to the objects so sorted.

In hyperbole the scheme is displaced downward. Expressions at the lower end of the scheme lack application and the scheme is exhausted without characterizing objects at the upper end of the realm. Thus, a miserable student is labeled 'adequate', and a reasonably good one 'superb'. No superlatives remain for characterizing the genuinely outstanding student, and there are, on this application of the scheme, no bad students.

Understatement is displacement upward. The bottom of the realm

1. *Beyond the Letter*, p. 16.

is unlabeled, while the top of the scheme lacks application. A good paper is labeled 'passable' and an outstanding one, 'quite good'. None is sufficiently good to merit the label 'brilliant' and, owing to the displacement of the scheme, genuinely bad papers defy description.

A consequence of the displacement that occurs in hyperbole and understatement is that under the metaphorical application of a scheme some of the objects in a realm go unlabeled. To avoid this we can introduce an intensifying adverb such as 'very'. In the case of understatement it attaches to the minimum label of the scheme; in the case of hyperbole, to the maximum. Since 'very' iterates, we can extend a scheme as far downward or upward as is required to cover the entire realm.

The use of hackneyed metaphors invites criticism of one's style. The use of mixed metaphors is a more serious matter. In a mixed metaphor separate schemes are simultaneously applied metaphorically to a single realm. Confusion results. In their metaphorical application, it is not clear how the predicates of the two schemes are supposed to relate to each other, and as a result it is not clear how their joint application sorts the objects in the realm. Consider the following (admittedly unfortunate) example:

> As high priest of foreign policy, he was captain of the ship of state.

The metaphorical application of 'high priest' grafts an ecclesiastical scheme onto a secular realm; that of 'captain of the ship of state', a nautical scheme onto a political realm. Each application is familiar enough. The difficulty arises from their joint application. For the relation of a high priest to congregation and clergy is not that of a ship's captain to passengers and crew. It is thus not obvious what sorting of the secular political realm is effected by the metaphor, nor what comparisons between objects in the literal and metaphorical realms are instigated. A mixed metaphor then is a semantic error, for its extension is likely to be indeterminate.

The classification of a token as literal or metaphorical depends on the system in terms of which it is interpreted. Different systems classify particular tokens differently. Under a system that construes the extension of a term narrowly, relatively few of its applications are literal, relatively many, metaphorical. Under one that construes its extensions more broadly, more of its applications are literal. According to a system that labels only animal appendages 'legs', all talk of table legs is metaphorical. According to a more liberal system, supports for animals and furniture alike fall under the literal application of 'leg'.

Where replicas have different extensions, it is the system under which they are classified that decides whether the difference is a matter of metaphor or ambiguity. If the application of a term to the objects in one domain precedes and informs its application to the objects in the other, the latter application is metaphorical. If the applications are semantically independent, the expression is ambiguous. It is not always obvious which is the case, and different systems are likely to yield different verdicts. Whether 'lame duck' is ambiguous or metaphorical depends on whether, according to the referential system in use, politicians who have failed to win reelection exemplify features of disabled water fowl.

3. METAPHORICAL TRUTH

Although it is often denied, correct metaphorical sentences are genuinely true and metaphorical expressions genuinely denote the objects to which they apply. Isaiah Berlin[2] classified thinkers as hedgehogs or foxes according as they relate everything to a single central thesis or pursue a variety of unrelated cognitive ends. Even though 'Plato is a hedgehog' is literally false, under Berlin's system it is metaphorically true; whereas 'Plato is a fox' is both literally and, under that system, metaphorically false. 'True' and 'false' then are not coextensive respectively with 'literally true' and 'literally false', nor is 'denotes' coextensive with 'literally denotes'.

This claim is consonant with Tarski's theory of truth.[3] A truth definition can be given for any interpreted extensional language, so long as its primitives are finite in number, and certain semantic terms do not belong to it. A truth definition is formally correct only if it yields no paradoxical sentences such as

This very sentence is false.

It is materially adequate if the sentences it yields are replacements for the following schema:

(T) X is true if and only if p.

where the name of a sentence replaces X and the sentence itself (or its translation into the metalanguage) replaces p. The interpretation of the primitives is given trivially by a list. Thus 'snow' denotes snow; 'white' denotes each white thing, etc. Nothing in Tarski's formal definition of truth for a language mandates any particular choice of primitives or any particular assignments of objects as their extensions. Any semantic system that satisfies the aforementioned formal requirements has a truth definition.

2. Isaiah Berlin, *The Hedgehog and the Fox* (New York: Simon & Schuster, 1953), p. 1.

3. Cf. Alfred Tarski, "The Concept of Truth in Formalized Languages", *Logic, Semantics, and Metamathematics* (Oxford: The Clarendon Press, 1956). Inasmuch as Tarski's account makes use of set theory, philosophers who share Goodman's nominalist scruples are not likely to find this impressive. But for those philosophers who take Tarski to have given a formally correct and materially adequate definition of truth, the discovery that it applies indifferently to literal and metaphorical sentences should be of some interest.

According to the account offered above, metaphorical systems (except those containing 'true', 'denotes', and the like) typically do so. Metaphor consists in applying a scheme to a new realm, or in applying it to its old realm in a new way. Any scheme that has a truth definition when interpreted literally can be given a truth definition when interpreted metaphorically. Whether snow is identified with solid crystalline precipitation or with cocaine, 'snow' denotes snow. And 'snow is white' is true if and only if snow is white. Since 'true' is a semantic predicate, a truth definition can be given only for an interpreted language. But whether the interpretation is literal or metaphorical is a matter of indifference.

Granted, more than the construction of a truth definition is required to show that a new application of a scheme is metaphorical rather than arbitrary. The construction of a truth definition explains what it is for the sentences of a system to be true, not what it is for them to be metaphorical. A complete account of metaphorical truth clearly requires both. Part of what is needed has been supplied already by requiring that the relations of inclusion and exclusion that obtain in the scheme's literal application also obtain in its metaphorical application. Another part must wait until the referential device of exemplification has been explained. The point here is that if we accept Tarski's account of what is required for a formally correct and materially adequate definition of truth for a language, there is no reason to deny that some metaphorical claims, even if literally false, are true.

Each system then is given its own truth definition. Under a literal system 'Plato is a hedgehog' is false; under a metaphorical one it is true. The fact that we define 'truth' for separate systems rather than for the language as a whole is no special cause for concern. Tarski recognized from the outset that, as it stands, an entire natural language cannot be given a truth definition. Regimentation is required to exclude paradox-generating semantic terms from the object language and to fix relations between primitive and nonprimitive terms. Alternative systems of regimentation take different terms to be primitive. Since primitive denotation determines ontological commitment, under different systems of regimentation a language is ontologically committed to different things. Under a system Quine favors, there are only physical objects in space-time; under one Davidson prefers, there are also events.

Ontological pluralism then is not ruled out from the start. Moreover, every attempt to give a single truth definition for English (or any other natural language) has fallen far short of its goal. A large range of sentences has typically been excluded from the scope of a truth-predicate: not just metaphorical sentences, but also 'metaphysical' sentences, evaluative sentences, and statements of propositional attitude. Since the formal requirements for a truth definition dicate no such exclusion, it is better to define 'true' for each system to which such sentences belong than to rule that they are to be altogether excluded from the range of a truth predicate because they fail to fit into a preferred regimentation of the language of science.

Empiricists argue that the primitive terms of the language must refer to sensations or sense data. Physicalists maintain that they must refer to whatever a correct physical theory takes to be primitive. Both contentions go beyond what is required for a formally correct, materially adequate definition of truth. Empiricism and physicalism are, of course, not just (or even primarily) theories of language. It may well be the case that a particular choice of primitives is best suited to each of their philosophical programs. But it has not been established that any such choice is required for a truth definition *per se*. All that can legitimately be required in advance is that the sentences it yields satisfy Convention (T). And Tarski's theory does so—for both literal and metaphorical systems.

Davidson[4] contends that a truth definition for a language yields semantic rules for that language. Because he thinks no such rules can be given for metaphors, he denies that metaphorical sentences are true.[5] But the "rules" that a truth definition yields for its primitive vocabulary are trivial and are equally satisfied whether a sentence is interpreted literally or metaphorically. So if we accept Davidson's contention that a truth definition gives semantic rules for the language or system to which it applies, there is no reason to deny that there are rules for interpreting metaphors.

To avoid semantic paradox, we need not banish all semantic terms from the object language. Only those coextensive with 'true', 'false', and 'denotes' need be excluded.[6] Specifically, the inclusion of 'literal(ly)' and 'metaphorical(ly)' in the object language gives rise to no paradox. If they are included in the object language, then there are semantic rules for metaphorical truth which precisely parallel those for literal truth.

$$\text{'}X \text{ is } p\text{' is metaphorically true} \equiv X \text{ is metaphorically } p.$$

just as

$$\text{'}X \text{ is } p\text{' is literally true} \equiv X \text{ is literally } p.$$

If 'literally' and 'metaphorically' are excluded from the object language, we are left with the original formulation of Convention (T):

4. Donald Davidson, "Semantics for Natural Language", *The Logic of Grammar*, ed. Donald Davidson and Gilbert Harman (Encino: Dickenson Publishing Co., 1975), p. 18. He makes the same point in a number of other papers as well.

5. Except, of course, metaphorical sentences like 'No man is an island' which are true under their literal interpretation. Cf. Donald Davidson, "What Metaphors Mean", *On Metaphor* ed. Sheldon Sacks (Chicago: University of Chicago Press, 1979), pp. 29–45.

6. If we are platonists, of course, we must also limit the sets we admit into our ontology so as to avoid the set theoretical paradoxes. How to choose among the various ways of doing so is not germane to the issue under discussion.

$$\text{'}X \text{ is } p\text{'} \text{ is true } \equiv X \text{ is } p.$$

But this is indifferent as between literal and metaphorical readings.

It might be replied that Davidson is concerned with rules for primitive denotation, not just with sentences that satisfy Convention (T). But the same point can be made for these. If 'literal(ly)' and 'metaphorical(ly)' are excluded from the object language,

'snow' denotes snow

is indifferent as between literal and metaphorical readings. If they are included,

'snow' literally denotes literal snow,

and

'snow' metaphorically denotes metaphorical snow.

The so-called rules of primitive denotation remain trivial. We no more know how to identify the stuff to which 'snow' applies metaphorically on the basis of the latter rule than we know how to identify the stuff to which 'snow' applies literally on the basis of the former.

Davidson is convinced that the understanding of each metaphor is a distinct achievement. Because on his account metaphorical sentences are typically false but suggestive, he contends that there is no general linguistic competence for metaphor. Discovery of what a metaphorical sentence suggests requires special insight into how a manifestly false sentence (or, less frequently, a trivially true one) functions, or how its author intends it to function in the context in which it appears.

The denial that understanding metaphor is part of our linguistic competence is misguided. The habits that constitute our competence to use and understand a term or scheme in its literal application determine what sorting it effects when applied metaphorically to an alien realm. A scheme can be applied metaphorically to practically any realm. But it cannot effect an arbitrary sorting of the objects in its new realm. Our competence with the terms of a scheme determines how they sort even when what they sort is new.

4. METAPHOR AS COGNITIVE

Davidson's view is based on the conviction that metaphor is noncognitive. This thesis is familiar enough. But it is difficult to maintain in light of some of the ways metaphors function in indisputably cognitive disciplines.

Boyd[7] has discussed the way in which the language of computer science has been applied metaphorically in cognitive psychology. Psychologists apply a scheme of organization that has proved successful in systematizing one domain in the hope of understanding another. He argues that the metaphors cannot be discounted as merely illustrative or decorative, for psychologists currently have no nonmetaphorical scheme capable of marking the same distinctions. The metaphorical scheme drawn from computer science then organizes the psychological realm in a way that no literal scheme does. If that mode of organization is of value to psychology, then at least until a coextensive literal scheme is developed, the metaphor is ineliminable.

The metaphor serves to focus research, one of whose goals is the discovery of correct literal descriptions of the human cognitive processes it characterizes metaphorically. Notice that the aim of that research is not to discover what the originator intended in using the metaphor. Cognitive scientists are engaged in solving a problem whose solution is no more known to the person who first posed it than it is to other investigators working in the field. The conviction that something important about human cognitive processes is captured by their metaphorical description in terms taken from computer science guides research into those processes, not into the intentions of the person who first voiced that conviction. Speakers' intentions are thus no more important in the interpretation of metaphorical claims than they are in the interpretation of literal claims.

The original author's claims are not authoritative. They may be amended, corrected, or rejected by other investigators employing the same metaphorical scheme. In science a metaphorical claim functions like any other hypothesis. It is articulated, clarified, disambiguated, and extended by diverse members of the scientific community. It does not reside in a single work, nor is it the property of a single author. Like a literal hypothesis, a metaphorical one will be incorporated into a scientific theory if it proves fruitful, explanatory, and (at least approximately) true.

There seems then to be no important difference in the cognitive roles of literal and metaphorical claims in science. Both are open to intersubjective scrutiny. Both can be contested, confirmed or disconfirmed by evidence, accepted and incorporated into a science or rejected as false, or as trivial, or as lacking in explanatory power. The computer metaphor, with its talk of inputs, accessing, retrieval systems, and the like, facilitates communication and verbal reasoning concerning human cognitive processes. The metaphor then both organizes the phenomena for investigation and provides a vocabulary with which to carry out that investigation. It is implausible, at best, to claim that a metaphor that plays these roles is not functioning cognitively.

7. Richard Boyd, "Metaphor and Theory Change", *Metaphor and Thought* ed. Andrew Ortony (Cambridge: Cambridge University Press, 1979), pp. 359–364.

These cognitive functions are not peculiar to scientific metaphors. In the arts, philosophy, politics, and everyday life, metaphors function analogously. The cognitive roles of metaphorical sentences thus seem to be much the same as those of literal sentences.

Metaphors have another cognitive function as well. Recall that a scheme determines a system of kinds according to which the objects in a realm are classified. The scheme does not provide a label for every set of objects. One function of a metaphor is to introduce a new mode of organization of the objects in the realm by classifying under a single label objects that are classed under distinct literal labels [MM, 126–7]. Metaphor thus increases our conceptual repertoire. It enlarges our stock of predicates for classifying the objects in a domain. This might, of course, be done without the use of metaphor. We can simply introduce a new literal taxonomy to effect novel groupings of those objects. But the problem is to discover which groupings are wanted. The metaphorical application of a scheme to a new realm employs a mode of organization that has already proved useful in systematizing another domain. We are comfortable with the terminology, even though its metaphorical application is new. A metaphor thus makes use of conceptual resources that we have already developed. It thereby facilitates comprehension and communication concerning the newly organized realm. At the same time it exemplifies similarities between its literal and metaphorical realms.

This is not to say that every true metaphorical sentence is cognitively valuable. Some, like some true literal sentences, are banal, boring, trite, or trivial. Others, although illuminating, are not suited to the cognitive purposes for which they are introduced. This, perhaps, is the case when evolutionary predicates are applied metaphorically in the social sciences. Even if they yield interesting descriptions of human behavior, those descriptions do not contribute to the cognitive goals of disciplines which seek to explain behavior conceived as action. But we should not expect that questions of the cognitive value or suitability of particular metaphors will be answered by a general theory of reference.

V EXEMPLIFICATION

1. SAMPLES

The samples we encounter are various, and the uses to which they are put diverse. The model home on a development site, the prototype of a jet plane, and the free bottle of shampoo which arrives in the mail are integral parts of sales campaigns. A sample problem worked out in a text is an illustration of characteristic problems and acceptable modes of solution in a given discipline. And an example of the way you can expect to be treated or of the sort of person you are likely to become, may serve as a promise or a threat. I am not concerned, however, to catalogue the different roles that samples play or the different enterprises of which they are a part. Rather, I want to determine just what it is for something to function as a sample.

Let us begin by considering a familiar sample—a chip of paint on a manufacturer's sample card. This particular chip is blue, one-half inch long, one-quarter inch wide, and rectangular in shape. It is the third chip on the left on the top row of a card manufactured in Baltimore on a Tuesday. The chip then instantiates each of the predicates in the previous two sentences, and many others as well. But it clearly isn't a sample of all of them. Under its standard interpretation, it is a sample of 'blue', but not of such predicates as 'rectangular' and 'made in Baltimore'. How does its relation to 'blue' differ from its relation to these other predicates? Its being a sample of 'blue' does not depend on its instantiation of the label being particularly conspicuous or striking as compared with its instantiation of other labels. Many ostentatiously blue things—such as electric-blue roller skates—are not samples of the predicate. Nor need the chip's instantiation of 'blue' be particularly noteworthy. If all the other samples on the card are circular, 'rectangular' is likely to be the more salient predicate. Even so, interpreted as paint samples usually are, the chip is a sample of 'blue', not of 'rectangular'.

There is some temptation to maintain that we should be able to identify the labels of which the chip is a sample "just by looking". Although this does not explain why it is a sample of 'blue' and not of 'rectangular', we at least have reason to deny that it is a sample of 'made in Baltimore'. But the proposal clearly won't do. It is notoriously difficult to distinguish between "observational" and "nonobservational" predicates, so the prospect of specifying what we can tell "just by looking" is not promising. In any case, the distinction, however we draw it, will not solve our problem. For there are samples of

71

just about any predicate we care to mention. The paint chip may be a sample of 'latex', 'mildew resistant', and 'long lasting' as well as of 'blue'. It may even be used by the Chamber of Commerce as a sample of 'made in Baltimore'.

There is no significant difference between the way the paint chip instantiates 'blue' and the way it instantiates such predicates as 'rectangular' and 'made in Baltimore'. The relevant difference between these predicates concerns what it does besides instantiating them. Something serves as a sample when it functions as a symbol for a label it instantiates [LA, 53]. It refers to that label and thereby acts as a representative of the stuff to which the label applies. The paint chip is then a sample of the labels it both instantiates and refers to. It is an aid in choosing house paint because we know that any label of which it is a sample applies equally to the rest of the stuff "of the same kind". If it is a sample of 'teal blue', 'semi-gloss', and 'washable', we know that buying "that kind of paint" is buying teal blue, semi-gloss, washable paint. But since it is not a sample of 'made in Baltimore', it carries no commitment regarding the place of manufacture of the rest of the paint "of that kind".

From the thesis that samples are symbols, it follows that a wide variety of objects not usually considered to be symbols sometimes function as such. The distinction between things that are samples and things that are not is not a hard and fast ontological distinction, but varies with circumstances and depends on the way in which the things are used.

A portion of cereal may simply be breakfast. In that case, it neither refers nor symbolizes. It does not function as a sample of anything. Then again, it may be a sample of vitamin-enriched, sugar-coated, Oat Toasties. If so, the consumer is supposed to project some of the labels it instantiates onto the rest of that brand of cereal. Among these, presumably, are 'vitamin-enriched', 'toasted-oat flavored', and 'sugar-coated', but probably not 'packaged in single-serving boxes', or 'arrives in the mail', and certainly not 'free'. In another context, however, it may function as a sample of the latter predicates, not the former ones. This might be the case if it is held up as an example of inspired marketing techniques. Manufacturers of quite different products might attempt to reproduce the Oat Toasties success, not by creating products to which 'vitamin-enriched', 'toasted-oat flavored', and 'sugar-coated' apply, but by designing their marketing campaigns around portions of their own products to which 'free', 'arrives in the mail', and 'packaged in single-serving boxes' apply.

Interpreting samples thus involves determining whether a given object functions as a sample at all, and if it does, discovering to which among the labels it instantiates it also refers. Even where there is no change in the labels it instantiates, variations in context may bring about changes in which of them it symbolizes. This is why in different contexts the same object can be a sample of quite different predicates.

The interpretation of samples, like the interpretation of denoting symbols, is thus relative to a semantic system [LA, 53]. Understanding how (and whether) something functions as a sample requires knowing something about the system in effect, and the role that object plays in the system. Some sample systems are highly standardized and easily learned. Under their normal interpretations, tailors' swatches and paint chips belong to systems of this kind. As a result, we have little difficulty identifying the labels they sample. Other cases are not so straightforward. It may be easy to recognize the Oat Toasties give-away as an example of inspired marketing. but difficult to say just what makes it so—difficult, that is, to identify the labels that, as inspired marketing, it serves as a sample of. Delineating the system to which those labels belong may well be a long and painstaking process.

In this chapter I discuss the semantics of samples. Exemplification, the relation of a sample to a label of which it is a sample, is widespread. Symbols function as samples, or have the semantic structure of samples, in art works, scientific experiments, and mathematical proofs, as well as in marketing campaigns. Moreover, interpreting samples is crucial to learning. But before all of this can be established, a good deal more has to be said about what exemplification is.

2. EXEMPLIFICATIONAL REFERENCE

When an object exemplifies a label, it both refers to and instantiates that label [LA, 53]. Let us call such an object *an exemplar*.[1] Exemplification then is like denotation in being a mode of reference, but it differs from denotation in direction [LA, 65]. Denotational reference goes from a label to the objects to which that label applies. Exemplificational reference goes from an object to labels that apply to it. If 'green' denotes grass, then 'green' refers to grass; if grass exemplifies 'green', then grass refers to 'green'. Exemplification is not, however, the converse of denotation. To denote an object, a term need only refer to it. But to exemplify a term, an object must both refer to and instantiate that term. Only if grass is (literally or metaphorically) green can it exemplify 'green'. Because it involves instantiation as well as reference, exemplification is but a subrelation of the converse of denotation [LA, 59].

An objection should probably be raised at this point. I said that exemplification is the relation between a sample and its referent. I also said that it is labels that are the objects of exemplification. But when we consider our unstudied talk about samples, it does not appear to be true that we take labels to be their referents. We speak of samples of blue paint, not of 'blue paint', and of Oat Toasties, not of

---

1. Philosophers have criticized Goodman's contention that works of art function as samples of the labels they exemplify. Although I'm not convinced of the validity of this criticism, I use the term 'exemplar' rather than 'sample' so as not to beg the question. In practical contexts, at least, exemplars are samples.

'Oat Toasties'. If ordinary discourse is to be our guide, it is the extension of a label, not the label itself that seems to be the referent of a sample. In that case, we must either take the position that extensions are the objects of exemplification, or abandon the thesis that samples symbolize by exemplifying.

But perhaps we are going too fast. We may be wrong to take ordinary discourse to be our guide in this matter. For our unstudied talk about samples may be but another instance of the confusion between use and mention that Quine so often decries. Are we just speaking with the vulgar when we speak of samples of blue paint rather than of 'blue paint'? Or do the vulgar have a point? I hope to show that a better theory results if we take labels rather than their extensions to be the referents of samples. Still, there are arguments favoring each interpretation. If our ordinary talk about samples betrays a confusion of use and mention, at least it is not a simple confusion.

One reason for preferring the thesis that it is extensions that are exemplified is the solution it affords to the problem of failure of reference. We know that failure of denotational reference occurs whenever there exists a denoting symbol whose denotation is null. If we want a fuller account of how such a symbol functions semantically (as we do, for example, in the discussion of fictive labels), we look to its non-null compounds. Is there a parallel problem for exemplificational reference? If so, exemplifying symbols exist, but the things to which they are supposed to refer do not. Since not every class is labelled, if we insist that labels are the objects of exemplification, there is a *prima facie* reason to think that such failure of reference will occur. In the case of denotation, failure of reference occurs because of the nonexistence of objects; should it occur in the case of exemplification, it will be because of the nonexistence of labels.

The problem can perhaps be seen if we consider the note produced by an oboeist to which other members of an orchestra tune their instruments. The note exemplifies a certain pitch, but which one? To simply identify it as an A is far too crass, for then all the musicians need do to play in tune is hit the right notes. In that case, the oboeist's action is superfluous. The reason that his action is not superfluous, of course, is that a more refined level of attunement is wanted than is to be achieved by simply hitting the right notes. And the note he produces sets the standard for that level of attunement. The problem (for a theory of exemplification, if not for an orchestra) is that we may have no sufficiently precise verbal classification of the note he produces. If what the note exemplifies is a pitch for which we can produce no adequate description, and if it is labels that are exemplified, then it seems that the oboeist's note is an exemplifying symbol that lacks a referent.

But this conclusion just won't do, for the note does set a standard of attunement which the musicians seek to match, and for which they can be legitimately faulted if they fail to match. If the note's exemplification is null, if, that is, the note fails to refer, it cannot perform its normative function. For in that case all notes to which musicians tune their instruments are co-referential, and a precise standard of attunement is not forthcoming.

If we treat sets as the objects of exemplificational reference, this problem does not arise. For there are many sets if any. The oboeist's note then exemplifies the set of all notes that match it. And no matter how refined our standard for matching that note, there will always be a nonempty set of sounds that satisfy that standard. Accordingly, if sets are the objects of exemplification, there is little threat of failure of exemplificational reference. For even if it exemplifies nothing else, a sample can still exemplify the unit set of which it is the sole member.

The threat of failure of reference is significantly diminished if we take sets rather than labels to be the objects of exemplification. To be sure, doubts can be raised about the wisdom of admitting sets into our ontology at all, but in any ontology that admits them there are likely to be a lot more of them than there are labels. Nevertheless, the semantic and set-theoretic paradoxes demonstrate that there are labels to which no sets correspond. Accordingly, there remains some prospect of failure of reference if the paradoxical locutions exemplify.

The difficulty appears if we consider Berry's paradoxical phrase: 'the least integer not nameable in fewer than nineteen syllables'. What set might it exemplify? Perhaps the set of paradoxical expressions. This raises no problems, but it also does nothing to explain the paradox, which results because the phrase is an integer-name containing only eighteen syllables. Since the phrase points up or refers to this disconcerting fact about itself, it apparently exemplifies the paradox. The phrase then refers to and is included in[2] some set that contains an integer that is both not nameable in fewer than nineteen syllables and nameable in eighteen syllables. But nineteen is greater than eighteen, so there is no such integer, and thus no set containing such an integer. We cannot then explain the paradox by appeal to exemplification if sets are the objects of exemplification.

If, however, it is labels that are exemplified, the paradox is easily explained. The phrase exemplifies, and thus instantiates, both 'the least integer not nameable in fewer than nineteen syllables' and 'an integer nameable in eighteen syllables'. But nineteen being greater than eighteen, an integer-name that instantiates both of these labels names no integer. And at least until we distinguish between integer-names and names of intergers, the existence of an apparently well formed integer-name that names no integer seems paradoxical.

Still, there are well-known ways of handling the paradoxes—ways that do not depend on exemplification. So perhaps the fact that they

---

2. When we speak of exemplification of sets, the exemplar must be included in the set it refers to. An inclusion requirement then replaces the instantiation requirement that obtains if it is labels that are exemplified.

cannot be explained by the exemplification of sets is no major criticism of the thesis that it is sets that are exemplified.

There is, however, another problem to which the exemplification of labels yields a better solution than the exemplification of sets. This one concerns coextensive labels. If sets are exemplified, then an object exemplifies a set regardless of how that set is identified. But this does not appear to be the case. 'Rational animal' is presumably coextensive with 'featherless biped'. Still, a naked marathoner might well exemplify the latter even though he seems not to exemplify the former. Again, even if teal-blue paint is manufactured only in Baltimore, the sample on the paint card exemplifies 'teal-blue paint', not 'teal-blue paint manufactured in Baltimore'. It seems preferable then to take the labels themselves rather than their extensions to be the referents of exemplifying symbols.

The focus on labels rather than on their extensions recalls the account of fictive terms developed above. Even though all and only unicorns are griffins, it is not the case that all and only unicorn-descriptions are griffin-descriptions. Similarly, even though all and only featherless bipeds are rational animals, it is not the case that all and only featherless-biped-exemplifiers are rational-animal-exemplifiers.

Taking labels to be the objects of exemplification yields a more sensitive semantic device than taking sets does. One person might exemplify 'featherless biped'; another, 'rational animal'; and yet a third, both labels. But because the labels are coextensive, if it is sets that are exemplified, each of the three exemplifies the same set. It is preferable then to take labels to be the objects of exemplification. But can we guarantee that the supply of labels will be adequate? Or are we forced to fall back on the exemplification of sets because they pose less of a threat of failure of reference? If, following Goodman [LA, 57], we recognize that not all labels are verbal, I suggest that we can assure an adequate supply of labels.

To show this, I want to begin by discussing the classification of verbal labels. Consider, for example, 'onomatopoetic'. This term applies to words like 'hiss', 'meow', and 'bobwhite' because their pronunciation reproduces sounds associated with their referents. It is clear than an appropriate replica of 'meow' might exemplify 'onomatopoetic', given that there is such a term in the language. But what should we say of the interpretation of that replica in a sublanguage that differs from English only in that it lacks the term 'onomatopoetic'? Obviously, the replica doesn't exemplify 'onomatopoetic', for that term simply isn't there to be exemplified. Are we forced to conclude that it doesn't exemplify at all? I think not. Instead, let us say that it exemplifies the makeshift predicate 'meow-predicate'.

Granted, until the system to which the new term belongs is developed further we don't know what else is denoted by 'meow-predicate'. Thus, we don't know whether the exemplified label groups together an interesting and important class of terms. Moreover, there is no reason to believe that all exemplifying replicas of 'meow' have the same reference. Accordingly, if all we know about 'meow-predicate' is that it is the referent of some exemplifying replicas of 'meow', we don't know whether it is ambiguous. Such, of course, is our epistemic situation with regard to any novel or unfamiliar predicate. The problem can be alleviated by characterizing the system(s) to which the term is to belong. And typically this isn't too difficult. If 'meow-predicate' in the sublanguage is supposed to be coextensive with 'onomatopoetic' in English, the requisite development of the system is reasonably straightforward. We might stipulate that meow-predicates are those, like 'meow', whose pronunciation reproduces sounds associated with their denotations. Or we might give a partial list of the expressions that are meow-predicates—'bow-wow', 'chug-chug', 'tweet-tweet', and so on.

Even if we don't have a recognized term like 'onomatopoetic' to fall back on, we should still be able to say something about the expressions classed under our newly coined term. And if it isn't enough to determine the extension of the term or settle the question of its ambiguity, still our uncertainty regarding such matters is not restricted to this kind of case. We are often equally uncertain about the interpretation of expressions that have an established place in our vocabulary. Psychiatrists, for example, may agree that a particular patient presents a textbook case of schizophrenia—that is, is an ideal exemplar of the label 'schizophrenic'—while passionately disagreeing about the extension of the term and about whether everyone in its extension suffers from the same disease.

For our purposes, however, it is not terribly important that the terms we coin be unambiguous or that they mark off interesting classes of expressions. What is important is that such compound terms are readily constructed. Therefore, for verbal systems at least, we need not worry about failure of exemplificational reference.

Failure of reference thus does not threaten when a verbal label is exemplified or when an exemplifying symbol is itself verbal. But what of cases, common in music and the visual arts, in which neither one is verbal? Sometimes, to be sure, we introduce onomatopoetic labels to denote and be exemplified by rhythms or tunes. Thus, the Lone Ranger theme song (or, for the more cultured, the final section of the William Tell Overture) goes 'ta da dum, ta da dum, ta da dum dum dum'. Analogously, we might introduce hieroglyphic elements into our written language in an effort to create labels to denote and be exemplified by symbols in the visual arts. Such moves will add to our stock of labels, but they are clearly inadequate to account for all but the coarsest exemplification by nonverbal symbols. We neither have nor know how to invent a verbal vocabulary sensitive enough to capture all of the nuances exemplified by musical and pictorial symbols.

Goodman suggests that we solve the problem by recognizing that there are nonverbal labels as well as verbal ones. Recognizing that some labels are nonverbal by itself causes no special difficulty. Portraits, photographs, diagrams, and maps are nonverbal-denoting labels whose interpretations are often straightforward. If we are reluctant to admit nonverbal labels as objects of exemplification, it is because the labels in question seem somewhat elusive and difficult to identify. Having admitted that they aren't verbal, I can't very well expect to be able to say what they are. But can I mimic them, sketch them, wave at them, or whistle them? Portraits, photographs, diagrams, and maps are at least easily pointed out. But where are we to look for the nonverbal labels exemplified by a still life or a sonata?

I suggest that the labels are typically to be found in the exemplifying symbols themselves. In exemplifying, a symbol in such a system functions as a label that denotes itself and the other things that match it. A painting, then, not only points up some of its own features but also heightens our sensitivity to other instances of the forms, patterns, colors, etc., that it exemplifies. We come to see things differently, reordering our visual experience in terms of the categories referred to by the work. "After we spend an hour or so at one or another exhibition of abstract painting, everything tends to square off into geometric patches or swirl in circles or weave into textural arabesques, to sharpen into black and white or to vibrate with new color consonances and dissonances." [WOW, 105]

Two symbols exemplify the same label if they match each other and refer to the same shared feature. E.g., separate sound sequences exemplify the same rhythm if they instantiate and refer to that rhythm. And we do not require a way to characterize that rhythm independently of its instances in order to recognize that they do so.

We can see now how symbols in such systems function normatively. The oboeist's note both denotes the musical sounds that satisfy a particular standard of attunement and serves as an example of what satisfying that standard consists in. And as we have seen, this is a standard that no verbal label captures.

There is then no danger of failure of reference. So long as the exemplifying symbol in such a system exists, so does its referent. Problems, however, remain in the interpretation of exemplificational symbols—in both verbal and nonverbal systems. It is to a discussion of these that I now turn.

3. INTERPRETATION

Even though exemplification and denotation differ in direction, the issues involved in interpretation are much the same. Exemplifying symbols are subject to vagueness and to ambiguity. Some refer uniquely while others are multiple in reference. Moreover, the basis for exemplification and thus the identity of the labels exemplified are sometimes uncertain. And to complicate matters even further, some symbols exemplify metaphorically as well as, or instead of, literally.

Still, none of these factors should present an insuperable obstacle to recognizing exemplification as a mode of reference. Or, at least, any that does tells equally against denotation.

Objects in the extension of a label match one another and so match any exemplar of that label. To identify a label that an object exemplifies requires ascertaining both the basis for matching and the limits on matching that object. If its referent is unfamiliar or obscure, we may have trouble saying what matches a given exemplar, or, to put it differently, what belongs in the extension of its referent. Unless we are familiar with the symbolic function of the oboeist's note, we will not know whether it is matched by notes like it in duration, in pitch, or in volume. And if the system for interpreting our textbook case of schizophrenia is sufficiently muddled, we may not know whether the patient is matched by others like him in behavior patterns, in brain damage, or in biochemical imbalance. We need then to be reasonably familiar with the symbols in a reasonably clear system in order to recognize the basis for matching its exemplars.

There is, in addition, the problem of the scope of an exemplifying symbol. Such a symbol may exemplify a label of any degree of generality. A single paint chip, for example, might exemplify 'blue', or 'deep blue', or 'teal blue'. If it is indeterminate how closely other objects must match it in order to be classed under its referent, an exemplar is vague. If our paint sample is sufficiently vague, there is no saying whether it is matched only by teal blue objects, or by dark blue objects in general, or by any blue object whatsoever. In that case, there is no saying which of the three labels is its referent.

The two problems are distinct. The identification of the basis of an exemplar concerns the standard for matching it; the identification of its scope, the limits on matching it. The usual basis for interpreting a paint sample is color: it exemplifies a color label and is matched by things that are like it in color. The scope of the sample determines the amount of color variation among the things that match it—that is, among the things that are denoted by the label to which it refers.

Moreover, even when interpreted in accordance with a single system, an object may exemplify a multiplicity of labels, both verbal and nonverbal, and of varying degrees of specificity. A tailor's swatch, for example, simultaneously exemplifies labels denoting fabric, pattern, color, and weave. Accordingly, from our identification of a single label that an object exemplifies, it by no means follows that our interpretation of that object is complete. For it may exemplify a variety of other labels as well. This is one of the reasons when aesthetic objects require sensitivity for their interpretation and reward repeated attention. The labels they exemplify are neither straightforwardly identified nor easily exhausted.

Interpreted according to different systems, a single object may exemplify different labels. If so, it is ambiguous [RR, 125]. Under one interpretation the sample on the paint card exemplifies 'teal blue'; under another it exemplifies 'made in Baltimore'. Under one interpretation an abstract painting exemplifies a pattern of light and shadow. Under another it exemplifies 'bourgeois decadence'. This speaks to the necessity of choosing an appropriate system for interpreting exemplifying symbols [WOW, 130]. For we may be as much in error if we interpret a symbol correctly under an inappropriate system as if we interpret it incorrectly under an appropriate one. The Party regular who fails to invoke a politically sensitive system for interpreting the painting may find himself in serious trouble regardless of the accuracy of his interpretation in other respects.

Nevertheless, the susceptibility of exemplifying symbols to ambiguity is not always a defect. Particularly in the arts, an object's ambiguity may contribute to its richness and power as a symbol. The depth and resonance of a poem like *The Wasteland* clearly derives in part at least from its susceptibility to a variety of interpretations. Although ambiguity is typically a vice in scientific treatises, it is often a virtue in works of art.[3]

It is important to recognize that ambiguity is not the same as multiple reference. A symbol that is ambiguous has different interpretations under different systems. One that has multiple referents refers to more than one label according to a single system. A tailor's swatch is not ambiguous merely because it exemplifies labels denoting fabric, pattern, color, and weave. For all of these belong to a single system for interpreting fabric samples. It is ambiguous, however, if it also exemplifies labels such as 'square', or 'tailor's swatch', or 'product of Hong Kong' when interpreted according to another system.

Still, the distinction between ambiguity and multiple reference should not be pushed too hard. For whether a symbol refers to different labels according to different systems or to several labels according to a single system depends on how we construe our systems. And they may be variously construed. Stravinsky's music might exemplify 'atonality' according to one system, and 'individualistic sedition' according to another. In that case it is ambiguous. But if the systems are construed differently, it might exemplify both labels according to a single system. In that case it refers unambiguously to both labels.

In order to exemplify a label, a symbol must instantiate it. This suggests that the range of exemplification is relatively narrow—first, because only symbols exemplify, and second, because they are required to satisfy any label that they exemplify. Music can exemplify only labels that are satisfied by sounds; literature only those that are satisfied by texts. Even so, the suggestion of narrowness is misleading. We have seen that anything that serves as a sample functions as a symbol. There is then no fundamental distinction between symbolic and nonsymbolic objects. Rocks, rutabagas, and rhinoceri, although ordinarily nonsymbolic, sometimes function as symbols. An object that has no history of symbolizing becomes a symbol just by being taken as a sample.

3. *Beyond the Letter*, p. 7.

Moreover, which labels an object instantiates depends on how that object is described and classified. This is the case whether the object in question is a symbol or not. And so long as we avoid paradox and contradiction, there is no limit to the symbol systems we can construct. Accordingly, even though music can exemplify only labels that apply to sounds, it is our creativity in constructing symbol systems that determines what labels these are and what else besides sounds they apply to.

Nor are the candidates for exemplification restricted to labels a symbol instantiates literally. As we saw above, metaphorical instantiation is genuine instantiation. Hence, a symbol may exemplify labels it metaphorically instantiates as well as ones it literally instantiates. A painting that literally exemplifies 'dark' may metaphorically exemplify 'disturbing'. And if it points up its own dismal prospects of gaining aesthetic acceptance, it may metaphorically exemplify 'dark horse' as well.

4. EXEMPLIFICATION IN THE ARTS

A symbol exemplifies a label metaphorically if it both refers to that label and metaphorically instantiates it. The same sculpture metaphorically exemplifies 'frenzied' as a work of art, 'a gold mine' as an investment, and 'a bomb' as a contribution to the decor. The sculpture then functions metaphorically in several different symbol systems at once.

Typically we are not interested in the whole motley of metaphors that a particular object exemplifies or instantiates. We are interested rather in those it exemplifies or instantiates as a symbol of a certain kind. That is to say, in those it exemplifies or instantiates when interpreted as a symbol in a particular system. The attributions of 'frenzied' to the sculpture and of 'joyous' to the symphony contribute to our understanding of them as works of art only if the metaphors function as aesthetic predicates.

We noted in the discussion of metaphor in the previous chapter that a scheme can be metaphorically transferred to practically any realm, and can be applied to an alien realm in a variety of ways. A drawing of a tightrope walker, for example, might exemplify 'precarious' as an aesthetic symbol and, if its monetary value is uncertain, as an investment. To know whether the metaphor is to be interpreted in one way or the other, we need to know what realm its scheme divides. And since the drawing in question belongs to both aesthetic and financial realms, knowing that the metaphor denotes the picture is not enough. By identifying the metaphor as an aesthetic label, its application is rendered determinate.

This is not to suggest that the realm is antecedently characterized by an adequate system of literal aesthetic labels. If we know that as a musical symbol the final movement of a symphony exemplifies 'joyous', that metaphor can serve as a touchstone against which to test our conjectures as to which literal labels are musically or aesthetically relevant. Indeed, one function of metaphor is to characterize recondite features for which no easy or obvious literal label is available.

A form of exemplification that is particularly important in the arts is expression. Thus a painting is said to express terror, a poem to express sadness, a trio to express bliss. To say that a work expresses a feeling is not to say that it evokes that feeling in its audience. Often the feeling that the audience experiences is quite different from the one that the work expresses. A work that expresses suffering may cause us to experience pity, and one that expresses indifference may cause us to feel rage. Moreover, a work of art does not fail to express such feelings even if, because of ignorance, or inattention, or insensitivity, the audience does not respond to the work. Nor need the work express the mental state of its artist. An actor's performance may express wonder even if, having played the same role for years, he is suffering from profound boredom. And Mozart's overriding emotion during the composition of many of the late works was, if history is to be believed, desperation over his financial plight. Still, the works do not express that desperation, and would not—even if performed before an audience afflicted with the same.

Rather than literally describing the artist or the audience, such labels metaphorically describe the work itself [LA, 85]. Characteristics of the work suggest the application of those labels. But the work, being strictly inanimate, does not literally instantiate them. When the fact that it metaphorically instantiates those labels contributes to the way the work functions as a symbol, the work refers to and thus exemplifies them. Expression then is a mode of metaphorical exemplification.

An objection might, and probably should, be raised at this point. I have been speaking of labels as the objects of exemplification. But in the previous paragraphs it was sadness, terror, bliss, and so on, that were said to be expressed. If expression is a mode of exemplification, then either so-called universals must be exemplified, or labels, expressed. Although I prefer the latter formulation, as it carries no suggestion of platonism, the two actually come to much the same thing. Recall one of Plato's formulations of the problem of universals: What is that which all just acts have in common by virtue of which they can be called 'just'? His answer: Justice. But we have found that all that the instances of a label need have in common in order to be called by that label is that the label actually apply to them. Accordingly, an action is an instance of justice if and only if the predicate 'just' applies to it. And a picture expresses sadness if and only if it expresses the predicate 'sad'.

Under what circumstances then does an object express such a label? We have already seen that expressed labels are metaphorically exemplified. But not just any metaphorical exemplification will do. An object expresses only those metaphorical labels that it exemplifies as an aesthetic symbol [LA, 87]. Thus, although the sculpture metaphorically exemplifies 'frenzied', 'a gold mine', and 'a bomb', it expresses only 'frenzied'. For in its exemplification of the other two labels, it does not function as an aesthetic symbol.

Although emotive predicates are often expressed, expression is not restricted to such labels. A poem may express 'plodding', or a painting 'graceful'. But there is a restriction on the metaphors that can be expressed by an aesthetic symbol. Only those that are imported from an alien realm count as expressed [LA, 86]. It might be perfectly proper to say ironically that a dancer's exquisitely graceful performance exemplifies 'clumsy'. Still, it does not express that label. For the metaphor results from reapplying a scheme to its home realm. On the other hand, one poem might express 'clumsy', and another one 'graceful', since these labels are imported from the realm of gesture and applied metaphorically to that of texts.

Given a symbol that metaphorically exemplifies a label from an alien realm, how are we to tell whether it expresses that label? We know that it does so only if the metaphor functions aesthetically. The problem is, how are we to tell *that*? Goodman has suggested five symptoms of the aesthetic:

> (1) syntactic density, where the finest differences in certain respects constitute a difference between symbols . . . (2) semantic density, where symbols are provided for things distinguished by the finest differences in certain respects . . . (3) relative repleteness, where comparatively many aspects of a symbol are significant . . . (4) exemplification, where a symbol, whether or not it denotes, symbolizes by serving as a sample . . . (5) multiple and complex reference, where a symbol performs several integrated and interacting referential functions, some direct and some mediated through other symbols. [WOW, 67–68][4]

I don't want to offer a detailed explication of them here, for each is discussed elsewhere in my text. But a couple of points about the nature of Goodman's proposal deserve mention. In saying that these are *symptoms* of the aesthetic, he does not maintain that they are infallible guides. English, for example, is semantically dense, and ungraduated meters are syntactically dense. Neither is supposed in general to be aesthetic. Goodman does suggest that the symptoms may be disjointly necessary and conjointly sufficient. That is, it may be the case that to function aesthetically a symbol needs to exhibit at least one of the symptoms, and that any symbol that exhibits them all is guaranteed to function aesthetically. But there is no suggestion that a symbol is more aesthetic the more of these symptoms it exhibits. His use of the term 'symptom' here is apposite. One patient may exhibit

---

4. Cf. also [LA, 252–53] and "Replies", *Journal of Aesthetics and Art Criticism* 39 (1981), pp. 277–278.

few symptoms of a disease even though he is suffering from a severe case, while another may show many of its symptoms and have but a light case. The symptoms of the aesthetic that Goodman identifies are then clues. He offers no decisive test for whether a symbol functions aesthetically and hence none for whether an exemplified metaphor is expressed.

Howard[5] suggests that a metaphorical label functions musically when its application is constant relative to a literal description in music theoretical terms. It is then left to music theorists to decide what the literal vocabulary appropriate for characterizing works of music is to be. He maintains that it includes labels denoting tones, pitches, harmonies, melodies, intervals, and rhythms. With obvious modifications this suggestion might be applied to the other arts as well. Whether it will suffice to identify the metaphors that are expressed by works in the different arts depends in large measure on the adequacy of their respective literal theoretical vocabularies. It is likely that it will work better for some arts than for others.

My aim is not, however, to espouse any particular method for identifying metaphors that function aesthetically. It is rather to emphasize that the characterization of a symbol as expressive is relative to its identification as an aesthetic symbol. Different methods for identifying aesthetic symbols are likely to yield different verdicts as to which metaphors are expressed.

Moreover, in order to express, a symbol must exemplify metaphorically. But we have seen that the application of a single label to a single range of objects might be classed as literal under one system and as metaphorical under another. There might be disagreement, for example, about whether 'rhythm' applies literally or metaphorically to poetry, and hence about whether it is exemplified literally or expressed. Systems of aesthetic labels that disagree about which applications of a term are literal and which are metaphorical are then likely to disagree about what labels their objects express.

Expression is thus doubly relative: it is relative to the identification of symbols as aesthetic, and to a partition between literal and metaphorical applications of labels to aesthetic symbols.

Since this is not a work on aesthetics, it might be wondered that so much effort is devoted to explicating a purely aesthetic device. The reason is this: 'Exemplification' is introduced as a technical term. One way to demonstrate that it is of more than narrowly technical interest is to show that it provides an explication of a significant body of discourse. 'Expression' is not primarily a technical term of this theory, but has its home in the vocabulary of aesthetics. Accordingly, explaining expression in terms of exemplification not only clarifies the semantic structure of a body of aesthetic claims but also demonstrates the importance of exemplification for semantic theory.

5. Vernon Howard, "On Musical Expression", *British Journal of Aesthetics* 11 (1971), pp. 277–278.

There is often fairly widespread agreement among critics as to what labels a work expresses, even though those labels clearly are not literally true of that work. The interpretation of expression as metaphorical exemplification of aesthetic symbols accounts for this. Labels expressed are metaphorically, not literally, true of the works that exemplify them. But as I argued in the last chapter, metaphorical labels are genuinely, even if not literally, true of the works that instantiate them. So the features a work expresses are genuine features of that work. And an object that exemplifies a label, literally or metaphorically, refers to that label. It is unsurprising then that the people who know how to interpret a work agree as to what it expresses. But since works of art are referring symbols, they require interpretation. It is therefore equally unsurprising that those who do not know how to interpret them disagree about what they express. Finally, because expression is exemplification by aesthetic symbols, the experts to whom we defer are those who understand art.

Justification for restricting the labels that count as expressed comes not from the theory of reference, but from aesthetics. The restrictions reflect critical practice and are justified if the metaphors that satisfy them are the ones that are significant in interpreting works of art.

The understanding and evaluation of a work of art depends on the proper identification of the aesthetic labels it literally exemplifies as well as of those it expresses. A quartet might exemplify melodic and harmonic labels, while a painting might exemplify labels denoting patterns of color and shape. If we fail to recognize the labels a work literally exemplifies, just as if we fail to recognize those it expresses, we fail to understand the work.

To function as a work of art is to function symbolically. Nonrepresentational works do not denote, and some of them may not express. But even these convey, point up, or make manifest some of the aesthetic labels they instantiate. That is, they exemplify those labels [WOW, 65].

This is sometimes denied. Formalists maintain that what is aesthetically important about a work of art is not what it refers to, but what it is. But surely they do not want to maintain that everything it is—e.g., owned by a man with a limp, first performed by a social democrat—is important to it as a work of art. There must be some way of singling out those things it is (or those labels it instantiates) as an aesthetic object.

Perhaps formalists might attempt to do so by considering only the predicates of a restricted vocabulary, such as that of music theory, that a work instantiates. But this will not do. First, there is bound to be a certain arbitrariness in the specification of the terms that are held to belong to the specialized vocabulary. Second, and more important, there is no reason to believe that every term of that vocabulary which is instantiated by a particular work will be important to its identity as an aesthetic object. For example, the exact proportion of quarter notes might be relevant to the way one piece functions musically but not to the way another one does. We cannot then obtain a general solution to the formalist's problem by imposing restrictions on the system of labels with which we are concerned. For the instantiation of any particular label may matter to the way one work functions aesthetically, but not to the way another one does.

The problem the formalist poses has no general solution. Each work determines which of the labels it instantiates are relevant to its own interpretation. It does so by singling them out, serving as a sample of them, referring to them. Formalists are right then to say that what matters aesthetically is what a work is. But they are wrong to deny that reference is involved. For the work refers to those among the things it is, to those among the labels it instantiates, that matter to its function as a work of art.

But there may be more to the formalist's thesis than this suggests. Instead of taking it to deny that certain works of art refer at all, suppose we take it to deny that they refer to anything outside of themselves. Since, as I argued above, exemplifying symbols in non-verbal media are often self-exemplifying, we are not bound to look beyond these works to discover the labels they exemplify. The formalist position can then be reconstrued as maintaining that (some of) the labels certain works of art exemplify are uniquely satisfied by those works or, even more strongly, that those labels are logically proper names and hence are in principle incapable of being satisfied by any other objects. The claim that certain works of art refer to nothing outside of themselves does not then undermine the thesis that those works function as symbols and that they do so by exemplifying—that is, by referring selectively to labels they instantiate.

I am neither called upon nor qualified to rule on the adequacy of formalist theories of art. My aim here is only to show the extent to which the formalist thesis is compatible with this account of reference. Still, I think Goodman has a point in holding the denial of the aesthetic importance of expression to be misguided [PP, 126–27]. Formalists insist that it is the structures of the work itself that are aesthetically significant. Their dismissal of metaphor is presumably grounded in the conviction that what is metaphorically attributed to an object cannot be genuinely true of that object. But we have seen that this is incorrect. Not all actual denotation is literal denotation. The structures that a work metaphorically exemplifies are actual structures of that work—often quite subtle structures for which no phrase in the literal vocabulary is quite adequate.

'Expresses' is part of the critic's vocabulary. But 'exemplifies', at least in the technical sense it has here, is not. When a critic says that a painting is cold, dark, and forbidding, he is apparently concerned with labels the work instantiates, not with those it exemplifies. But is this a correct description of critical practice? Certainly only some of the labels a work instantiates are recorded by the critic—presumably those that are pertinent to understanding and evaluating it as a work of art. If the critic is insensitive to the distinction between the labels whose instantiation matters aesthetically and those whose instantiation does not, his remarks are apt to be dismissed as an unfocussed motley. The labels on whose instantiation the understanding and evaluation of a work of art depend are those it exemplifies as a work of art. Whether he uses this terminology or not, it is to these that the good critic directs our attention.

5. EXEMPLIFICATION IN THE SCIENCES

In the foregoing discussion we restricted our attention to the aesthetic labels an object exemplifies. This allowed us to say something about the way works of art function semantically and, by implication at least, about aesthetic epistemology. The fruitfulness of this approach in the aesthetic realm suggests that we might do well to proceed similarly in our investigations of other realms. Instead of seeking to identify all the labels a particular object exemplifies, regardless of the diversity of systems to which those labels belong, let us focus on exemplification within a single system. This approach will prove valuable in investigating the role of exemplification in logic and mathematics as well as in the empirical sciences.

In logic and mathematics, exemplification is crucial. Whether an argument is valid, for example, depends on the labels it exemplifies when interpreted as a logical symbol. One that exemplifies 'modus ponens' is valid; one that exemplifies 'ignoratio elenchi' is not. Moreover, the former also exemplifies 'valid'; the latter, 'invalid'.

This might be doubted. It might be thought that the logical status of a body of sentences turns only on the logical labels it instantiates. It need not also refer to those labels. To see that this is incorrect, consider various alternative ways in which the same sequence of sentences might be construed—as an elocution exercise, as the script of a monologue, as a list of sentences of increasing difficulty to be translated into Serbian. Under none of these construals does the question of its logical form even arise. That question does arise, however, as soon as the sequence of sentences is considered as an argument. And a sequence of sentences coalesces into an argument by exemplifying a label that denotes its logical form. Reference by that sequence to a logical label it instantiates brings the logical relations among its constituent sentences into focus. Lacking such reference, we have only a list.

The question of validity is at the heart of the logical evaluation of an argument, so it is unlikely that a logical symbol will instantiate 'valid' or 'fallacious' without also exemplifying that label. But it is not the case that an argument exemplifies every logical label that it instantiates. That it is expressed in Polish notation, for example, may be simply incidental. On the other hand, if Polish notation affords a particularly perspicuous way of exhibiting the structure of the argument, this too might be exemplified.

Formalization and axiomatization are valued highly in logic and mathematics. It is not plausible to account for this by the increased ease of calculation they allegedly afford. In certain areas, notably arithmetic and syllogistic logic, calculation was already sufficiently easy that little was to be gained from making it even easier. In any case, whether a method of calculation is counted easy or not seems to depend more on our familiarity with it than on any features of its formalism. Nor it is obvious how, for example, the ability to derive arithmetic from Peano's axioms is supposed to make it easier to balance one's checkbook. Indeed, axiomatization of a branch of mathematics often reduces the primitive vocabulary and restricts the permissible rules of inference. It might well thereby increase the difficulty of making particular calculations. But if knowing what labels are exemplified is as important in mathematics as it is in the arts, it is easy to see why formalization and axiomatization are so highly regarded. For by means of formalization and axiomatization, relations between symbols and the mathematical labels they exemplify are rendered perspicuous. And the reason why reaxiomatization of a branch of mathematics is often fruitful is that under different axiom systems the exemplification of different mathematical labels is often exhibited. Indeed, unless a difference in emphasis results, reaxiomatization seems a pointless exercise.

Not all of the labels exemplified by mathematical symbols are literal. Such metaphors as 'elegant' and 'economical' are exemplified by mathematical symbols in much the way that 'peaceful' and 'forbidding' are exemplified by aesthetic ones. In this case, however, the metaphors are constant relative to the mathematical, not to the aesthetic, labels the symbols literally instantiate. A proof might exemplify 'elegant', for example, even though inscribed in a nearly illegible hand on a torn and dirty envelope.

One of the desiderata in axiomatizing any branch of mathematics is economy of the basis. Here again the exemplification of mathematical labels affords the explanation. For the power of its mathematical techniques is clearly exhibited by a system in which rich results are derived from a relatively improverished basis.

Symbols that differ significantly in other respects may nevertheless exemplify the same mathematical labels. This is what makes it possible to recognize different formulations of the same proof and different proofs of the same theorem. Of course whether two strings of symbols count as different formulations of the same proof, as different proofs of the same theorem, as proofs of different theorems, or as no proof at all, is a function of the systems in terms of which they are interpreted. In mathematics, as elsewhere, interpretation is relative to a symbol system.

It should be evident by now that exemplification plays a major role in the way mathematical and logical expressions symbolize. Instead of adducing further evidence of this, I want to turn to some of the ways exemplification functions in the empirical sciences.

One way is in determining what counts as evidence. Something counts as evidence for or against a theory if it serves as a sample of a label whose satisfaction is relevant to the truth or falsity of that theory. But to serve as a sample is to exemplify, so evidence concerning a theory exemplifies labels pertinent to its truth or falsity.

An illustration may help to make this clear. Optical and electromagnetic phenomena instantiate some of the same labels. So long as these phenomena were believed to be determined by distinct scientific laws, such coinstantiation was regarded as a curiosity. But with the Maxwell equations, optics was incorporated into electromagnetic theory. As a result, optical phenomena came to serve as evidence for or against electromagnetic hypotheses. With the introduction of the Maxwell equations, then, optical phenomena came to refer to, and hence to exemplify, the electromagnetic labels that they were already known to instantiate.

Interpreting an experiment requires knowing what labels it exemplifies. For an experiment functions as an example of a theory,[6] referring to those among its descriptions that are pertinent to the theory it tests. A single experiment might be interpreted in one context as confirming a hypotheses of physics, and in another as attesting to the accuracy of a measuring device, a hypothesis of instrument theory. Although the two interpretations agree about the labels the experiment satisfies, they disagree over which among them are exemplified.

There is a methodological requirement that to be scientifically acceptable an experiment must be repeatable. Clearly we cannot and need not produce a duplicate that matches the original experiment in every respect. Certain features of the experiment—e.g., having been performed by an assistant professor hoping to get tenure—are irrelevant to its role in confirming or disconfirming a theory. What is required is that its duplicates match the original in every respect that is pertinent to the theory being tested. That is, to be counted a duplicate, an experiment must exemplify the same labels as the original when both are interpreted as tests of the same theory. Which labels these are vary from case to case. But the standard for duplication is neutral and allows for wide variation in the other labels the various experiments instantiate.

Indeed, such variation is desirable. To the extent that duplicates of an experiment instantiate the same unexemplified labels as well as the same exemplified ones, there is a danger that their agreement will be misleading. For that agreement may be due to some shared feature that is not exemplified under the theory's interpretation of the experiments. Instead of seeking to reproduce the original experiment "as closely as possible", then, it is methodologically preferable to perform a variety of experiments that reproduce the features that the original exemplifies but that differ from the original and from one another in those that are not exemplified.

In the empirical sciences, as in the mathematical sciences, infer-

6. Sir George Thompson, "Some Thoughts on Scientific Method", *Boston Studies in the Philosophy of Science II* ed. Robert Cohen and Marx Wartofsky (New York: Humanities Press, 1965), p. 85.

ence patterns or argument forms are exemplified. Labels such as 'theorem' which are exemplified in mathematics are also exemplified in the more formalized branches of empirical science. In other branches such labels as 'inference to the best explanation', 'teleological argument', or 'argument ad hominem' might be exemplified. These labels describe relations between statements of evidence (or, more broadly, reasons) and the hypotheses they are adduced to support. For research reports, textbook presentations, and the like to exemplify such labels, the proper description of the evidence must be chosen. An enzyme might be correctly described in one way in an argument that exemplifies 'teleological reasoning' and in quite another, equally correct way in one that exemplifies 'reductive biochemical analysis'. The choice among accurate descriptions of the evidence thus depends not only on the hypothesis for which it is evidence, but also on the form the argument relating evidence to hypothesis is to exemplify.

6. EXEMPLIFICATION IN ETHICS

Exemplification has a number of roles in ethics as well. It is worth mentioning a few of them. One need not espouse an emotive theory of meaning to recognize that ethical evaluations have an emotive dimension. Thus, e.g., if disconnecting the respirator that keeps a patient alive is described as 'killing him', the action is brought to exemplify morally blameworthy labels. If it is described as 'ending his suffering', it is brought to exemplify morally praiseworthy labels. It is an important feature of moral life that a single action instantiates both descriptions. Choosing the correct characterization of an action is thus critical to evaluating its moral worth.

That ethical deliberation involves such a choice is often overlooked by moral theorists. E.g., one formulation of Kant's categorical imperative is "I ought never to act except in such a way that I can also will that my maxim should become a Universal law."[7] How are we to determine which of the indefinitely many descriptions of an action yields its maxim? What is interesting is that Kant seems not to take this to be a problem. He apparently thinks that we need only consider an action from the moral point of view for its moral character to stand out. That is, when considered from the moral point of view, the action is taken to exemplify its own moral description.

If it is tacitly assumed that actions exemplify their own moral labels, it is easy to see why ethical theorists ignore the problem of identifying the appropriate descriptions of the actions they are concerned to evaluate. And if each action instantiates but one moral label, there may be no real difficulty. But if an action instantiates several moral labels, we need a way to determine which one is exemplified.

---

7. Immanuel Kant, *Grounding for the Metaphysics of Morals* trans. J. W. Ellington (from Carus). (Indianapolis: Hackett Publishing Co., 1981), p. 14.

And if an action exemplifies several moral labels, the problem becomes serious. The relation between its exemplification of those labels and its overall moral evaluation then deserves consideration by ethical theorists.

Discussions of moral character are also illuminated by appeal to exemplification. Iris Murdoch[8] describes the following case: A mother-in-law, M, believes her daughter-in-law, D, to be vulgar, undignified, and tiresomely juvenile. Although D's behavior does not change, M, after considerable effort, revises her opinion. She now takes D to be refreshingly simple, spontaneous, and delightfully youthful. Murdoch maintains that even though M behaved properly throughout, she is a better person for having changed her mind.

To make this out, we have to consider the relations between M's two descriptions of D. If D instantiates just one of them, then M either replaces a false belief with a true one, or a true belief with a false one. If the former, M's progress seems mainly epistemic; if the latter, M comes to delude herself. It is not obvious that either change is morally progressive.

Suppose, however, that D belongs to the intersection of the two descriptions. Then both of M's characterizations are true. In that case M's change of opinion consists in her coming to interpret D as exemplifying the more admirable of the two descriptions she instantiates. It is interesting to consider whether this sort of change of opinion makes one a morally better person.

One last function of exemplification in ethics deserves mention. Writers like Jane Austen and Henry James are sometimes said to be moralists.[9] Certainly they are not thought to have written tomes to rival the *Nicomachean Ethics* or the *Critique of Practical Reason*. Such works function denotively for the most part, describing (correctly or incorrectly) various features of the moral realm. The novels of Austen and James, however, function not denotively, but exemplificationally. They are characterized as moral works because they metaphorically exemplify certain aspects of the moral life. And since their doing so contributes to our moral understanding, such a characterization is accurate.

Exemplification in the arts, in the sciences, in ethics, and elsewhere, is a source of emphasis. Any object has indefinitely many accurate descriptions. Our problem is to select the ones that are appropriate to the various enterprises in which we are engaged. Often this requires determining what labels an object exemplifies when interpreted according to one or another symbol system. But if we are to maintain that exemplification is a source of emphasis, we must take

8. Iris Murdoch, *The Sovereignty of the Good* (London: Routledge & Kegan Paul, 1970), pp. 17–18.

9. Alasdair MacIntyre, *After Virtue* (Notre Dame: University of Notre Dame Press, 1981), pp. 222–26.

pains to insist that what is emphasized is not always what is prominent. The most outstanding characteristic of a painting might be its
price, and that of a chemical reaction its smell. But neither is likely to
be emphasized. Under reasonable interpretations the painting might
exemplify and thus emphasize some subtle configurations of light and
shadow, and the reaction some recondite feature of benzene. Discovering what something emphasizes then is not a matter of identifying its most obvious characteristics, but involves knowing how to
interpret it as a symbol. This frequently requires sensitivity to what it
exemplifies as well as to what, if anything, it denotes.

Sentences, as we saw, do not denote. Nevertheless, they may refer
by means of literal and/or metaphorical exemplification. Some of
Shakespeare's sentences, for example, literally exemplify particular
rhythms and rhyme schemes; and some of Joyce's, the wordings and
cadances of Catholic prayers. Such sentences often exemplify
metaphorically as well. Frequently the social status of a Shakespear-
rean character is expressed in his mode of speech: the nobleman
speaks in verse; the baseborn, in prose. So speeches that literally instantiate or exemplify 'verse' or 'prose' can serve to express the
speaker's station.

Nor is exemplification by sentences exclusively a literary matter.
The sentences of a call to arms are likely to exemplify 'patriotic' and
those of a eulogy, 'mournful'. A professor's sentences might
exemplify such labels as 'convoluted', 'pompous', and 'boring', while
his teaching assistant's explications of them exemplify 'clear', 'co-
gent', and 'to the point'. Interestingly, the exemplification of certain
syntactic and semantic patterns in the sentences of brain-damaged
patients is important in the diagnosis of different types of asphasia.[10]

Questions, commands, and exclamations can exemplify as well.
The question, 'Don't you think we should ask permission first?' often
expresses 'timid'. The command, 'Halt, or I'll shoot!' might express
'determined' or 'resolute'. And the exclamation, 'You've been playing
with poisonous snakes!' is likely to express 'horrific'. Notice that
statements, exclamations, and questions that correspond to the same
phrase can differ in exemplificational reference. The question, 'Are
you well?' might express 'anxious' or 'concerned' in a context in
which the statement 'You are well' expresses 'relieved'. And since
differences in the word order of a statement and a corresponding
question normally result in differences in rhythm, in contexts in which
rhythmic labels are exemplified, corresponding statement and question typically exemplify different labels.

Exemplification depends heavily on context. So we are unlikely to
find significant general correlations of the form: Whenever a state-

10. E.g., sentences consisting of vague circumlocutions are symptomatic of anomia;
syntactically rich but semantically garbled sentences are symptomatic of Wernicke's
aphasia; and sentences in which nouns and uninflected verbs are plentiful but logical
and grammatical particles few are symptomatic of Broca's aphasia. These different
types of aphasia are correlated with lesions in different areas of the brain. Cf. Howard
Gardner, *The Shattered Mind* (New York: Vintage Books, 1974), pp. 52–113.

ment exemplifies p, there exists a corresponding question that exemplifies q. To a statement that exemplifies any one label, there correspond a number of questions. And in different contexts these questions might exemplify any of a number of different labels, or none at all.

To understand how a text functions symbolically then, we cannot limit our attention to the referential functions of its component words and phrases. We must also discover what labels are literally and metaphorically exemplified by its sentences, paragraphs, chapters, and by the work as a whole.

7. LEARNING FROM EXPERIENCE

Learning from a sample involves learning to identify and project the labels that the sample exemplifies. Given a sample problem worked out in a textbook, what we need to discover is how the solution to this problem is supposed to help us solve others. We need to learn then what features of the problem and its solution are projectible, and onto what class of cases they are to be projected [WOW, 135].

When, for example, the conjugation of a verb such as 'parler' is presented in a French text, the point is not just to instruct the student in the conjugation of this particular verb; rather, it is to instruct him in the conjugation of all regular '———er' verbs. To master his task, the student has to learn which features of its conjugation are peculiar to 'parler', and which are characteristic of '———er' verbs in general. That is, he has to learn what labels the conjugation of 'parler' exemplifies as a sample '———er' verb. Further, he has to ascertain that the sample is fair. For if it is not, the labels it exemplifies will not be representative of the class onto which they are to be projected [WOW, 134]. If he has the misfortune to take 'aller' to be representative of '———er' verbs in general, he will go badly wrong. Since 'aller' is an irregular verb, the labels its conjugation exemplifies are not projectible onto other cases. Finally, the student must learn onto what class of cases the labels exemplified by the sample are to be projected. If he thinks that the class includes all French verbs, all regular French verbs, or even all French verbs whose infinitives end in '———er', he will be in error.

Learning to conjugate regular verbs in this way is learning to solve a problem in induction. And the questions the student must answer are characteristic of inductive problems generally. Given a sample, we must identify the labels it exemplifies, discover whether it is a fair sample of those labels, and (if it is) determine onto what other objects the labels exemplified by the sample are to be projected.

We determine the proportion of cashews in a barrel of mixed nuts by taking a sample from the barrel and measuring the proportion of cashews in it. By interpreting the sample in light of our question we bring it about that the sample exemplifies the proportions of the various kinds of nuts it contains. But before we can project those proportions onto the mixture as a whole, before we can legitimately maintain that the proportion of cashews in our sample gives a basis for predicting the proportion of cashews in the mixture, we must ascertain that the sample is fair. How are we to do that?

We might treat a sample of the mixture as fair only if the proportion of cashews in it is equal to the proportion of cashews in the entire mixture. The difficulty is that typically we don't know what that proportion is. Indeed, the point of taking the sample is to discover something about the mixture as a whole. But we can do so only if the sample is fair. And if the only way to determine that it is fair is to compare the proportions it exemplifies with those of the whole from which it was taken, then sampling is otiose. What we had hoped to learn by studying the sample must already be known to insure that the sample is fair.

Granted, in this case we might laboriously count out all the nuts in the barrel, so our original question might be answered anyway. But typically we do not have this option. Whenever we are concerned with something indefinite in extension—as we are, for example, when we want to discover the proportion of pollutants in the air or of binary stars in the galaxy—our only approach is inductive. But induction carries no guarantees. No feature of a sample or of the way it is taken suffices to insure that the labels it exemplifies are instantiated by the whole onto which they are projected. Accordingly, if this is our standard of fairness, where induction is involved we have no way of knowing that our samples are fair.

Of course we do not and should not conclude from this that all samples are equally fair. Instead, we invoke a different standard of fairness. According to this one, a sample is fair if it is fairly taken [WOW, 135]. Our sample of nuts is then counted fair if it is fairly taken, even if the proportion of cashews in it differs from the proportion in the mixture as a whole. This standard of fairness is the one we use when we acknowledge the calls of an unbiased umpire to be fair even though we realize that lack of bias confers no immunity against error.

But what makes fairly taken samples fair? We cannot maintain that they yield outcomes that are fair accordingly to our earlier standard, for there is no assurance of that. All we can say is that the samples we count as fair are those that are taken in accordance with our current best methods of sampling [WOW, 135]. Fairly taken samples then reflect the state of the art of sample-taking.

These methods, of course, change over time as we discover biases and sources of error and invent strategies for avoiding them. A sample counted fair today may be dismissed as biased tomorrow. An early method of sampling mixed nuts might involve nothing more than skimming a handful off the top and determining the proportions of the different kinds of nuts in the handful. But if we learn that heavier nuts settle on the bottom during shipment, we will stir the mixture before sampling or take samples from different levels. Thereafter, the samples that had been deemed fair according to the earlier test will be disregarded as biased.

Even if it is not feasible to compare the sample to the whole to insure its fairness, at least we can compare it to other samples. In this way, it might be thought, we have a more "objective" test of fairness—one that is grounded in the stuff being sampled, not just in our methods of sampling. Agreement among samples is certainly desirable, but it does not prevent systematic bias. Skimming nuts off the tops of lots of barrels might yield consistent results which nevertheless differ significantly from the proportions of nuts of different kinds in those barrels.

We count a sample as fair then when it is fairly taken. And whether it is fairly taken depends not on the accuracy of its results, which cannot be guaranteed, but on its compliance with our current best sampling techniques. And all we can say in support of the techniques we call fair is that we know none better.

Finally, we have to determine over what range of objects the labels exemplified by a fairly taken sample are to be projected. Is our handful of nuts representative of the nuts in the barrel, of barrels of mixed nuts sold by Nut House, Inc., or of mixed nuts in a particular price range? Clearly, any of these is possible. What is crucial is that the answer to this question is intertwined with answers to our earlier questions. If we are concerned only with nuts in a particular barrel, a sample might exemplify such labels as 'stale' and 'broken'. That same sample, interpreted as a representative of nuts in a particular price range, may well not exemplify these labels. And dipping into a single barrel is a fair method of sampling the nuts in that barrel, but a broader sample is required if we are to project over barrels sold by Nut House, Inc. The labels that a sample exemplifies, the fairness of the sample, and the range of things onto which those labels are to be projected are thus interdependent.

According to the theory of reference I am offering, exemplification is a fundamental semantic notion. If so, it might be wondered that we are not more aware of it. Put bluntly, if exemplification is so basic, why wasn't it noticed earlier? Why did we have to wait for Goodman to discover it?

I have maintained that exemplification is pervasive. It plays a central role in the arts, in the sciences, and in ethics, in investigating, learning, sampling, and selling. If we lack an awareness of exemplification, it apparently does not interfere with these practices. But it does result in our giving rather peculiar accounts of them. In our ignorance of exemplification then we are in the position of Molière's *bourgeois gentilhomme* who had been speaking prose for forty years without realizing it. And like him, perhaps, we need a philosopher to explain to us what we have been doing all along.

We require an account of exemplification, not to engage these practices, but to explain them. Without such an account, we may be able to get on quite well with these activities, but we will be unable to produce adequate semantic theories to explain what they involve.

VI THE STRUCTURE
OF SYSTEMS

Names and numerals, drawings and diagrams, maps and musical scores are all symbols. Each symbolizes by referring, indeed by denoting. But they plainly refer in different ways. Some of their differences are the result of their referring to different sorts of things. Thus, musical scores denote the sound of high C, but not Puget Sound or the South China Sea. A map, on the other hand, may denote such sounds and seas, but no sounded C's. Other differences, however, are due to differences in the structures of the systems to which such symbols belong. It is the latter that I want to investigate in this chapter. The syntactic structure of a system determines how its symbols are to be identified. The semantic structure determines how their referents are to be identified. I will show that the syntactic and semantic structures of the system to which a sign belongs are largely determinative of its symbolic powers and limitations.

1. SYNTAX

The utterances and inscriptions, gestures and tones we perceive and produce are various. Let us call all such items *marks* [LA, 131]. Some are evidently without significance—random whistles, waves, ink blobs, and infant babbles. Others form the basis of our symbol systems. The difference is not grounded in any perceptual or "intrinsic" features of the marks. It is due, rather, to the fact that marks of the latter sort do, and those of the former sort do not, belong to characters [LA, 131]. For characters are the classes of marks whose relations to one another determine a syntax. A mark that belongs to no character has no place in a syntax.

No two marks are alike in every respect. So if we are to say that distinct marks belong to the same character, we must be able to distinguish between their constitutive and their contingent features.[1] Then any marks alike in constitutive features belong to the same character, or are character-indifferent, however much they may differ in other respects.

The partition into constitutive and contingent features is effected by an alphabet. Marks that are composed of exactly the same alphabetic

---

1. Talk of "features" here is just a manner of speaking. In more rigorous terms the distinction between constitutive and contingent features is a distinction between labels that a mark instantiates: those that are syntactically significant are constitutive; those that are not, contingent.

elements in exactly the same combination—marks, in short, that are spelled alike—are character-indifferent. Because such marks belong to the same character, they can be freely exchanged for one another without syntactical effect. It follows that any mark that has a spelling can be replicated, and any scheme that has an alphabet can recognize distinct marks as replicas of one another. An alphabet, of course, need not consist of letters. Numerals, and the dots and dashes of Morse code, for example, admit of syntactic replication. As I am using the term 'alphabet', they too belong to alphabets.

What is it about an alphabetic scheme that grounds the distinction between constitutive and contingent features of a mark? Briefly, it is that the syntax of such a scheme groups marks into characters that are disjoint and finitely differentiated. Because syntactic disjointness and finite differentiation are important features of alphabetic schemes, I will discuss each of them in some detail.

If a symbol system is syntactically disjoint, none of its marks belongs to more than one character [LA, 133]. It is not, of course, always easy to identify the character to which a particular mark belongs. The marks we seek to schematize do not come nearly sorted, but resemble and differ from one another in a multitude of ways. No matter what standard we establish for membership in a character, there are bound to be marks whose syntactic classification is difficult to decide.

Partition into disjoint characters is not found in the marks themselves, but is imposed on them by a syntactic scheme. That scheme in effect mandates that no mark is to be considered syntactically significant unless and until it is classed as belonging to one and only one character. According to a different scheme, the very same mark might belong to several nondisjoint characters. And according to a third, it might belong to no character at all.

Consider a mark

whose syntactic classification is not obvious. It might belong to the first letter of the alphabet, or alternatively, to the eighth. If contextual cues are insufficient to decide the question, we can simply stipulate that it is to belong to one character or to the other. The syntactical disjointness of our scheme is thereby preserved. But what happens if we try to have it both ways—insisting that the mark belongs to both the first and the eighth letters of our alphabet? If some of its replicas are A's and others are H's, and the system remains syntactically disjoint, the two characters merge. In that case, all A's are replicas of all H's, for all replicas of a mark in a syntactically disjoint system are replicas of each other. The system has an alphabet, but it is not the one we are used to. If, however, A's and H's are not all replicas of one another, then the characters of the system properly intersect. Two marks belonging to a single character are then not freely interchangeable, for each may belong to an additional character from which the other is excluded. Thus ⟋⟍ is substitutable for A, and for H, but A is not substitutable for H. Such a system is not syntactically disjoint.

That the characters of an alphabet scheme be finitely differentiated or articulate requires this: "For every two characters K and K', and every mark m that does not actually belong to both, determination that m does not belong to K or that m does not belong to K' must be theoretically possible" [LA, 135–36]. We can explicate 'theoretically possible' in any reasonable way. If, e.g., we take the requirement to be one of current technological possibility, then our current technology must provide a means for identifying the character to which m belongs. If we take it to be one of physical possibility, then there must be some physical state, condition, or magnitude that determines the character to which m belongs, and so on. What is excluded by this requirement is any system whose characters are ordered in such a way that it is in principle impossible to ascertain that a mark belongs to one rather than another of them. And alternative readings of 'theoretically possible' invoke different principles to decide the case. But there are some systems that will be excluded by every reading.

Syntactically dense systems, for example, are always excluded, for they provide for an infinity of characters so ordered that between any two there is a third [LA, 136].[2] Accordingly, it is impossible to assign some marks exclusively to any one character, for they might with equal warrant be assigned to any of a variety of others. Moreover, no refinement of measuring or classifying techniques will improve the situation. Inevitably, there will be competing candidates, and no basis for rationally deciding among them. Such systems lack alphabets, for there are cases in which it is impossible to identify the character to which a mark belongs.

A syntactical scheme may be finitely differentiated even if its characters are infinite in number. Arabic fractional notation is a scheme of this kind. And a syntactical scheme whose characters are finite in number may nevertheless lack finite differentiation. A scheme consisting of just two characters lacks finite differentiation if one character comprehends all marks exactly 3 cm. in length and the other comprehends all marks whose length is not 3 cm. For no matter how precise our measuring techniques, there are bound to be marks whose syntactic classification eludes us. We will have no basis for saying that such marks are *exactly* 3 cm. long rather than ever so slightly longer or shorter.

I have been speaking only of atomic characters, but of course there are compound characters as well. A character is compound if the marks that belong to it are composed of marks that belong to other characters [LA, 142]. Thus, 'JBE' belongs to a compound character,

---

2. A system *provides for* an infinity of characters if its formation rules allow for the construction of infinitely many syntactically significant marks any two of which belong to distinct characters.

since it consists of inscriptions of 'J', 'B', and 'E'. The latter inscriptions are atomic, as they consist of no further marks.

Needless to say, not every combination of atomic marks belongs to a compound character. Each system has its own rules for generating compound marks out of atomic ones. Still, it is important to distinguish between configurations of atomic marks that belong to characters but lack application, and configurations of atomic marks that belong to no character. The former is a semantic matter; the latter, a syntactic one. An inscription that consists of letter inscriptions strung out left to right belongs to a compound character of our system. One that consists of letter inscriptions piled one on top of the other does not.

The existence of compound characters does not affect the syntactic disjointness of an alphabetic system. For even though every inscription of 'JBE' contains an inscription of 'J', no inscription of 'JBE' belongs to the same character as an inscription of 'J'. That is, no 'JBE' is a replica of any 'J'.

Syntactic disjointness and finite differentiation are plainly independent of one another. The scheme mentioned earlier according to which all marks 3 cm. in length belong to one character, and all other marks belong to another character is disjoint but not finitely differentiated. No mark belongs to more than one character, but there are marks whose character classification is impossible to decide. And the scheme according to which the mark

belongs to two characters of the Roman alphabet is finitely differentiated but not disjoint. The characters of the scheme are clearly different from one another, so membership in a character is determinate. But a single mark belongs to more than one of them.

The syntactic features of disjointness and finite differentiation perform different functions. The former insures that all marks correctly adjudged to belong to the same character are mutually substitutable. The latter insures that it is possible to adjudge correctly that two marks belong to the same character. Discursive languages, Arabic numerical notation, and standard musical notation satisfy these requirements.

Representational systems—those to which paintings, drawings, sculptures, and some diagrams belong—do not. These are syntactically nondisjoint and dense throughout. A single mark may belong to several characters at once. And between any two characters there is a third. Moreover, no insertion of additional characters in normal position will destroy density [LA, 136].[3] In such systems there is no basis

3. "A scheme is syntactically dense if it provides for infinitely many characters so ordered that between each two there is a third. Such a scheme may still leave gaps, as when the characters correspond to all rational numbers that are either less than 1 or not less than 2. In this case, the insertion of a character corresponding to 1 will destroy

for assigning a mark exclusively to one character rather than to any of indefinitely many others. Nor is there any basis for assigning different marks to the same character. Since marks in representational systems cannot be reliably judged to be syntactic replicas of one another, none can be freely substituted for any other.

In syntactically dense and nondisjoint systems then, there is no general distinction between the constitutive and the contingent features of a sign. That is, there is no general criterion to determine what features of a sign are syntactically significant. This is not to say that all features of such signs are constitutive. Some—e.g., the paper on which a map is printed, the location of a painting—are plainly contingent. The difficulty is that the distinction must be drawn on a case-by-case basis. For the paper on which a picture is sketched and the location of a monument may well be constitutive features of these signs.

Let us look now at a case Goodman considers. A momentary portion of an electrocardiogram and a Hokusai drawing of Mt. Fujiyama are symbols in syntactically dense systems, each consisting of a black line on a white background. Suppose the configurations of black on white are the same in both cases. Are we to say that the two marks are syntactically identical? Surely not. The only features that are constitutive of the electrocardiogram are the relation of each point on the line to the x and y axes. In particular, the color, thickness, shading, and intensity of the line, the color of the background, and the texture of the paper on which the line is drawn are contingent features of the electrocardiogram. But all of them are constitutive features of the drawing. The cardiogram then symbolizes along fewer dimensions than the drawing does. The drawing is replete; the diagram, attenuated [LA, 229–30].

We cannot, however, draw a sharp distinction between the pictorial and the diagrammatic by differentiating between replete and attenuated symbols. For repleteness is a matter of degree. A map on which lakes and rivers are represented in blue, forests in green, and prairies in pale yellow is more replete than the cardiogram, but less so than the drawing. There is then a continuum from the diagrammatic to the pictorial, from the attenuated to the replete.

2. SEMANTICS

Traditional musical scores, Arabic fractions, and the words and phrases of ordinary discursive language all belong to symbol systems that are syntactically disjoint and finitely differentiated. There are, however, important semantic differences among these systems.

Discursive languages typically contain ambiguous expressions. In

---

density. When no insertion of other characters in their normal position will thus destroy density, a scheme has no gaps and may be called *dense throughout*'' [LA, 136].

some cases syntactic replicas differ in extension. In others, a single utterance or inscription has more than one extension. Such languages are highly redundant as well. That is, they contain a variety of expressions that agree in extension. As a result, a term in such a language does not always determine a unique compliance class; nor a compliance class, a unique term.

Nor is redundancy the sole source of semantic nondisjointness. The compliance classes of a discursive language properly intersect. So a single object belongs to indefinitely many compliance classes. A gorilla, for example, belongs to the extensions of 'animate', 'powerful', 'gentle', 'gray', 'larger than a squirrel', 'heavier than an acorn', 'furrier than an elephant', etc. Given an object, we cannot derive a unique compliance class to which it belongs, for the object complies with a host of expressions whose extensions diverge.

Moreover, the compliance classes of a discursive language are dense throughout. That is, they are so ordered that between any two there is a third, and no insertion of others in normal position will destroy density [LA, 153]. The language thus sets no limit on the precision our descriptions can achieve. Our semantic resources are bound to outrun our ability to make discriminations. There will inevitably be cases in which we have no basis for saying with which of a number of mutually exclusive predicates a given object complies.

Consider the problem of saying what color a damson plum is. We might call it 'purple', 'dark purple', 'halfway between dark purple and deep purple', 'halfway between dark purple and the shade that is halfway between dark purple and deep purple', and so on. English contains the resources to continue refining our descriptions *ad infinitum*. But of course we do not have the ability to recognize infinitely fine differences in color. There are then predicates of the language whose application to a given object we have no way to ascertain. Once our ability to discriminate is exhausted, we have no justification for taking one rather than the other of a pair of mutually exclusive terms to denote the object.

To be sure, with the aid of technology we can extend our ability to make discriminations. Nevertheless, there will remain cases in which even our most refined discriminatory techniques afford no basis for deciding which of several mutually exclusive predicates applies to a given object.

In summary, a discursive language is syntactically disjoint and finitely differentiated. It is semantically nondisjoint, dense throughout, and ambiguous.

Consider now the semantics of a system that uses Arabic fractions to measure weight in fractions of an ounce. The system is unambiguous. Each term has one and only one compliance class. '3/4 oz.', for example, denotes all and only those things three-quarters of an ounce in weight. The system is redundant. Many expressions—'3/4 oz.', '6/8 oz.', '9/12 oz.', . . .—have the same compliance class. And because it is redundant, the system is not disjoint. But redundancy is the only violation of semantic disjointness. Although different expressions have the same compliance class, no object belongs to more than one compliance class of the system. A system in which only fully reduced Arabic fractions are used to measure weight in fractions of an ounce is semantically disjoint.

Both systems are semantically dense throughout. They assign to distinct compliance classes objects so close to one another in weight that no measurement can determine that their weights are not identical. The point here is logical, not technological. It is not simply that we currently have no device sensitive enough to measure all the distinctions that the system admits. It is rather that however sensitive our measuring device, there will always be further differences in weight which it is incapable of distinguishing. If it is accurate to within a thousandth of an ounce, it will fail to distinguish between objects whose difference in weight is a ten-thousandth of an ounce. And if it is accurate enough to measure these, there remain objects whose weights differ by but a hundred-thousandth of an ounce, and so on.

What happens if we impose a limit on the weights our system discriminates? Suppose the smallest unit the system admits is 1/1000 oz. Under this system objects whose weights differ by less than 1/1000 oz. belong to the same compliance class. Obviously, "judgment calls" will be required to decide borderline cases. And unless instruments for measuring small differences in weight are developed, technological difficulties remain. But the structure of this system is quite different from the structures of previous ones, for this system is finitely differentiated semantically. That is, for every two characters of the system, and every object that does not actually comply with both, it is theoretically possible to determine that the object in question does not comply with one or that it does not comply with the other [LA, 152]. Here, as in the case of finite syntactic differentiation, there is a variety of ways of explicating 'theoretically possible'. And depending on which explication is chosen, different systems count as semantically differentiated.

It should be clear that semantic disjointness and finite semantic differentiation are independent features of a system. The system that measures weight in fully reduced Arabic fractions of an ounce is semantically disjoint, but not semantically differentiated. No two characters have any compliant in common, but there are cases in which it is impossible to determine with which of several mutually exclusive characters a given object complies. And a system that measures both weight in Arabic fractions of an ounce up to some limit, and length in Arabic fractions of an inch up to some limit is semantically differentiated, but not disjoint. It is possible to determine with what characters a given object complies, but that object complies with more than one character. It may, for example, comply with both '3/4 oz.' and '7/10 in.'[4] Semantic disjointness insures that each object

4. Notice that separately the two subsystems are disjoint. Nothing complies with more than one weight character nor with more than one length character. Moreover, a system whose characters are all conjunctive— . . . oz. & —— in.—is likewise disjoint. For to comply with a character an object has to be both some particular weight and

complies with at most one character of the system. Finite semantic differentiation insures that it is possible to ascertain the characters with which each object in a realm complies.

If a system without ambiguous expressions is syntactically and semantically disjoint and finitely differentiated, that system is a notation [LA, 156]. Its syntax insures that it is possible to discover the unique character to which each of its marks belongs. Its semantics insures that it is possible to discover both the unique compliance class to which each of the objects in its realm belongs and the unique character with which each of them complies. Each character of a notation then determines a unique compliance class; and each compliant, a unique character.

3. NOTATIONS

The syntactic and semantic requirements on a notation are severe. We must investigate the extent to which they are satisfied by actual symbol systems.

One system that qualifies as a notation is the United States postal service system of zip codes. Each zip code applies only to the mailing addresses of a single region, so the system is unambiguous. Moreover, each mailing address has but a single zip code. The system is thus semantically disjoint. And the boundaries between regions are drawn in such a way that it is possible to ascertain the zip code of any mailing address in the United States. The system is then semantically differentiated as well. The semantic requirements on a notation are thus plainly satisfied by the zip code system.

The syntactic requirements are also satisfied, for the characters of the system are numerals. Since no inscription belongs to more than one character, the system is syntactically disjoint. And if an inscription belongs to a character of the system, it is possible in principle to identify that character. The system is then syntactically differentiated as well. Granted, the postal service is frequently faced with illegible inscriptions. But this in no way affects the syntactic disjointness or finite differentiation of the system. For regardless of the difficulty in deciphering it, a mark cannot be treated as an inscription of a zip code unless and until it is recognized as an inscription of a single identifiable character. Inscriptions that prove entirely indecipherable are simply excluded from the system. They are not counted as zip codes.

The syntax and semantics of postal codes are, perhaps, of limited general interest. I discuss them because the system is familiar and simple enough that its notational features are easily shown. But it should not be thought that only simple, utilitarian systems are notational. Goodman has shown that the system in which music is traditionally scored comes close to satisfying the requirements for a nota-

---

some particular length. But if the system considers ounces and inches separately, it is nondisjoint. For in that case its compliance classes properly intersect.

tion. Since that system is a rich and subtle one, we would do well to review his argument [LA, 179–87] in some detail.

The traditional system for scoring music is symbolically complex. Its characters include notes, staves, clefs, key and time signatures, as well as verbal indications of tempo. All satisfy the syntactic requirements for a notation. For each inscription belongs to at most one character, and none is admitted to be musically significant unless it is possible to identify the character to which it belongs.

Of course, there are cases in which it is difficult to determine the character to which a particular mark belongs. A quarter-note inscription, for example, might be so positioned that it is hard to tell whether it is an F-note or a G-note. Still, it cannot be both. And it cannot be considered a mark of the notation unless the musical character to which it belongs can be identified.

It is when we consider whether scores satisfy the semantic requirements for a notation that complications arise. Some characters, such as staves, are syncategorematic. For these, there is no question of semantic interpretation. Others can be shown, on reasonable construals, to satisfy the semantic requirements for a notation. Yet others must be excluded from the score proper, if the score is to be notational.

A musical note is a character whose inscriptions determine pitch by their position on a staff, and relative duration by their shape. Both raise difficulties for the thesis that scores are notational. Let us begin by considering the difficulties that concern pitch.

In piano scores, for example, there is redundancy with respect to pitch. Inscriptions that belong to separate characters are alike in denotation [LA, 181]. Thus, e.g., the C-sharp half note directly above middle C and the D-flat half note directly above middle C are coextensive. Since the system is redundant, it is not semantically disjoint. From a compliant, a unique character cannot be derived.

Instead of concluding that piano scores are non-notational, what happens if we relax the requirements on notationality to admit redundant characters? In that case, inscriptions with identical compliants are not all syntactic replicas of one another. But redundant characters have identical compliance classes, so it remains true that each individual belongs to at most one of the system's compliance classes. Rather than defining a score syntactically as a single character in a musical notation, we can define it semantically as a set of coextensive characters. A score then determines a work in that its compliance class consists of all and only performances of that work. But there are several distinct characters in the system that denote the members of that class. Relaxing the requirements on notationality this far seems to do no significant damage.

There may be a more serious problem than the discussion has so far indicated. If C-sharp and D-flat are in general alike in denotation,[5]

5. Strictly speaking, C-sharps and D-flats in piano scores do not all denote members of a single compliance class of musical notation. It is rather the C-sharp and the D-flat that belong to the same octave and agree about relative duration that do so. To avoid

then a system containing both characters is merely redundant. But this is not the case. In violin scores, for example, C-sharp and D-flat differ in extension. And in general, different characters in violin scores have different compliance classes. This suggests that there is a greater threat to semantic disjointness than redundancy. For it now appears that some tones (viz., piano tones) that comply with C-sharp also comply with D-flat, and others (violin tones) that comply with C-sharp do not comply with D-flat. If this is the case, then the compliance classes of the notes C-sharp and D-flat properly intersect, and semantic disjointness is gone for good.

There is, however, a reasonable construal that avoids this difficulty. Since music is played on one instrument or another, we might consider the specification of the instrument that is to play the notes to be part of the score. C-sharp and D-flat taken by themselves are then semantically incomplete symbols that lack denotation until an instrument is specified. Piano C-sharp compliants are identical to piano D-flat compliants. Violin C-sharp compliants are distinct from violin D-flat compliants.[6] And since no piano tones comply with violin notes, and no violin tones with piano notes, the compliance classes of piano C-sharp and violin C-sharp do not intersect. Thus, except for redundancy which was shown to be harmless, the semantic disjointness of musical notation is preserved [LA, 182].

The full range of musical sounds is, of course, dense. Does this mean that musical scores lack finite semantic differentiation? Surely not. For the question of semantic differentiation turns on the way those sounds are classed together as compliants of a single note, not on whether there are discernible or indiscernible differences among compliants. Music scored for the piano recognizes but one tone between C and D; music scored for the violin, two. The sounds from a dense realm are thus forced into a limited number of compliance classes.

It has been argued that these compliance classes are disjoint. Consequently, no sound actually belongs to more than one of them. If they are finitely differentiated, then for any sound that complies with a character, it is possible to identify the character with which it complies. And in fact it is. Even when our ears aren't sensitive enough to determine that a given violin tone falls within the limits the system imposes on D-flat, the length of the resulting sound wave, or the

---

needlessly complicating the discussion, I make no mention of the octave or of the relative duration of the notes in question.

6. This is controversial: a tone of 333 vibrations per second, for example, might be taken to comply with both. It is not clear, however, whether this amounts to saying that the tone *actually* complies with both or that it falls within the limits of deviation from genuine compliance that is ordinarily permitted in practice. If the former, the semantic disjointness of the system is lost. If the latter, it is preserved. To the extent that notationality is valued, we should, *ceteris paribus*, prefer the latter interpretation [LA, 182n].

number of vibrations per second is sufficient to decide the case. The system sets definite conditions on compliance with its notes, and it is in principle possible to discover whether the conditions are satisfied.

The differences in relative duration marked by characters in musical notation clearly satisfy the requirements of unambiguity and semantic disjointness. The difficulty, if there is one, arises with the requirement of finite semantic differentiation. If the sequence: whole note, half note, quarter note, . . . is infinite, then the system lacks finite differentiation. For then "by tying note-signs together we can construct characters for notes differing in duration by less than any given fraction of a beat" [LA, 182]. Differences in duration of compliants of some of the system's characters are so small that it is impossible to identify the unique character with which a sounded note complies.

In fact, of course, no one writes music in which differences in the durations of compliants of different notes are vanishingly small. By convention, the shortest relative duration is marked by the 1/128th note. The question of notationality turns on how such a convention is to be interpreted. If it is simply a rule of thumb—practical, perhaps, if most musicians cannot clearly articulate smaller fractions of a beat—then so far forth the system has the capacity to make infinitely fine distinctions in duration. It lacks finite semantic differentiation, and so is not a notation. If, however, this convention (or some other, tacit or explicit) genuinely sets a lower bound on the differences in relative duration, the system is finitely differentiated semantically. There is inevitably some limit in practice. If we elevate it to a limit in principle, we can retain the benefits of notationality for musical scores [LA, 183].

Scores written with basso continuo and those written with free cadenza contain characters that are more general than individual notes. In each case a set of parameters is indicated within which compliant performances must fall. These parameters are broad enough that compliant performances are not note-for-note identical with one another. Generality, of course, is no bar to notationality. A difficulty arises, however, if the same passage complies with a score in which each note is individually specified and one written with basso continuo (or with free cadenza). That passage, it seems, belongs to compliance classes that properly intersect. And unless we can tell which characters appear in the score, we will be unable to tell what other performances belong to the work. A score, of course, still determines the performances that are its compliants. But because the system is not semantically disjoint, a compliant performance does not determine the score [LA, 183–84].

Deriving a score from a performance requires knowing what notational system is in effect. And there is no reason to suppose that a single notational system has a monopoly on a particular realm. So perhaps the best way to handle the problematic performances is to recognize that they comply with scores of two distinct systems. In one, each sounded note is individually scored; in the other, certain passages are indicated more generally. If no performance complies with more than one character of each, both systems are notational. Then scores in both notations can be derived from a single performance. The two scores, of course, define different works.

One final area in which the notationality of musical scores is threatened is in verbal indications of tempo — 'largo', 'allegro', 'presto', and the like. This vocabulary apparently contains indefinitely many terms of varying scope. We find, e.g., 'andante', 'andante allegro', 'più andante', 'meno andante', 'molto andante', 'andantino', and 'andante espressivo'. The terminology evidently lacks semantic disjointness, for a given movement might comply with several of these terms. Moreover, since the tempo of a movement can be prescribed with any desired degree of precision, finite semantic differentiation is wanting as well. Finally, some of these terms are ambiguous. In some applications 'andantino' denotes a slower tempo than 'andante'; in other applications, a faster one.

Finite semantic differentiation of notes was achieved by imposing a limit on permissible differences in relative duration of different notes. It might likewise be achieved here if we impose a limit on permissible differences in tempo. But the conventions concerning the vocabulary of tempo are not so clear as those concerning relative duration, so it may be difficult to decide whether such an imposition is sufficiently faithful to the antecedent usage of that vocabulary.

It doesn't much matter how (or whether) we decide this question. For the absence of finite semantic differentiation is not the main barrier to interpreting the vocabulary of tempo as a notation. The absence of semantic disjointness is. And apparently no construal of that vocabulary as semantically disjoint retains any hint of fidelity to the way the terms are actually used.

It should not be thought that tempo is somehow peculiarly unsusceptible to notation. For metronomic indications of tempo are plainly notational. Nor is it because verbal indications of tempo are relative terms that they cannot be construed notationally. For the syntactic and semantic criteria for notationality can be satisfied by relative terms. A notation can, e.g., specify that a half note is to be half as long as a whole note without having to specify the absolute duration of either. The claim that the terminology of tempo is non-notational has to do more with the terminology than with tempo. As it is used, the vocabulary of tempo is semantically nondisjoint, nondifferentiated, and ambiguous. Accordingly, its use is not captured by an interpretation that satisfies the criteria for notationality.

Goodman suggests that we concede that the terminology of tempo is nonnotational, but that we preserve the notationality of musical scores by denying that verbal indications of tempo are properly part of a score [LA, 185]. Instead they serve as advice from the composer as to the speed at which the piece should be played. If this is the case, then they play no part in the identification of a performance as an instance of a particular work. Regardless of the extent of its deviation from the suggested tempo, an otherwise faithful performance must be counted compliant with its score, and so an instance of the work. Of course, if the composer's advice is good, serious deviation in the matter of tempo is reason to consider a performance a particularly poor instance of the work.

Why go to all this trouble? Does it matter so very much whether musical scores are notational? In fact, it does. Music is a multiple medium. That is, diverse performances are instances of a single work. These performances may be remote from one another in time and place, and may differ from one another in a host of other ways as well. We thus need a criterion of work identity in order to ascertain what performances are instances of a given work. This is what a score provides. From any performance it is possible to derive the score with which it complies; and from any score, to derive the compliant performances. It is thus possible to discover that two performances belong to the same work by discovering that they comply with the same score.

A musical work is then the class of performances that comply with a given score. The score, in effect, prescribes the respects in which different performances of the work must agree [LA, 128].

At various points in the discussion we had to choose among alternative interpretations of musical scores, all of which seemed reasonably faithful to the way music is actually written. And at some points the arguments for our choices even seem somewhat strained. The justification for the choices we made lies in the primary function of a score: "the authoritative identification of a work from performance to performance" [LA, 128]. If scores belong to a notational system, they can perform this function. If they violate any of the conditions on notationality (save the one forbidding redundancy), they cannot. If either of the syntactical conditions is violated, it will be impossible to tell whether inscriptions are replicas of each other, and thus copies of the same score. If any of the semantic conditions is violated, it will be impossible to identify the score with which a performance complies, and thus impossible to tell whether diverse performances comply with the same score.

There may, of course, be an easier, more natural way to construe musical scores as notational. If so, it is certainly to be preferred. The point here is simply that to sacrifice notationality for ease and naturalness is to give up a good deal—for it is to render scores incapable of performing their primary function.

If compliance with a score is what defines a performance as an instance of a work, then we are forced to a conclusion for which Goodman has become notorious: A performance with a single wrong note is not, strictly speaking, an instance of the work [LA, 186]. Certainly we are not accustomed to judging performances so harshly. Should we relax our formal standard for being a performance of a work in order to bring it into agreement with our practice? Or should we retain our standard for strict compliance, but agree that performances that comply with a score to within some reasonable margin of error are to be treated as performances of the work that the score defines?

There are two problems with the former alternative: First, there seems to be no nonarbitrary way to decide which errors and how many of them are to be tolerated before a performance is excluded from a work. Second, and more important, if we relax our formal standard, the structure of the system is radically altered. And it is altered in such a way that the score is unable to define diverse performances as instances of a single work. If each performance differs from its predecessors by but a single note, performances sufficiently remote from one another in a series might be so unlike each other that there is no score with which they even approximately comply.

It is better then to accept the original standard and to allow the exigencies of different situations to decide how strict we will be about applying it. This seems reasonable, not only because the score can then serve its primary purpose, but also because it reflects our willingness to adjust our tolerance for error with differences in context. We might, for example, be willing to recognize as a performance of a given work the sequence of sounds emitted when the local high school orchestra sight reads the score for the first time. But should the same sequence of sounds be produced by the Boston Symphony Orchestra in concert, we might be quite unwilling to acknowledge it as a performance of the work. If both verdicts are reasonable, then simply relaxing our standard by permitting a few wrong notes will not accommodate our various "intuitions" as to what performances ought to be treated as instances of a work.

Discussion of the relation between scores and performances was undertaken out of an interest in musical notation as a symbol system. Strict compliance of performance with score is required if the score is to identify a performance as an instance of a work, and to identify distinct performances as instances of the same work. And since music is a multiple medium, the capacity to make such identifications is clearly desirable. But strict compliance with a score is no measure of aesthetic merit. If the sequence of sounds prescribed by the score is sufficiently awful, deviation from the score may be aesthetically welcome. In any case, there are other factors that go into the aesthetic evaluation of a work—e.g., what the work exemplifies and expresses. Excellence in these may compensate for a few wrong notes, and lack of excellence in them need not be overridden by strict compliance with a score.

The differences between a discursive language such as ordinary English and a notation are semantic. A discursive language contains ambiguous expressions; a notation does not. A discursive language is semantically nondisjoint. Its compliance classes properly intersect. A notation is semantically disjoint. Each of its compliants belongs to a unique compliance class. And a discursive language is semantically dense. Thus, there are cases in which it is impossible to determine to which of a number of mutually exclusive compliance classes a given object belongs. A notation is semantically differentiated. In every case it is theoretically possible to identify the compliance class to which an object belongs.

Because discursive languages are not semantically disjoint, every selection of objects belongs to indefinitely many properly intersecting compliance classes. Indeed, "the objects in any given selection comply with some English description that has as its other compliants any other given objects" [LA, 202]. Accordingly, in projecting from a given selection to a wider class of objects we have to choose among the various compliance classes to which the selected objects belong. All emeralds examined to date belong to the compliance class of 'green' and to that of 'grue'. But 'green' and 'grue' are not coextensive, so any generalization regarding the color of emeralds requires a choice between them. I am not concerned here to discuss the way such choices are to be made. I want only to note that the necessity of making them is a consequence of the nondisjointness of discursive language. A selection of objects does not determine a unique compliance class onto which it is to be projected.

Projection from selected compliants of characters of a notation involves no such choice. In effect, the choice has been made in advance in designing the system. Because a notation is semantically disjoint, nothing belongs to more than one of its compliance classes. And because it is semantically differentiated, it is possible in every case to discover the compliance class to which a selected item belongs. There is then but a single class of a notation onto which an instance can be projected [LA, 201–03].

It follows that from a single compliant of a notation the character (or, if the system is redundant, the coextensive characters) it instantiates can be derived. Thus, it is possible to derive its score from a single performance of a musical work. Of course, a performance of the entire piece is required to derive the complete score. The beginning of the piece plainly does not determine what comes next. Still, the derivability of a unique character (or a unique set of coextensive characters) from a single compliant is a remarkable and important feature of notational systems. The fact that a single performance determines a score, and a score each compliant performance is what allows for the authoritative identification of a musical work from one performance to the next. "Identity of work and of score is retained in any series of steps, each of them either from compliant performance to score inscription, or from score inscription to compliant performance" [LA, 178]. This feature is not shared by the characters and compliants of discursive language. A mountain lion, for example, instantiates 'native to North America', a label that is also instantiated by a mountain laurel. The latter, however, also instantiates 'flowering plant', a label that is manifestly not instantiated by the former. A chain connecting characters and compliants of a notation always links the same (or coextensive) characters with the same compliants. One connecting characters and compliants of a discursive language can go on indefinitely without repeating characters or compliants.

Devising *a* notation for a domain is simple enough, for the criteria for notationality are purely formal. But devising one that suits our symbolic purposes is often difficult, sometimes impossible.

In constructing a notation for a field like music, we are constrained not only by the formal criteria for notationality, but also by our antecedent classificatory practices. These serve as a touchstone against which to measure the adequacy of any proposed system. For the most part, performances that are antecedently recognized as instances of a single work should turn out according to our notation to be so. Certainly some of our initial judgments can be revised in the interest of systematization. But substantial agreement with them is required if a notation is to define works in a given field. Unless its verdicts generally agree with our antecedent classifications of musical performances, a notation is inadequate to define musical works. The characters of such a notation do not qualify as musical scores.

Dance, like music, is transient and temporal. It frequently involves many performers at once and the same dance is apt to be performed by different dancers on different occasions. These features, it would seem, make a notation for the dance desirable. Moreover, even without a notation, we recognize distinct performances as performances of the same work. So we have an antecedent classification against which to measure the adequacy of any candidate notation.

A number of systems have been developed to record works in the dance—e.g., the Banesh system, the Eshkol-Wachmann system, and Labanotation. Goodman suggests [LA, 211–18] that Labanotation is one that comes as close as is practicable to satisfying the criteria for notationality. To the extent that its compliance classes accord with our antecedent classifications of performances as instances of a single work, it is then a theoretically adequate notation for the dance. And if there are other theoretically adequate systems as well, the choice among them must be made on aesthetic or practical grounds.

Interestingly, the applicability of Labanotation is not restricted to the dance. Its domain is human movement generally, and it has been used in the behavioral sciences, in physical therapy, and in such sports as figure skating and diving. The question whether the same movement has been repeated—a question that is relevant in all of these fields—has a determinate and discoverable answer only if movements are catalogued in terms of semantically disjoint and finitely differentiated categories.

If it is to define works in a particular field, a notation must be reasonably faithful to our antecedent practice of identifying such works. But there are works that we identify on the basis of criteria that cannot be captured by a notation. A painting, for example, retains its identity as a particular work regardless of the syntactic and semantic changes it undergoes. It may fade, chip, be restored, be interpreted as denoting and exemplifying different things in different eras. Yet it remains the selfsame work. The identification of a painting as a particular work depends on a matter of historical fact. Only the object with the requisite history is the work in question. Thus, the only painting that is the *Mona Lisa* is the one painted by Da Vinci. Since the criteria for work identity supplied by a notation are syntactic and semantic, not historical, a notation is incapable of reflecting our practice of identifying works on the basis of their history. So long as the practice remains the same, there is no prospect of developing a notation for the authoritative identification of works in painting.

Fidelity to antecedent practice is a requirement on notations suited to certain purposes. It is not a requirement on notations as such. In some cases the adequacy of a notation is independent of the ways its domain has previously been organized. Consider a system in which the final digit of the Social Security number under which a person last worked determines the day of the week on which he is to apply for unemployment benefits. The system is notational: The final digit of each Social Security number is determinate and identifiable; no digit has more than one compliance class; each applicant belongs to exactly one compliance class; and in every case it is possible to discover the class to which an applicant belongs. But there is no antecedent classification of the jobless which the system is required to reflect. All that is wanted is a system in which approximately the same number of applicants are processed on each day of the week. So the system is adequate if its compliance classes are about equal in size. It matters not at all who belongs to each class.

Music belongs to a dense field of sound; dance, to a dense field of movement. Plainly a domain need not be composed of recognizably discrete individuals to be a candidate for a notation. Disjointness and finite differentiation are imposed on fields of reference, not found in them.

Whether it is possible to devise a notation in a given case depends not on the nature of the domain, but on our purposes in symbolizing it. It is these that determine whether we can make do with a system in which ambiguity is precluded, and in which each mark belongs to exactly one identifiable character, and each compliant belongs to exactly one identifiable compliance class.

4. WORKS

The problem of identifying diverse items as instances of a single work arises in other media as well as in music and the dance. And the solution is not always the same.

Novels, essays, and poems are written in discursive languages. Such languages satisfy the syntactic criteria for notationality, but not the semantic ones. Each utterance and inscription belongs to at most one character, and it is possible in principle to determine which one.

But the compliance classes of a discursive language are neither disjoint nor finitely differentiated, and some terms are ambiguous. As a result, a literary work cannot be identified as the compliance class of a text in the way that a musical work is identified as the compliance class of a score.

Because a discursive language lacks finite semantic differentiation, it contains mutually exclusive terms that are so related that it is impossible to determine with which of them a given object complies. Accordingly, there are cases in which it is impossible to tell whether a particular object complies with a text. Because such a language lacks semantic disjointness, every object belongs to a host of properly intersecting compliance classes. Thus a single object might comply with several noncoextensive texts. And because such a language contains ambiguous expressions, distinct classes of objects might comply with the same text. Therefore, if literary works are compliance classes of texts, then there are cases in which it is indeterminate whether something is an instance of a work, cases in which the same thing is an instance of several works, and cases in which a single text defines more than one work.

But of course the identity of a literary work is not determined by the membership of its compliance class.[7] Otherwise, all manuscripts alike in denotation would define the same work. And an event—a lunar landing or a military coup—would become a work of journalism as soon as it was reported in the newspaper. The identity of a literary work resides, rather, in the text itself. Anything spelled exactly like a true copy of *Pride and Prejudice* is an instance of that work. The syntactic features of the language in which it is written thus suffice to identify the various instances of a literary work.

A literary work is then a character in a discursive language—a most comprehensive class of syntactic replicas [LA, 209]. This of course includes research reports, résumés, and recipes, as well as novels, essays, and poems under the rubric 'literary'. Nothing concerning the aesthetic classification or the aesthetic evaluation of a work is suggested by my use of the term. Although my usage may be somewhat broader than the ordinary application of the term, there should be no major difficulty. Just as a true copy of *Pride and Prejudice* is an instance of Austen's great work, a true copy of *The Origin of Species* is an instance of Darwin's. The question of how literary works are to be classified in terms of genre is something I leave aside.

Certain consequences of a purely syntactical criterion for membership in a work should be noted. First, only *true* copies of an instance of such a work are themselves instances of that work. A copy containing a single misprint or spelling error is not, strictly speaking, an instance of the work. One wrong letter in the verbal media is thus as serious as one wrong note in music. And the argument for accepting

---

7. There are, to be sure, theories of literature according to which a text defines more than one work—namely, those which maintain that the reader determines the work. But under no plausible theory does the compliance class of a text determine a work.

such a strict standard in principle and exercising reasonable tolerance in applying it in practice parallels the one given for music.

A second consequence is this: because it is spelled differently from the original, a translation of a literary work is not strictly an instance of that work. This consequence is, perhaps, surprising. But the philosophical problems concerning translation are notorious. Certainly translation is a semantic matter—a matter of how to paraphrase claims made in one language adequately in another. And since there is no clear standard for adequacy of paraphrase, if the criteria for the identity of a literary work have to comprehend translations of that work, the problem of discovering such criteria seems intractable. We do not, in any case, regard paraphrases of a work in its own language as instances of that work. To have read the *Classics Illustrated* version is not to have read *Pride and Prejudice*. It seems best to extend this policy to translations, and to deny altogether that paraphrases of a literary work are instances of it.

There is, to be sure, a looser use of the term 'work' according to which translations of a work count as instances of it. It is tempting to adopt a double standard here: to employ a syntactic criterion (sameness of spelling) to identify instances of a literary work in the home lanaguage, and a semantic criterion (translation) to identify its instances in other languages. This accords well with our practice. The difficulty is that translations of a given work into a given language can differ substantially. So French translations of *Pride and Prejudice* need not be spelled alike. They need not be true copies of one another to be counted instances of the work.

Because the identity of a work is located differently in literature from the way it is in music, the relation between what is seen and what is heard is also different. Inscriptions and utterances are alike instances of a literary work. For as we saw in Chapter II an utterance is a syntactic replica of every inscription with the same spelling. And any replica of a true copy of a literary work is itself an instance of that work. But an inscription of a score is not an instance of a musical work. The relation between score and performance is semantic, not syntactic. And the score defines, but does not belong to, the work. Every instance of a musical work is audible, while some instances of a literary work are audible, others visible.

Drama is an intermediate case. Plays are written in discursive language, but instances of dramatic works are performances, not scripts. Should we say then that a script, like a score, prescribes its compliant performances—prescribes, that is, the performances that are instances of the work? If so, we shall have to construe compliance somewhat differently from the way we have done so far. For a dramatic performance plainly does not comply with its script if that script is interpreted as characters in the language ordinarily are. No one, for example, is actually murdered during a typical performance of *Macbeth*, even though under the standard interpretation of English it is murders that comply with descriptions of murders.

The dialogue of the play does, however, comply with a script when the script is interpreted as a character in sound-English—that is, in a system in which "ordinary English alphabetic notation is correlated with sound events according to the usual practice of pronunciation" [LA, 144]. The dialogue of a play then belongs to an approximately notational system[8]—one in which utterances belong to the compliance classes of inscriptions. For a performance to be an instance of a particular dramatic work, the words uttered by the actors must comply exactly with the words inscribed in a true copy of the script.

A difficulty arises since dramatic scripts do not consist exclusively of dialogue. They typically contain stage directions and often descriptions of costumes, scenery, and props as well. These function not as expressions in a sound language, but as expressions in an ordinary discursive language. An actor complies with the stage direction 'exit stage left' by exiting stage left, not by emitting an utterance of "exit stage left". Such directions and descriptions are non-notational, for their compliance classes are neither disjoint nor finitely differentiated. In leaving the stage, an actor might be complying with 'exit', 'exit stage left', 'exit slowly', 'exit slowly and deliberately', etc. A performance thus does not determine a unique set of stage directions.

It does, however, determine a unique dialogue (or, if there are homonyms, a set of coextensive dialogues). Accordingly, if we are to identify a dramatic work as the compliance class (in a sound language) of a script, we must locate the identity of the script in the dialogue. We can then treat stage directions and descriptions of scenery, props, and the like as we treated verbal indications of tempo in musical scores. They function as advice as to how a work is to be played, but they are constitutive of neither score nor script [LA, 210–11].

Such an interpretation of dramatic scripts is not unreasonable. Performances in modern dress, without props or scenery, are counted as performances of *Macbeth* so long as the actors utter the dialogue of that play.

If infinitely many monkeys were to type for an infinitely long time, one would eventually produce a replica of *Pride and Prejudice*. And if those monkeys were to bang on pianos instead of typewriters, one would eventually play the *Moonlight Sonata*. The monkeys in question would produce genuine instances of these works. For an item is an instance of a literary work if it is spelled the same as other instances of that work. And an item is an instance of a musical work if it complies with the work's score. In neither case need there by any special historical, causal, or intentional relation to the original manuscript or author of the work. Arbitrarily generated items having the

---

8. 'Approximately' because discursive languages contain homonyms. Accordingly, it is not always the case that an utterance complies with a unique character in a sound-language. The approximation to notationality is closer in Spanish that it is in English, for Spanish contains fewer homonyms [LA, 207n]. In any case, a sound-language containing homonyms is merely redundant, for more than one character has the same compliance class. But redundancy, as we saw, is no major defect in notationality.

requisite notational features are genuine instances of such works. Works such as these, and the arts to which they belong are *allographic* [LA, 113], for the history of an item's production is irrelevant to its identification as an instance of such a work.

The situation is different in the case of painting. No matter how long those monkeys went on brushing paint onto a canvas, none would ever produce the *Mona Lisa*. Why not? It is tempting to answer, "Because someone else already painted the *Mona Lisa*." But the fact that someone else already wrote *Pride and Prejudice* proved no reason to deny that a monkey might produce a genuine instance of that work. Why should painting be different? Unlike literature, painting is not a multiple medium. The closest copy of the *Mona Lisa* is not an instance of the work. Moreover, to identify an object as a particular painting requires discovering that object's history. To be the *Mona Lisa* is to be the very thing that Da Vinci painted. Such a work is *autographic* [LA, 113], for its identity depends on its history of production. And when a work of art is autographic, the art is autographic as well.

Consider now the case of infinitely many monkeys engaged in print making. Might one of them produce an instance of *The Three Trees?* Print making, like literature and music, is a multiple medium. But like painting, it lacks a notation. To identify a print as an instance of a particular work requires ascertaining a matter of historical fact. To be an instance of *The Three Trees* a print must be taken from Rembrandt's plate. But if we look at the way we identify prints as instances of a particular work, we see that there is no requirement that the artist make the actual impression. So if the monkeys had access to Rembrandt's plate (and if they didn't ruin it first), they could produce an instance of the work. Lacking the plate, however, even with infinite time and resources, they could not.

Print making, like painting, is an autographic art. The only way to discover whether a print is genuine is to ascertain the history of its production. No resemblance to known instances of the work suffices, for the print in question might be a good copy or a clever forgery. Moreover, a decided lack of resemblance to known instances is not always reason to exclude a print from a work. Prints from the same plate may differ markedly in color, paper, sharpness of line, quality of impression, and so on. And what makes a print an instance of a particular work is the fact that it was taken from a particular plate [LA, 118–19].

One major difference between autographic and allographic works is this: Autographic works are subject to forgery; allographic works are not. "A forgery of a work of art is an object falsely purporting to have the history of production requisite for the (or an) original of that work." [LA, 122] Since the authenticity of an allographic work does not depend on its history, such a work cannot be forged.

We must take care to interpret this claim correctly. Certainly an item alleged to be an unpublished manuscript of Jane Austen's, or a first edition of *Pride and Prejudice,* might turn out to be a forgery. For the author and edition of a literary work are matters of historical fact. But whether something is an instance of *Pride and Prejudice* at all depends on its spelling, not on its history. Anything spelled like a true copy of the work is an instance of the work; anything spelled differently is not. There is then a decisive test for the authenticity of such works—one that is indifferent to matters of history.

It is not only in the arts that authenticity is decided on historical grounds. There are other artifacts whose authenticity is determined by their history of production as well. This is the case, for example, for currency and couture: nothing is a genuine dollar or a genuine Dior unless it was produced in the appropriate circumstances. There are social categories whose application depends on matters of historical fact as well. E.g., whether a person is a British peer, a Catholic priest, a U.S. citizen depends on specific facts of his history. There are also labels whose application turns on historical facts in certain sciences—geology, paleontology, evolutionary biology. Thus, e.g., for a ridge to be a moraine, it must have been deposited by a glacier. And for animals to belong to the same species, they must be descendants of a common ancestor. Just what facts about an item's history determine its authenticity plainly vary from case to case. Still, the dependence on historical facts to determine authenticity suggests that these categories too can be considered autographic.

In that case it is reasonable to ask whether such items, like autographic works of arts, are subject to forgery. In fact they are. Currency, of course, is frequently counterfeited. And there is a thriving, if illegal, industry in counterfeiting clothing whose designer or manufacturer is renowned.

Social roles like the ones I mentioned are subject to imposture in a way that other social roles are not. Anyone who plucks chickens, for example, is *ipso facto* a chicken plucker. But a person who represents himself to be a priest, and engages in priestly activities is, nevertheless, not a priest unless he has been ordained. Otherwise he is an impostor. Of course, someone might lie about being a chicken plucker just as he might lie about being a priest. The difference is this: what determines whether a man is a chicken plucker is whether he does what chicken pluckers do—namely, pluck chickens. But his doing what priests do is not what determines whether a man is a priest. That is determined by the occurrence or nonoccurrence of a specific event in his past—his ordination.[9] A person can live the life of a priest without being one. But a person who lives the life of a chicken plucker *is* one.[10]

9. Cf. Israel Scheffler, "Ritual and Reference", *Syntheses* 46 (1981), p. 425.

10. According to Kripke's account, proper names are autographic. To be the referent of a proper name, a person has to be the very individual who was denoted on the occasion when the name was introduced into the language. Cf. "Naming and Necessity", p. 302. Thus, an impostor who represents himself to be Saul Kripke is someone who fradulently alleges to have been so denoted. That is, he fradulently represents himself to have the history required to be the genuine referent of that name.

There are opportunities for forgery in the historical sciences as well. A famous example is the Piltdown man—a collection of bones fraudulently alleged to be the remains of a prehistoric man. And if there are no mock mongooses or mock moraines, it is perhaps because no one has yet developed the techniques for or an interest in forging such items. Still, the possibility of forgery is there. For whenever the authenticity of an item depends on its history, there is a danger that a copy might be produced, and its history faked.

I said earlier that the authenticity of an allographic work is independent of its history. On what then does it depend? It depends on the semantics and/or the syntax of the symbol system to which the work belongs. For a work to be allographic it must belong to a symbol system that has certain notational features. It is these features that allow for the authentication of works without consideration of their history of production.

A notational scheme differentiates between constitutive and contingent features of marks, ruling that marks with the same spelling are alike in constitutive features and are thus syntactically equivalent. When the authenticity of an item as an instance of a work is attested on strictly syntactical grounds, as it is in literature, that item is a mark, and the work a character in a notational scheme. For only in a notational scheme are syntactical features determinate and verifiable. Accordingly, only in such a scheme is it determinate and verifiable that an item has or that it lacks the constitutive syntactic features required for membership in the work.

A notational system differentiates between constitutive and contingent features of its compliants, as well as those of its characters, ruling that items that belong to the same compliance class are alike in constitutive features and are thus semantically equivalent. When the authenticity of an item as an instance of a work is attested on semantic grounds, as it is in music, the item is a compliant and the work a compliance class of a notational system. For the character with which an item complies is uniquely determined and verifiable only in a notational system. So only in such a system is it determinate that an item has or that it lacks the constitutive semantic features required for membership in the work.

Any adequate classification of items as works and instances of works should be reasonably reflective of our antecedent practices. But our practices are various, and there is no reason to expect a single general schema or overarching rationale to reflect the ways we classify works of widely different kinds. It is interesting and important, however, that the criteria we use to identify works and their instances in music, drama, and literature cannot be used to identify works and their instances in painting, sculpture, etching, and the like. For the latter belong to systems that lack the requisite notational features. Since the systems are syntactically dense throughout, it is impossible to determine exactly which characters the marks in such works belong to.

Certain works—abstract paintings, drawings, sculptures, etc.—

lack a denotive component altogether. They refer entirely by means of exemplification. Representational works, on the other hand, have a denotive component, so the issue of their semantic structure should be addressed. Representational works, like literary works, belong to systems that are semantically nondisjoint and dense throughout [LA, 151–4]. As a result, it is possible for an object to comply with several intersecting symbols of the system and impossible to say just which ones they are. Moreover, symbols in a representational system are often ambiguous. This is the case not only in works like those of Escher in which symbols have more than one literal interpretation, but also in works in which symbols have a literal interpretation and a metaphorical, allegorical, or figurative one.

The impossibility of identifying works in the visual arts allographically follows directly from the structure of the symbol systems to which they belong. Unlike literary works, they cannot be identified syntactically, for there is no way to determine the characters to which their marks belong. And unlike musical and dramatic works, they cannot be identified semantically, for there is no way to determine the characters with which they comply. Moreover, since we have no basis for treating distinct objects as semantically equivalent or distinct marks as syntactically equivalent, no replacement of compliants or marks preserves work identity.

Syntactic and semantic density are not, of course, restricted to works of art. Police sketches and photographs of wanted criminals, although devoid of artistic pretensions, are likewise dense. Perhaps less obviously, so are topographical maps and levels of mercury in ungraduated thermometers. Indeed, any system for measuring absolute position on a continuum—that is, any analog system—is syntactically and semantically dense throughout [LA, 160].

The virtue of such a system is that it imposes no limit on the precision of our measurements. The cost is that it sacrifices determinateness of reading. However careful we are in deciding that, e.g., the character to which an analog instrument points is K, there will always be some K' within small ϵ of K to which the instrument might with equal justice be said to point.

In science, dense systems tend to be replaced by articulate ones. Because reproducibility of experimental results and community-wide agreement are so important in science, the unlimited precision of a dense system may be outweighed by the indeterminateness of its assignment of a mark to a character and of a referent to a compliance class. The more determinate an experimental result, the easier it is to ascertain whether that result is reproduced. And a discipline that seeks agreement across a community is more likely to achieve its goal the less it leaves to the differing sensibilities of its various members. Since we can set as fine limits on the precision of an articulate system as we like, the benefit to science of a system that sets no limits at all may not be worth the cost in disputes among scientists.

5. EXEMPLIFICATIONAL SYSTEMS

Exemplification, as we saw, is reference by a symbol to a label that applies to that symbol. And just as the interpretation of a denotational symbol depends on the structure of the system to which it belongs, so does the interpretation of an exemplificational symbol. Moreover, the questions of differentiation, disjointness, and repleteness that arise for denotational systems also arise for exemplificational ones. The identification of and relations among the symbols that make up an exemplificational scheme are syntactic matters; the identification and organization of the labels that belong to its exemplificational realm, semantic matters.

When we are dealing with exemplification in a traditional symbol system, the issue of syntax is reasonably straightforward. Works in the visual arts[11] and in representational diagrams are syntactically nondisjoint and dense throughout. It is impossible to determine the characters to which their marks belong, and impossible to ascertain whether distinct marks are syntactically equivalent. Characters in verbal, numerical, and notational systems are syntactically disjoint and finitely differentiated. It is possible to determine the unique character to which each mark belongs, and to recognize syntactically equivalent marks.

For samples of other kinds, questions of syntax may be harder to decide, since they do not typically belong to systems that are known to have or known to lack an alphabet or a notation. Still, the same criteria apply in these cases. If it is determinate and uniquely decidable exactly what the exemplifying symbol is, the symbol is syntactically disjoint and finitely differentiated. In such cases it is possible to identify replicas of a sample—namely, any other samples that in the same context belong, and can be recognized to belong, to the same symbol. If it is not possible to decide what character a symbol belongs to, the system lacks finite syntactic differentiation. And if the symbol belongs to more than one character, the system lacks syntactic disjointness.

When we turn to the semantics of exemplificational systems, things are apt to become complicated. We saw earlier that a single symbol can exemplify several different labels. A fabric sample simultaneously exemplifies labels denoting color, texture, pattern, and weave. And a sample serving of cereal might in one context exemplify 'vitamin enriched' and in another, 'inspired marketing'. Multiple reference and context dependence are thus characteristic of exemplification.

It is often the case that an exemplified label can plausibly be incorporated into distinct realms or fields of reference. A berry that exem-

---

11. I follow common usage in taking the visual arts to consist of painting, etching, sculpture, and the like. This usage is not without drawbacks, however, as there are other arts whose apprehension and appreciation involve vision. We read books, after all, and watch movies, dances, and plays.

plifies 'green' symbolizes in one way in a system in which 'green' is opposed to 'ripe', and in quite another way in one in which 'green' is opposed to other color predicates. To understand how a sample symbolizes we need to determine the composition of its field of reference. We need, that is, to know what labels besides the one exemplified belong to that field.

Finally, we need to know how the labels that make up the realm are sorted by the exemplificational scheme. Since different sortings of the realm might be effected by different schemes, discovering this may be difficult. The musical realm, for example, might be sorted into the disjoint and finitely differentiated tones of the chromatic scale, or into a nondisjoint and dense field of sounds. Identifying a symbols's exemplificational realm then is not sufficient to determine the semantic structure of its system.

The identification of a symbol's exemplificational realm and the discovery of the way its scheme sorts the labels in that realm can be difficult matters. Even so, the criteria that determine the semantic structure of an exemplificational system parallel those that pertain to denotational systems.

An exemplificational system is finitely differentiated semantically if it is determinate which labels each of its symbols exemplifies. That is, it is finitely differentiated if for every symbol s and every label L of the system it is possible to determine that s does or that s does not exemplify L. At the opposite extreme, if the labels are so ordered that between any two there is a third, the system is semantically dense. And if no insertion of additional labels in normal position would destroy density, it is dense throughout. Since finite semantic differentiation is lacking in such systems, it is impossible to determine exactly which labels a particular sample exemplifies.

An exemplificational system is semantically disjoint if no two characters exemplify the same label. It is nondisjoint if it has two characters both of which exemplify some one label.

Perhaps these distinctions will become clearer if we look to cases. A system in which the only labels that sample eggs exemplify are 'white' and 'brown' is semantically disjoint. It is finitely differentiated semantically if in every case it is possible to determine whether a sample egg exemplifies 'white' or 'brown', these being the only labels in the exemplificational realm. Suppose, however, that there are sample eggs whose color is such that it is impossible to say whether they instantiate 'white' or 'brown'. In that case the system lacks finite semantic differentiation. A sample instantiates whatever labels it exemplifies. And if it is impossible to determine which of a system's labels a sample instantiates, it is impossible to determine which of them it exemplifies. Moreover, if undecidable cases are inevitable, regardless of the number of labels we introduce between 'white' and 'brown', the system is dense throughout.

A caveat should be entered here. Even though a symbol instantiates every label it exemplifies, it is not the case that everything that instantiates a label exemplifies it. Accordingly, we might enforce finite semantic differentiation on our exemplificational system by ruling that no egg whose color is undecidable can function as a sample.

In determining the semantic structure of an exemplifying symbol, a good deal hangs on the way we construe its exemplificational system. And there are samples whose systems can, without undue strain, be variously construed.

It is customary, perhaps, to take the paint chips on a sample card to exemplify labels from a dense field of color. But the chips might equally be construed as exemplifying only the twenty-seven colors of paint available from the XYZ Paint Company. The point of the sample card is to assist prospective customers in choosing a paint. So it is not unreasonable to construe the card so that each chip exemplifies one of the twenty-seven color labels, and so that it is possible in each case to identify the one that is exemplified. In that case the chips belong to a finitely differentiated semantic system.

The ascription of a sample to an exemplificational system is, of course, constrained by antecedent practice. To be sure, we can modify our practices in the interest of theoretical efficiency, economy, or elegance, but we are not free to ignore those practices entirely. As we have seen, there are samples that can be reasonably interpreted as symbols in quite different exemplificational systems. In such cases, there is no factual basis for deciding that the ascription of the sample to any one of those systems is exclusively correct. Still, it should be obvious that systems with different semantic structures have different virtues. And for specific purposes the ascription of a sample to a system with one semantic structure may be decidedly better or more fruitful, even if no more correct, than its ascription to a system with a different structure.

Nor should it be thought that every exemplifying symbol is subject to such legitimate alternative interpretations. Understanding a work of art involves discovering which of the labels in a dense field of reference its symbols exemplify. This is true in music as well as in the literary and the visual arts, for a musical performance exemplifies not its score, but labels from a dense field of sound. Since the field of reference of an aesthetic object is dense, for any label K which we take a symbol to exemplify, there is another label K' which is at least as good a candidate for the symbol's exemplificational referent.

Moreover, aesthetic symbols are relatively replete. So it is always possible that besides the referents we have already identified, it exemplifies yet other labels which, so far forth, we have overlooked. We can never conclude that our understanding of such a work is correct and complete, for it is always open to us to reconsider whether a better interpretation of the work results if a symbol is taken to exemplify some different label K' instead of K, or some additional label L as well as K. And as our sensitivity increases we find ourselves better able to discriminate among closely related labels and to make more refined judgments as to which labels are actually exemplified.

Parallel remarks apply to the difficulty of classifying marks, such as those in the visual arts, that belong to a syntactically dense and non-disjoint scheme. The issue there, however, is how the marks that make up the work are themselves to be identified, not how their referents are to be identified.

Disagreements among critics about what a work of art exemplifies or expresses are sometimes adduced as evidence that art is not cognitive or that aesthetics is not objective. But legitimate, long-term disagreements are to be expected when the subject under discussion involves reference in a dense, nondisjoint, and replete system. If a work of art is at all subtle, critics are likely to disagree about whether particular labels are exemplified or merely instantiated by it. And where two labels K and K' are sufficiently close, different interpreters may disagree as to whether a better interpretation of the work results if it is taken to exemplify K or if it is taken to exemplify K'. This is not, of course, to say that we can take a work to exemplify any label we like. But if K and K' are sufficiently close, differences between them may be difficult to discern. And even if discerned, deciding which of the two, if either, the symbol refers to and instantiates may remain problematic.

Because legitimate, long-term disagreements regarding reference are to be expected in systems that are dense, nondisjoint, and replete, science places a premium on disjointness, finite differentiation, and attenuation. For community-wide agreement and reproducibility of results are cognitive values of science—values that are more likely to be realized in systems in which it is possible to determine exactly what those results are.

Recall that an experiment exemplifies those among the labels it instantiates that are relevant to a theory's confirmation or disconfirmation. If they belong to a disjoint and finitely differentiated system, it is possible to tell which labels an experiment exemplifies, and whether subsequent experiments exemplify the same ones. In a dense system, on the other hand, it is impossible to determine that an experimental result has been reproduced. For it is impossible to tell exactly what labels the original experiment exemplifies, and impossible to tell whether subsequent experiments exemplify exactly the same, or indiscernably different ones.

Science favors controlled experiments—experiments in which the variables are so related that the effects of altering one at a time can be observed. Such experiments exemplify labels in a nonreplete or attenuated system. The cognitive utility of controlled experimentation is plain: if an experiment exemplifies a unique label, its result is quite clear; whereas, if a number of factors are tested together, and a number of labels simultaneously exemplified, it may not be obvious how each contributes to the outcome of the experiment.

It is a commonplace that our claims to scientific knowledge have to be tempered with fallibilism. Even the most strongly supported, widely accepted assertions of current science may be rationally rejected in the future. So scientific experiments, like works of art, are subject to reconsideration to see whether a better interpretation results if they are taken to exemplify different labels. But scientists do not typically decide among rival interpretations by looking ever more deeply into a single disputed experiment. Instead, they try to resolve the dispute by discovering the interpretation under which the experiment can best be incorporated into a comprehensive account of a wide range of theoretical and experimental evidence. And even though acceptance is provisional and rational consensus subject to revocation, it is expected that disputes concerning the proper interpretation of an experiment will be resolved. Indeed, if, in the long run, no resolution is reached, the disputed experiment will be thrown out. The failure of the scientific community to reach accord will be attributed to some defect in experimental design rather than to the differing sensibilities of different interpreters.

Scientific and artistic communities thus differ in their attitudes toward long term disagreements in interpretation. And these attitudes are reflected in their preferences for symbol systems with different syntactic and semantic features.

VII QUOTATION

1. VERBAL QUOTATION

Our language contains expressions that denote linguistic items as well as expressions that denote nonlinguistic ones. We make reference to sonnets and syllogisms, to the name of Smith's cat and to the title of Brown's book. We saw that by substituting various terms for P and Q in the schemata 'P-picture' and 'Q-description', we can manufacture labels of labels at will.

The latter locutions may have appeared a bit artificial. They seem not so much to be found in our everyday language as grafted onto it to avoid ontological commitment to fictive entities. There is, however, a device for generating certain labels of labels that is a familiar part of ordinary language—namely, quotation. Among the expressions that are counted as P-labels are quotations, direct and indirect, of P. Since quotation is a common device, and one that has interesting and important referential features, I want to consider it in some detail.

Quotation is a device for mentioning an expression rather than using it. When we *use* a term, we refer to its referent. When we *mention* it, we refer to the term itself. In a sentence like

1.1 There are no snakes in Ireland.

a certain country is denoted. If we enclose that sentence in quotation marks,

1.2 "There are no snakes in Ireland"

we denote not a country, but a sentence. Of course, there are other ways to denote that sentence. E.g.,

1.3 1.1

1.4 The assertion that there are no snakes in Ireland

1.5 The claim that snakes aren't native to Ireland

1.6 The sentence displayed at the beginning of the paragraph.

(1.2)–(1.6) are not sentences, but terms. If we compare them with one another, certain features of quotation begin to emerge.

(1.2) and (1.3) are names. Each is an indivisible singular term that denotes the sentence. (1.4), (1.5), and (1.6) are not names, but predicates—general terms that describe the sentence. Moreover, (1.2) and (1.4) contain syntactic replicas of the sentence. That is, they contain inscriptions that are spelled exactly the way the original sentence is spelled. (1.4) and (1.5) contain paraphrases of the original. Within each is a general expression whose components have the same primary extensions and some of the same secondary extensions as the corresponding components of the original sentence. (1.3) and (1.6) contain neither replicas nor paraphrases of the original.

Of the five, (1.2) is the only direct quotation. (1.4) and (1.5) are indirect quotation. (1.3) and (1.6) denote the sentence without quoting it. Evidently, both denotation and containment are required for quotation. A term that directly quotes an expression names that expression and contains a syntactic replica of it between quotation marks. A term that indirectly quotes an expression describes that expression and contains a semantic paraphrase of it. It has no quotation marks, but may be introduced by a phrase like 'said that . . . '.

Neither denotation alone nor containment alone is sufficient for quotation. (1.3) and (1.6) denote the sentence without quoting it. And

> 1.7   There are no snakes in Ireland because St. Patrick cast
>   them out.

contains the sentence but plainly does not quote it. The original sentence is used rather than mentioned in (1.7).

Nor are denotation and containment jointly sufficient for quotation. As Goodman notes,

> the twentieth letter of the alphabet

both denotes and contains the letter 't', but does not quote it [WOW, 46]. For quotation, an additional requirement has to be satisfied. "Replacement of the denoted and contained expression by any other of the language results in an expression that denotes the replacing expression" [WOW, 46]. Let us call this the *generality requirement*. Goodman's example raises difficulties only for direct quotation, for single letters that lack interpretations are not subject to paraphrase. But the point is a general one. The requirement thus applies to indirect as well as to direct quotation. In the case of indirect quotation, the replacing expression describes the expression it denotes. In the case of direct quotation, it names that expression.

Quotations denote utterances and inscriptions. Since denotation is not transitive, quotations do not in general denote the things that their referents denote.

> 1.8   Harold said, "There is a dragon in the bathtub"

is true or false depending on what Harold said. Its truth value is unaffected by the identity of the occupant of the bathtub. The ontological commitment of quotations is thus to utterances and inscriptions. (1.8) is ontologically committed to utterers and utterances, not to dragons and bathtubs. A quotation of P is a P-label—a P-name in the case of direct quotation, a P-description in the case of indirect. It denotes certain P-mentions, not the entities, if any, that those P-mentions in turn denote.

A direct quotation contains a syntactic replica of the expression it denotes; an indirect quotation contains a semantic paraphrase of the one it denotes. Thus quotations are not subject to failure of reference, for replication and paraphrase are reflexive. The containment requirement insures that there is at least one thing in the extension of each quotation—namely, the inscription that is contained within the quotation itself.

The difference between replication and paraphrase is central to the difference between direct and indirect quotation. Paraphase is a semantic device, and a fairly loose one at that. Typically a term is paraphrased by another that has the same primary extension and some of the same secondary extensions. But there is no general standard for saying which secondary extensions have to be shared, or how many of them. Indeed, there are cases in which our paraphrases do not even agree in primary extension. We sometimes substitute a precise term for a vague one, or a vague term for a precise one. We might, for example, substitute 'myocardial infarction' for 'heart attack' when conferring with a cardiologist, and 'heart attack' for 'myocardial infarction' when reporting that conference to the patient. The two expressions are not coextensive, for there are coronary conditions besides myocardial infarctions that are commonly called heart attacks. If exact agreement in primary extension is required in paraphrase, indirect quotation is of no use in eliminating vagueness and ambiguity. For then each vague term has to be replaced by an equally vague one, and each ambiguous term by one that shares its ambiguity. It seems best then to admit that the primary extension of an expression and that of its paraphrase in indirect quotation sometimes diverge. The limits on permissible paraphrase thus vary considerably with differences in circumstance. Accordingly, there may be disagreement as to whether an utterance that denotes another contains a paraphrase of it, and thus disagreement as to whether the utterance indirectly quotes or merely reports it.

Since paraphrase is semantic, indirect quotation is restricted to expressions that have semantic interpretations. We can indirectly quote terms and sentences but not, for example, nonsense syllables. We can, to be sure, paraphrase fictive expressions—e.g., substituting 'wizard' for 'sorcerer'—for although their primary extensions are null, their secondary extensions are not.

The value of indirect quotation is plain. We can convey the gist of a remark without knowledge of, or commitment to, its precise wording.

We can disambiguate ambiguous utterances and render vague ones more precise. And we can exhibit or obscure various features of an utterance. If, e.g., we substitute 'pornography' for 'adult entertainment', a suggestion of disreputability is conveyed. For 'pornography' exemplifies 'disreputable label', and 'adult entertainment' does not.

Of course, it is not true that every label exemplified by a paraphrase is instantiated by the expression that it paraphrases. A longwinded speech might be paraphrased by one that exemplifies 'pithy'. In some cases the selection of an appropriate paraphrase is an effective way to show than an indirectly quoted expression instantiates a particular P-label. In others, an indirect quotation may substantially misrepresent the expression it quotes by containing a paraphrase that exemplifies important P-labels that the original does not.

Direct quotation has neither the latitude nor the restrictions of indirect quotation. The containment requirement for direct quotation is syntactic replication—exact sameness of spelling. We can no more substitute 'Eire' for 'Ireland' in (1.2) than we can substitute 'Anger' for 'Ire' in 'Ireland'. On the other hand, direct quotation is not restricted, as indirect quotation is, to expressions that have semantic interpretations. Anything that has a spelling is replicable, and thus is a candidate for direct quotation. We directly quote a string of nonsense syllables—phligourdenik bznourq—by enclosing a replica in quotations marks thus: 'phligourdenik bznourq'. By placing nonsense syllables within quotation marks we create genuine English terms to denote them. These terms are not nonsensical even though their referents are. If we can produce a replica, we can directly quote an expression we don't understand. E.g., "The fully hydrated sulfides A_x $(H_2O)_z MS_2$ with small alkali cations Li^+ and Na^+ yield hydrates with bilayers of water due to higher hydration enthalpy of the guest ions."[1] We can't indirectly quote an expression we don't understand, for we are, presumably, ignorant of the primary and/or secondary extensions of at least some of its terms. We saw that when we enclose an expression in quotation marks we create a term to denote that expression. If we are speaking English at the time, the term we create is an English one. This is the case even if we do not understand the original expression, indeed even if the original is gibberish. If we restrict our attention to a single language, these features are unexceptionable. But they have a disconcerting consequence when it comes to translation. Consider the problem of the following sentence:

1.9   Alphonse a dit, "Il n'y a pas de serpents en Irlande."

(1.9) directly quotes Alphonse's utterance. So its translation must do so as well. Thus, (1.9) is to be translated into English as

1. U. Röder, W. Müller-Warmuth, and R. Schöllhorn, "^{1}H and ^{7}Li NMR Studies on the Dynamics of Water and Cations in Quasi-Two-Dimensional Electrolyte Layers of Hydrated Chalcogenides", *Journal of Chemical Physics* 75 (1981), p. 413.

1.10   Alphonse said, "Il n'y a pas de serpents en Irlande."

The quotation in (1.10) is an English name of Alphonse's utterance. But as Church remarked, names of this sort convey little to the English speaker who knows no French.[2] The quotation marks of direct quotation hermetically seal off their contents.

Of course, we regularly translate expressions that appear within quotation marks. Ordinarily (1.9) would be translated as

1.11   Alphonse said, "There are no snakes in Ireland."

The use of quotation marks here is deviant. For (1.11) contains an English paraphrase of Alphonse's utterance, not a replica of it. Strictly speaking then, (1.11) contains an indirect quotation of that utterance. Translation of what appears within quotation marks thus yields an indirect quotation. In translation, however, the constraints on permissible paraphrase are normally severe.

The capacity for quotation is the result of certain identifiable syntactic and semantic features of verbal symbol systems. Syntactic disjointness and finite differentiation allow for containment of one character in another and for replication of one mark by another. Semantic nondisjointness, particularly in the form of redundancy, is what allows for paraphrase. And the inclusion of letters, words, phrases, etc., in the universe of discourse is what makes denotation of linguistic items possible.

2. PICTORIAL QUOTATION

Goodman has raised question of quotation in the nonverbal media [WOW, 47–56]. Some works of art plainly allude to others. But it is less obvious when, if ever, one such work can be said to quote another. Investigation of this question in instructive, for it discloses certain differences in the referential capacities of various symbol systems

We saw that a quotation denotes a symbol and contains a replica or a paraphrase of that symbol. It is, moreover, the result of the application of a general rule or procedure for generating symbols that denote other. Investigation of this question is instructive, for it discloses certain differences in the referential capacities of various symbol systems.

Quotation is a form of denotation, so we need only consider works that denote—that is, representational works. Such works are obviously capable of denoting paintings, photographs, prints and the like as well as nonpictorial objects such as tables and chairs. There is a clear semantic difference between a picture that denotes a second picture and one that denotes the referent of the second. How is this

2. A. Church, "On Carnap's Analysis of Statements of Assertion and Belief", *Analysis* 10 (1950), pp. 97–99.

difference captured pictorially? What is the difference between, say, a picture of Victoria with a portrait of Albert, and a picture of Victoria with Albert himself?

When a picture is depicted, it is typically shown surrounded by a frame, placed on an easel, or hanging on a wall[3] [WOW, 47]. So although pictorial systems lack quotation marks, there are pictorial devices that function analogously. Since we can represent any picture by drawing a framed picture that denotes it, both the denotation and the generality requirements on quotation can be satisfied within a representational system. The difficulty in maintaining that pictures quote comes with the containment requirement.

A direct verbal quotation contains a syntactic replica of the expression it denotes. But symbols in the visual arts lack replicas, for the systems to which they belong are dense throughout. Since it is impossible to identify the characters to which the marks in such a system belong, no marks can be considered replicas of each other. It follows that no symbol in such a system can contain a replica of any other.

We might conclude that because syntactically dense systems lack the resources for replication they lack the capacity for direct quotation. Or we might alter the containment requirement so that a work that denotes another and contains a "framed" instance of it counts as a direct quotation of it. In that case multiple works in the visual arts are candidates for direct quotation. Thus a film, for example, contains another if a print of the latter is included in each print of the former. If the film also denotes the work whose instance it contains, and some general framing condition is satisfied, it directly quotes that work. By this standard, the end of *Casablanca* is directly quoted at the beginning of *Play It Again, Sam*. Notice that even if we accept this modification in the containment requirement for direct quotation, the distinction between autographic and allographic media is preserved. A direct allographic quotation contains a symbol whose spelling is the same as the symbol it denotes; a direct autographic quotation contains a symbol the relevant features of whose history of production are the same as those of the symbol it denotes.

When we turn to works in the singular arts, such as drawing and painting, direct quotation seems out of the question. Since these works have no replicas, and each has but a single instance, there appears to be no way in which such a work can be contained in another. To be sure, drawings and paintings contain copies of other works. Should we relax the conditions on direct quotation even further and concede that works that contain copies of other works can directly quote them? Or is copying closer to paraphrase? If so, such works are better said to indirectly quote the works they denote. There are difficulties with each alternative.

---

3. This, of course, is not an exhaustive list of the conventions for picturing pictures, but a couple of examples of the ways in which artists indicate pictorially that a picture rather than its referent is denoted or mention-selected by another.

In every case it is determinate whether one symbol contains an instance or a replica of another. But it is not always determinate whether a symbol contains a copy of another. For there is no set standard for how closely or in what ways a copy of a work has to resemble the original. In this respect copying is like paraphrasing. An expression and its paraphrase typically have to agree in primary extension and in some secondary extensions. But no general rule determines which secondary extensions or how many of them the two expression have to share. Just as there are cases in which it is indeterminate whether one expression paraphrases another, there are cases in which it is indeterminate whether one pictorial symbol is a copy of another.

Still, copying cannot be straightforwardly construed as pictorial paraphrasing either. We can paraphrase only expressions that have denotive or mention-selective interpretations. For only such expressions have primary and secondary extensions. Copying, however, is not so restricted. A painting can as easily contain a copy of an abstract work as a copy of a representational one. Our standard for counting one pictorial symbol a copy of another is sometimes agreement in denotation (with or without agreement in certain secondary extensions) and sometimes agreement in exemplification.

Whether to construe copies as analogues of replicas, of paraphrases, or of neither seems to be a matter of choice. If we take them to be analogous to replicas, singular autographic arts will be capable of direct quotation; if analogous to paraphrases, they will be capable only of indirect quotation; and if analogous to neither, they will be incapable of quoting the works to which they refer.

The distinction between direct and indirect quotation is clearly marked in writing, for only direct quotations are enclosed in quotation marks. We saw that pictures that denote other pictures are represented as placed on easels or as surrounded by frames, etc. These devices clearly indicate that a work is denoted or mention-selected. But they do not quite function as quotation marks. For the same devices are used whether the denoted work is quoted directly or indirectly, and even in cases in which it is not quoted at all. A picture that contains a copy of another with a frame drawn around it quotes the work it denotes directly or indirectly or not at all, depending on our interpretation of pictures of frames, easels, and the like. These devices indicate that a picture is mentioned pictorially. But beyond that they indicate nothing about what form its mention takes.

Certain references by works to other works in the visual arts are thus in some respects like verbal quotation. But the correspondence is not exact. The containment requirement on quotation is satisfied in verbal systems by symbols that syntactically replicate or semantically paraphrase the symbols they denote. There is a variety of ways in which the requirement can be said to be satisfied in pictorial systems. Some works contain copies that agree with the works they denote in primary and in some secondary extensions. Others contain copies that exemplify some of the same labels as the works they denote. None of these works contains a replica of the work it denotes, for symbols in syntactically dense systems admit of no replicas. Moreover, although there are a number of ways to indicate pictorially that a picture is denoted, it seems not to be the case that direct and indirect quotation are signalled by separate pictorial devices as they are signalled by separate linguistic devices. It seems reasonable to extend the notion of quotation to pictorial systems, but it is not clear that the distinction between direct and indirect quotation can be fruitfully extended.

3. MUSICAL QUOTATION

The difficulties concerning musical quotation are somewhat different. First off, a quotation denotes the symbols it quotes, and music typically doesn't denote. This, perhaps, is reason to think musical quotation unusual. But of course some musical passages do refer to others. Prokofiev's *Classical Symphony* refers to genuinely classical works. A passage in Schubert's Ninth Symphony refers to a passage in Beethoven's Ninth. Tschaikovsky's *1812 Overture* refers to the fire of cannons, the peal of church bells, and the French and Russian national anthems. And *leitmotiven* refer to operatic characters, subjects, and events. The problem is saying when, if ever, such works and passages quote.

The *Classical Symphony* refers to classical works by exemplifying some of their general stylistic features. Schubert's symphony refers to Beethoven's by means of a passage that has pretty much the same melody as the one that dominates the final movement of Beethoven's work. It is the difference between these two modes of reference that leads music theorists to consider the latter a case of quotation. In what sense does Schubert's work quote Beethoven's?

Quotation involves containment as well as reference. Perhaps the issue will be clarified if we look at the way the containment requirement is satisfied in music. To avoid needless complications, I limit my discussion to passages scored in standard musical notation. Then one passage contains a replica of a second just in case the score of the first contains a replica of the score of the second. If the first passage also denotes the second, it directly quotes the second passage.

The criterion of syntactic replication is severe. A musical passage does not directly quote a passage it denotes if, for example, the two passages are scored in different keys, or in different modes. Schubert's work then does not directly quote Beethoven's. Indeed, little of what is considered musical quotation is direct quotation, for little involves syntactic replication.

If a passage that is substantially like the one it denotes differs from that passage in mode, instrumentation, or whatever, should we say that it indirectly quotes that passage? This suggestion is not without drawbacks. Explicating what it is for one passage to be *substantially like* another is likely to be a tricky business. So is identifying the respects in which one passage can differ musically from another and still quote it. But the main problem is this: indirect quotation involves paraphrase. And paraphrase is a matter of denotation. Although it is reasonable to say that a piece that quotes another functions denotively, there is no reason to think that the denoted piece does so as well. But unless the denoted piece has a primary and/or secondary extension, there is nothing to paraphrase.

To be sure, some music denotes or mention-selects, and thus is subject to paraphrase. E.g., a piccolo trill that denotes a bird call might be paraphrased by a recorder trill that denotes the call of the same bird. And a *leitmotif* that mention-selects a certain operatic character might be paraphrased in a different work that mention-selects the same character. But since musical denotation is comparatively rare, so are musical paraphrase and indirect quotation. Schubert's reference to Beethoven thus seems to be neither direct nor indirect quotation.

I said earlier that our accounts should accord reasonably well with actual practice. The problem here is that there are different practices that substantially disagree about what counts as quotation. The clearest cases of quotation—verbal quotations—contain replicas or paraphrases of the expressions they denote. But most of the musical passages that theorists recognize as quotations contain neither. Is it a mistake to apply the standards for verbal quotation to musical cases? Or should we conclude, contrary to the claims of music theorists, that music almost never quotes? There are a couple of ways in which the problem might be adjudicated.

We might take paraphrase to be a matter of likeness of reference generally instead of just likeness of primary and secondary extension. In that case, symbols that are sufficiently alike in exemplificational reference are paraphrases of each other.[4] Then a musical passage that differs from the passage it denotes in key or mode or whatever indirectly quotes that passage so long as the two exemplify enough of the same musical labels. And just as there is no general rule to determine which and how many secondary extensions have to be shared by an indirect verbal quotation and its referent, there is none to determine which and how many musical labels have to be jointly exemplified by an indirect musical quotation and its referent. According to this account, the passage in Schubert's symphony indirectly quotes a passage in Beethoven's because it denotes Beethoven's passage and exemplifies sufficiently many of the same melodic labels as that passage.

There is, however, a verbal device that seems closer to the passages that are called musical quotations than either direct or indirect quotation—namely, onomatopoeia. An onomatopoetic expression—such as 'buzz', 'purr', or 'twang'—denotes sounds that have auditory characteristics (or, more exactly, instantiate auditory labels) that the expression exemplifies.

4. Cf. V. Howard, "On Musical Quotation", *The Monist* 58 (1974), pp. 307–318.

We have seen that a musical quotation need not be scored the same as the sound sequence it denotes, as would be required for strict analogy to direct verbal quotation. Nor need it agree with the sequence in primary and in (some) secondary extensions, as would be required for strict analogy to indirect quotation. What a musical quotation is required to do is, rather, to exemplify some of the auditory labels of the sequence it denotes.

I want to suggest then that in musical quotation, restatement, paraphrase and the like, a musical passage functions onomatopoetically to denote a sound sequence certain of whose auditory characteristics it exemplifies. In that case, the musical quotation of musical passages and that of nonmusical sounds are fundamentally alike. The *1812 Overture* quotes *La Marseillaise* by means of a passage that denotes *La Marseillaise* and both is and exemplifies its being a *La-Marseillaise*-sound. And it quotes cannon fire by means of a passage that denotes cannon fire and both is and exemplifies its being a cannon-fire-sound.

Both verbal onomatopeia and musical quotation have the form:

S denotes *R* and *S* is, and exemplifies its being an *R*-sound.[5]

In music, as in language, there are a variety of permissible substitutions for *R*. And the scopes of different replacements for *R*-sound vary considerably. Some musical passages may be all but indistinguishable from the sounds they quote; others maybe as different from them as the pronunciation of 'bow-wow' is from the sounds actually emitted by barking dogs.

Of course the fact that one sound exemplifies auditory labels instantiated or exemplified by another does not establish a referential connection between the two in music any more than it does in language. Successive utterances of the *Pledge of Allegiance* do not denote each other, nor do successive performances of *The Star-Spangled Banner*. And sounds that seem antecedently dissimilar, such as the pronunciation of 'bow-wow' and the barks of dogs may be brought to sound alike by being brought into a referential relation. That an onomatopoetic expression and its referent sound alike may thus be the cause of the referential connection between the two or the consequence of it.

Does construing musical quotation as onomatopoeia amount to denying that it is genuine quotation? Or does it amount to claiming that onomatopoeia is a form of quotation? I'm not sure. Nor do I think it matters very much so long as we recognize the respects in which onomatopoetic symbols resemble and those in which they differ from direct and indirect quotation.

5. Cf. V. Howard, "On Representational Music", *Noûs* 6 (1972), p. 44. In my discussion of onomatopoeia and of musical quotation generally I am indebted to Howard's work. Howard does not, however, identify musical quotation with onomatopoeia.

If onomatopoeia is treated as a form of quotation, then it satisfies the containment requirement on quotation by containing an audible expression that exemplifies auditory labels instantiated by the sound sequence it denotes. And it satisfies the generality requirement in that any expression that denotes a sound and exemplifies sufficiently many of the auditory labels instantiated by that sound, onomatopoetically quotes that sound.

A problem that was deferred earlier remains to be faced—namely, that of determining when the denotation requirement on musical quotation is satisfied. No matter how containment is construed, it does not entail denotation. For a musical passage that contains another may use the contained passage or mention it. And unless the passage is mentioned, it is not denoted. Thus, e.g., Brahms' *Variations on a Theme from Haydn* contains, but does not refer to Haydn's theme: the theme is used but not mentioned.

Verbal systems contain quotation marks to signal direct quotation and expressions like 'said that . . .' to signal indirect quotation. Pictorial systems do not clearly distinguish between direct and indirect quotation. But by portraying a picture as framed or as placed on an easel, they indicate clearly that it is mentioned by the work that contains its portrayal. Music contains neither specific devices to signal quotations nor more general framing devices to indicate that passages are mentioned.

We could, of course, introduce quotation marks or a framing device into standard musical notation. Such marks would function somewhat as quotation marks function in language. For quotation marks appear in inscriptions, but are unsounded. An utterance of

3.1   Beth said there are no snakes in Ireland

is ambiguous as between the direct quotation that reports Beth's actual words,

3.2   Beth said, "There are no snakes in Ireland"

and the indirect quotation that reports the gist of her remarks,

3.3   Beth said [that] there are no snakes in Ireland.

Unsounded punctuation marks could likewise be inserted into scores to indicate musical reference.[6]

Still, it is not clear how much benefit is to be gained from the introduction of such a device. Here the difference between verbal and musical systems is critical. In language, written and spoken expressions that are spelled alike are replicas of each other, and are

---

6. Goodman reports that this is sometimes done [WOW, 51n]. But this is based on hearsay and he can give no examples. Neither can I.

instances of the same work. But a musical score is not a replica of the performances it prescribes. Nor is a score an instance of a musical work. A character in a musical score that is without audible consequence seems to make no difference to the identity of the work the score defines. That is to say, the same compliance class of performances is prescribed by a score that contains that character and by an otherwise identical score that does not. So if the issue of musical quotation concerns reference by a musical work, not reference by a musical score, the introduction of unsounded quotation marks or of an unsounded framing device avails us nothing.

It seems then that the evidence that a musical passage mentions another should be audible. It should, that is, be discernible in performance, without recourse to the title, the score, or the history of the work. Plainly, musical performances contain nothing so explicit as quotation marks. But this is not to say that they give absolutely no indication whether a passage is used or mentioned. Howard suggests that musical passages that mention others occur in recognizably secondary contexts.[7] He maintains that denoting passages are conspicuously displayed against the primary musical context of the works within which they occur.

Frequently the passage, theme, or style that is denoted is a familiar one. But familiarity is neither necessary nor sufficient for reference. The *1812 Overture* denotes a portion of *La Marseillaise* whether or not its audience is acquainted with that piece. And Brahms' *Variations on a Theme from Haydn* does not denote Haydn's theme even when performed before an audience of Haydn scholars. Indeed, instead of presupposing familiarity with the denoted work, the musical setting of a passage that functions denotively often creates an air of familiarity by presenting the passage as a familiar tune.

Howard's account of secondary musical contexts is vague, and I know of no way to substantially improve on it. This may just be ignorance on my part. Or it may be that the indications of musical denotation are themselves sufficiently vague that we cannot significantly increase the precision of our account without sacrificing its accuracy.

What constitutes a secondary musical context evidently varies from case to case. And since there is no general device to single out musical quotations, greater sensitivity is required to recognize them than is required to recognize verbal or pictorial quotations. Moreover, there is likely to be significant disagreement as to whether particular passages quote. Since there is no clear measure of how different a secondary context has to be from the primary context against which it is displayed, there are likely to be cases in which the differences are small and it is unclear whether particular passages are used or mentioned.

Some musical passages quote the sound sequences they denote; others refer to them without quoting. The difference lies in the fact

7. "On Musical Quotation", pp. 315–316.

that quotation is subject to a containment requirement to which other types of reference are not. As we saw, the containment requirement on musical quotation can be variously construed. And under different construals the same musical passages will be alternatively interpreted as quotations or as nonquotational reference. Accordingly, even when it is plain that one passage refers to another, it is not always whether the one quotes the other.

We found that the criteria for verbal quotation—syntactic replication, denotational paraphrase—can be strictly applied to music only at the cost of denying that many of the passages normally held to be musical quotations actually function as such. To recognize these passages as quotations, we have to interpret 'quotation' more broadly, either by counting onomatopoeia as a type of quotation, or by taking paraphrase to be a matter of agreement in reference generally, not just in primary and secondary extensions. In that case, expressions that exemplify sufficiently many of the same labels are exemplificational paraphrases of each other, and one of them can indirectly quote another.

The motivation for broadening the interpretation of 'quotation' comes from an attempt to explicate musical quotation. But the adoption of either suggestion has consequences beyond the musical realm. If onomatopoeia is construed as a type of quotation, then onomatopoetic expressions in language as well as those in music quote the sounds they denote. If joint exemplification of enough labels is sufficient for paraphrase, then exemplificational systems generally have the capacity for paraphrase. And systems—be they verbal, pictorial, mimetic, or whatever—which have symbols that both exemplify and denote typically have the resources for indirect quotation. Accordingly, in deciding which, if either, of these suggestions to accept, we should not focus exclusively on music. We should consider their effects on the interpretation of other symbol systems as well.

VIII COMPLEX AND INDIRECT REFERENCE

Not every symbol is purely denotational or purely exemplificational. Certain symbols have a number of integrated and interacting referential functions. In this chapter I discuss some cases of complex and indirect reference. The cases I consider are interesting in their own right, and are common enough to require explication by any adequate general theory of reference. Moreover, they serve as useful illustrations of the phenomenon of complex reference. But there is no suggestion that these cases are the sole instances of complex reference, or that my discussion constitutes an exhaustive account of the ways denotation and exemplification interact.

1. REPRESENTATION-AS

Like the unreconstructed notions 'picture of' and 'description of' discussed in Chapter III, 'picture as', 'description as', and 'representation as' are ambiguous. In describing Napoleon as a greedy child, for example, I might simply be describing his personality during the early part of his life. In that case, the mode of reference is simply denotation. I might, however, describe the adult Napoleon as a greedy child—perhaps in characterizing his imperialistic ambitions. Then my description does not denote his personality during his childhood, for the description is not inapplicable should it turn out that the child Napoleon was unusually generous. It is this latter sort of description-as that is semantically complex. It involves denotation and exemplification at once.

Ordinary description is a matter of denotation. Fictive description is a matter not of what fictive terms denote, but of what terms denote them and, typically, are exemplified by them. In *description-as* both denotation and exemplification come into play. When I describe the adult Napoleon as a greedy child, my description denotes Napoleon and exemplifies 'greedy-child-description'. A parallel account applies to depiction-as. A picture of Christ as a lamb denotes Christ and exemplifies 'lamb-picture'.

Representation-as is involved in the explication of certain other symbolic devices. A caricature of Churchill as a bulldog is a picture that denotes Churchill and exemplifies both 'Churchill-picture' and 'bulldog-picture'. Goodman argues that realism in the arts depends on habituation or tradition, not on fidelity to the object depicted [LA, 34–39]. Even so, our habits and traditions are likely to be such that a

141

picture that exemplifies both of these labels will be fairly remote from the bulldog-pictures and Churchill-pictures we consider realistic. A good deal more needs to be said about the ways caricatures differ from other nonrealistic pictures, but a discussion of this would take us too far afield.[1] My point here is simply to suggest that caricature is a special case of representation-as.

Analogy is a device for pointing up likenesses among things normally held to be quite different. Thus, for example, the atom is said by analogy to be a miniature solar system. This is a clear case of description-as: a description that denotes the atom exemplifies solar-system-description. Even though 'solar system' does not literally denote the atom, the analogy brings it about that solar-system-description denotes and is exemplified by a description that does denote the atom.

The description of the adult Napoleon as a greedy child, the picture of Churchill as a bulldog, and the description of the atom as a solar system are all metaphors. But a representation need not be metaphorical to be a case of representation-as. A man is described as a wily and resourceful politician whenever a description that denotes him exemplifies 'wily-and-resourceful-politician-description'. Plainly, many literal descriptions of politicians satisfy this requirement.

What are we to say of descriptions of Hamlet as a man of reflection? Obviously we cannot say that they denote Hamlet and exemplify 'man-of-reflection-description', for the term 'Hamlet' is fictive, its denotation null. Rather, describing Hamlet as a man of reflection is classifying Hamlet-descriptions among the descriptions which exemplify 'man-of-reflection-description' [LA, 30]. The semantic structure of description-as is the same whether we are dealing with fictive or factual descriptions. But in the case of factual description-as we are typically concerned with what is exemplified by descriptions that denote nonlinguistic entities—Napoleon or the helium atom—while in the case of fictive description-as we are concerned with what is exemplified by descriptions that denote linguistic entities—e.g., the Hamlet-descriptions that occur in Shakespeare's play. Parallel remarks plainly apply to the distinction between factual and fictive depiction-as.

2. ALLUSION

Allusion is a form of referential action at a distance. One thing alludes to another by referring to it indirectly. The simplest cases are these: (1) a alludes to b by denoting something c that exemplifies b; and (2) a alludes to b by exemplifying something c that denotes b. Frequently in allusions of the latter type c not only denotes b but also

1. For such a discussion cf., Stephanie Ross, "On Caricature", *The Monist* 58 (1974), pp. 284–293.

is exemplified by it. But this need not be the case. A symbol that *b* plainly instantiates can serve as a vehicle for allusion even if *b* does not exemplify it. Schematically then the two simplest cases look like this:

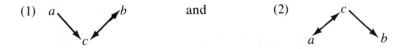

(1) *a*   *b*   and   (2)   *c*
         c   *a*   *b*

Lines with single arrows indicate denotation;
those with double arrows, exemplification.

In more complicated cases, referential chains are longer: *a* alludes to *b* by denoting or exemplifying something that in turn denotes or exemplifies something that . . . denotes or exemplifies *b* [RR, 126–32].

Let us consider some sample cases. I might allude to the enormous scope and complexity of a philosophical work by calling it 'Hegelian'. For 'Hegelian' denotes the works of Hegel which, whatever else they do, manifestly exemplify 'enormous in scope and complexity'. The allusion here depends on a chain of reference that proceeds from a term to its instance and thence to another term, thus:

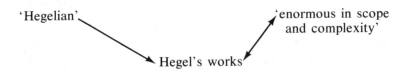

'Hegelian'   'enormous in scope
                                    and complexity'
                Hegel's works

In other cases, the chain goes from an instance to a label it exemplifies and from there to another instance of the label. Thus, e.g., a tiger exemplifies labels such as 'fierce and cunning'—labels that are also instantiated (and perhaps exemplified) by the football team that takes the tiger as its symbol.

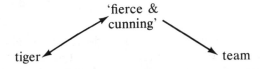

                'fierce &
                 cunning'
tiger   team

Longer and more complicated chains are easily discovered. The pictures of tigers on the players' helmets refer to the team by denoting tigers who exemplify 'fierce and cunning' which in turn is instantiated by the team.

What of the team whose symbol is the lion? It might seem that the same sort of chain is operative here—that lions exemplify labels such as 'courageous and aggressive' that are also instantiated and perhaps exemplified by the football team. But whatever may be true of the team, this account will not do. For lions, as it turns out, do not even instantiate, much less exemplify, 'courageous and aggressive.' They are, for the most part, cowardly, lazy beasts. Even so, our lion-stories typically exemplify some 'courageous-and-aggressive-labels'. That is to say, lion-stories mention-selectively exemplify 'courage and aggressive'. The chain of reference thus proceeds not from actual lions to the courageous and aggressive football team but from lion-mentions.

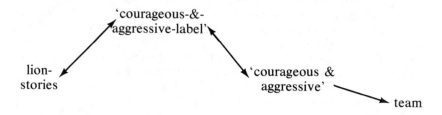

Suppose, however, that the team whose symbol is the lion turns out not to be courageous and aggressive either. Then the chain of reference goes not from lion-stories to the team, but from lion-stories to team-descriptions.

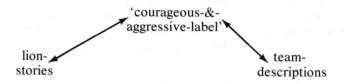

The lion-stories exemplify 'courageous-and-aggressive-label' which in turn is exemplified by certain team-descriptions. These team-descriptions, however, no more denote the team than the lion-stories in question denote actual lions.

Perhaps the chain of reference linking tigers to the fierce and cunning football team is longer than it first appeared, involving tiger-stories and team-descriptions as well as the links we have already identified. This suggestion is plausible, for when an allusion is also

grounded in a stereotype, the stories and descriptions that are re-
sponsible for that stereotype may be integral to the referential chain.
But we should not conclude that such stories and descriptions are part
of every chain of reference. For, particularly in the case of novel allusions, there may be no mediating stories or descriptions with the
requisite exemplificatory features.

Frequently, more than one chain of reference links a symbol with
the object to which it alludes. So both the chain that includes tiger-
stories and the one that does not may serve to explicate ways the tiger
symbolizes the team. And the lion may turn out to be an ironically apt
symbol for the cowardly, lazy team. For two chains secure the allusion: one linking lion-stories and team-descriptions via 'courageous-
and-aggressive-label'; the other linking actual lions and the team itself
via 'cowardly and lazy'.

I have been speaking as though the intermediate links of the
referential chain are always explicitly identified. Of course this is not
the case. Exactly which symbols serve as intermediate links need not
be obvious. So if an allusion is at all subtle, both the length of the referential chain and the identity of the intermediate links may be uncertain.

The symbolic features of a work that count as stylistic are those
that associate it with one particular artist, region, period, or school
rather than another. These features, Goodman maintains [WOW, 32],
may be a function of what the work denotes, what it exemplifies, or
what it expresses. In the arts, stylistic features often serve as vehicles
for allusion. By sharing the stylistic features that normally associate
works with a particular artist, region, period, or school, n, a symbol
can allude to genuine works of n.

Certainly not every symbol in the style of n alludes to works of n.
Some simply instantiate the style; these are either genuine works of n
or accidental likenesses. Others are imitations or forgeries. The
difference is that unlike instances, likenesses, imitations, and
forgeries, stylistic allusions refer to the works whose stylistic features
they share.

How are we to tell whether a work just instantiates or imitates a
particular style or whether it also alludes to works in that style? There
is no single answer. In some cases a work that alludes on the basis of
features associated with an artist, region, period, or school, n, also
exemplifies features that call attention to the fact that it is not itself a
work of n. The tension between these two sets of features can be an
indication of stylistic allusion. E.g., that an epistolary novel about
contemporary America stylistically alludes to the epistolary novels of
the eighteenth century may be marked by a tension between the
eighteenth-century style and the twentieth-century subject matter of
the work. But a work that stylistically alludes to works of n need not
exemplify, or even instantiate, 'is not an n'. *Don Quixote,* for example, is a chivalric romance that alludes stylistically to works of chivalric romance. It is itself then one of the works to which it alludes.

In some cases, such as parody, stylistic allusion may be marked by an exaggeration of the features characteristic of the works alluded to, or by the combination of those features with a ridiculous or inappropriate subject matter. Both are evident in *Don Quixote*.

There are a number of other ways in which stylistic allusion makes itself manifest. Nevertheless, cases remain in which it is uncertain whether stylistic allusion occurs. A single work is then subject to rival interpretations. According to some it simply instantiates or imitates a particular style; according to others, its instantiation or imitation of a style serves as a vehicle for allusion to works in that style.

3. METAPHORICAL LIKENING

In a metaphorical application, a term denotes the objects in its metaphorical extension and recalls the objects in its antecedent literal extension. In Chapter IV I explained metaphorical denotation. But I postponed a discussion of what is involved in metaphorical likening since the requisite analytical apparatus had not yet been developed. I can now take up that discussion, for the chains of reference which were needed to explain allusion are what is required to explain metaphorical likening as well. Indeed, the way a metaphor recalls the objects in the literal extension of a term is by alluding to them [RR, 128–29]. A metaphor then denotes the objects in its metaphorical extension and alludes to those in its literal extension.

Let us begin by considering a fairly simple example:

Phil is a whippet.

The chain of reference is as follows: 'whippet' literally denotes whippets, animals who exemplify a label such as 'small but fast' which is also exemplified by Phil. The chain then goes from the term to its literal extension, from there to a label exemplified by the objects in both its literal and its metaphorical extensions, and on to its metaphorical extension. Schematically,

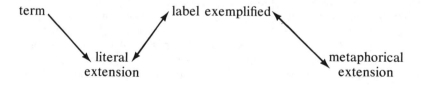

The joint exemplification of the labels in question need not antedate the metaphorical application of the term. A metaphor can effect a likening of the objects in its literal and metaphorical extensions by causing certain characteristics of those objects to be brought to the

fore—by, that is, bringing the objects to exemplify some of the labels they instantiate.

To be sure, not every metaphorical likening is effected by so simple a chain. Suppose a philosopher informs his students that Hume's *Treatise* is a gold mine. Typically, the expression 'gold mine' applies metaphorically to sources of great wealth or profit. Still, it is unlikely that he is claiming that the rewards of the *Treatise* are financial. A longer chain is needed to connect his metaphor to the literal extension of the term. 'Gold mine' then literally denotes gold mines which exemplify a label such as 'highly profitable'. This label is also exemplified by the sources of wealth to which the term 'gold mine' is ordinarily metaphorically applied. These in turn exemplify 'very rewarding', a label that is likewise exemplified by Hume's *Treatise*.

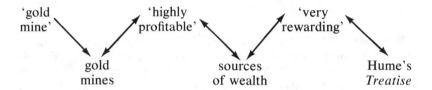

'gold mine'   'highly profitable'   'very rewarding'

gold mines   sources of wealth   Hume's *Treatise*

In this case the chain of reference involves a previous metaphorical application of the term.

There are other complicated chains as well. The referential chain correlated with the metaphorical application of a fictive term does not involve what the term denotes, but a group of expressions that denote it—namely, those the fictive term mention-selects. The chain of reference for 'David is a Don Juan' has the following form: The term 'Don Juan' exemplifies 'seducer-description', a label of labels that is also exemplified by 'seducer', which in turn is exemplified by David [RR, 129].

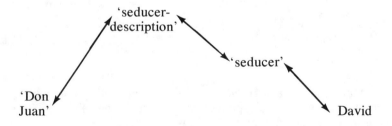

'seducer-description'

'seducer'

'Don Juan'   David

A similar chain is in effect when a metaphor depends on a false stereotype. Consider

The mobster's gorillas, Smith and Jones, were sent to enforce the contract.

Here 'gorilla' metaphorically denotes Smith and Jones who exemplify a label such as 'brutal'. No such label, however, is exemplified by the individuals in the literal extension of 'gorilla', for they are gentle, peaceable animals. Nevertheless, 'brutal' is typically mention-selectively exemplified by fictive gorilla-stories, and 'brutal-label' exemplified by them. So the metaphor's chain of reference looks like this:

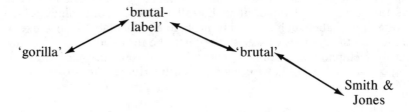

How are we to identify the labels that are the vehicles for metaphorical likening? Sometimes there are several candidates. Suppose I announce, "The guy who shares my office is a troglodyte". A number of labels might be jointly exemplified by my office mate and the individuals in the literal extension of 'troglodyte'—e.g., 'stupid', 'loutish', 'primitive', 'subhuman'. Individually and in combination these labels can serve as vehicles for metaphorical likening. Moreover, my office mate, I am forced to admit, is not literally subhuman. So a full explication of how 'troglodyte' functions metaphorically in this context requires explaining how 'subhuman' does. The relevant chain of reference might be diagrammed as follows:

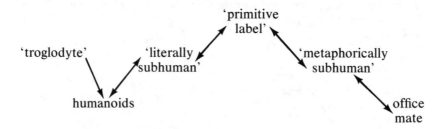

There may then be a number of referential chains connecting the metaphorical and literal applications of a term, and links in some of them may themselves involve metaphors.

Relations between the metaphorical and the literal extensions of a term often depend on contextual factors. The term 'rat', for example, is usually applied metaphorically on the basis of certain character flaws. But in a discussion of physical appearances, it might be applied metaphorically to a person with a long pointy nose, beady eyes, and an unpronounced chin. With a shift in context comes a shift in the predicates that need to be exemplified by the metaphorical and literal referents of the term.

Exactly what labels belong to a particular chain of reference may be uncertain. Whether, e.g., my office mate and literal troglodytes jointly exemplify 'loutish' is open to dispute. Perhaps 'uncouth' or 'uncivilized' is closer to the mark. And contextual cues may be too weak to decide among rival chains. If I say of a sneaky, beady-eyed person, "He's easily recognized, for he's a rat", there may be no telling whether his appearance, his personality, or both are vehicles for metaphorical likening. Moreover, regardless of the referential chains we have already identified, there remains the prospect of identifying yet others. So although a chain of referents can explain a particular likening of the metaphorical and literal references of a term, no chain or group of chains can be considered to constitute a literal paraphrase of the metaphor. For we are never in a position to maintain that the chains we have identified exhaust the metaphor.

Often the metaphorical application of a term effects a novel sorting of the objects in its domain. The objects it groups together do not constitute the extension of any simple literal predicate of the language. Once we recognize how metaphorical and literal applications of a term are linked by a chain of reference, the explanation of this is not difficult.

We saw that in the simplest cases objects in the metaphorical extension of a term exemplify some of the same labels as the objects in its literal extension.[2] But not every collection of objects has a literal predicate associated with it, so there need be no literal term that applies to just the objects in the realm of the metaphor that exemplify the labels in question. If there is not, the application of the metaphor brings about a novel sorting of the objects in its realm.

An example may be helpful here. Consider

Fred is nothing but a coat rack.

The main function of a coat rack is to hold up coats so that they don't fall on the floor. Accordingly, Fred and those things that are literally nothing but coat racks jointly exemplify 'functions mainly to keep coats from falling on the floor'.[3] Fred, we may conclude, and other people who are metaphorically nothing but coat racks, do little—their primary contribution to the greater good being to hold their own coats up. Certainly there are literal predicates that apply to such people—

2. To avoid needlessly complicating the discussion, I consider only the simplest cases. The point is the same for more complicated ones.

3. As applied to people, this plainly involves an element of exaggeration. (Indeed, even as applied to literal coat racks 'nothing but a coat rack' stretches the point. For even the most utilitarian of coat racks instantiates some other labels besides 'coat rack'.) And exaggeration, as we saw, is a form of metaphor. So the chain of reference linking Fred to literal coat racks is not completely mapped out. It is, however, sufficiently delineated for the presented discussion.

'ineffectual', 'inconsequential', 'of little account', 'noncontributing member of society', etc. But not everyone who instantiates these literal predicates, indeed not even everyone who exemplifies them, exemplifies 'functions mainly to keep his coat from falling on the floor'. So not everybody in the extension of these literal predicates is in the extension of the metaphorical one. And if I am correct in thinking that 'nothing but a coat rack' effects a novel sorting of the human population, there is no simple literal term[4] that denotes all and only those people who are metaphorically nothing but coat racks.

A metaphor then can effect a novel classification of objects in its realm. Of course the same could be done without metaphors by coining a new literal term. Still, there is the difficulty of deciding what new classifications are wanted. I suggested in Chapter IV that such metaphors enable us to make use of conceptual resources we have already developed. But it should not be thought that the use of such metaphors is exclusively a matter of cognitive efficiency. For they enrich the language in another way as well. They effect a likening of the objects in their literal and metaphorical extensions by bringing those objects to exemplify some of the same labels.

An especially apt metaphor may evoke a shock of recognition. Even though its object does not belong to its literal extension, its application to that object seems peculiarly apposite. In some cases such a metaphor evokes aftershocks as well. In addition to the primary chains of reference that go from the metaphor to the literal application of the term, we find chains that go in the opposite direction—from the literal back to the metaphorical application. The metaphor then prompts a reconsideration of the objects in the term's literal extension as a result of their being likened to those in its metaphorical extension.

Consider

> If they don't surrender, we'll turn their country into a parking lot.

The primary chains of reference go from parking lots under construction to the country in question. 'Turn [it] into a parking lot' applies metaphorically to the country in question because (supposing the enemy fails to surrender) we will cause it to exemplify such labels as 'leveled', 'flattened', 'demolished',—labels that are also exemplified during parking lot construction. But that the total destruction of a country can be described metaphorically as turning it into a parking lot provokes us to think about what goes on in parking lot construction. Secondary chains of reference then go from the destruction of

---

4. We could in principle, I suppose, list the names of all and only the people who are metaphorically coat racks. That list would be coextensive with the metaphorical term. I speak of a *simple* literal term to avoid objections based on the possibility of making lists like this and to avoid objections based on the possibility of constructing literal predicates that are convoluted, gerrymandered combinations of literal general terms.

countries to the construction of parking lots. These chains depend on
the joint exemplification of a different group of labels—labels like
'devastated', 'ravaged', and 'laid waste'. The metaphor then brings it
about that during parking lot construction, the terrain exemplifies
these labels.

Metaphors often reverberate as well. Related metaphorical terms
work together to heighten the likening of their literal and metaphorical
subjects. In Plato's *Republic,* for example, there are a number of
places in which 'seeing' serves as a metaphor for understanding or
knowledge. The metaphor is prominent in the myth of the cave, the
allegory of the sun, and the introduction to the discussion of justice in
the state. It is underscored when 'sun', a term that literally denotes
the source of light, is applied metaphorically to the Form of the Good,
the source of knowledge; when what is seen in sunlight is likened to
what is known, and what is seen in twilight, reflected in water, or as a
shadow is likened to matters of opinion; and when 'shortsighted'
serves as a metaphor for the inability to recognize justice in the individual. And given Plato's conviction that the knower is like the
known, the foregoing metaphors receive further support from the
myth of the metals; for only in the guardians, the most knowledgeable
citizens of the republic, is there said to be gold, the brightest, most
sunlike of the metals.

Let us look at the ways some of these metaphors interact. To avoid
overly complicating the discussion, I consider only the most central
ones, and these only schematically. It should be evident how to fill in
the details and how to extend the account to other related metaphors.

Even for a relatively simple system of metaphors like this, the network of referential chains is fairly intricate. 'Sunlit objects' serves as
a metaphor for what is known, as both sunlit objects and what is
known exemplify such labels as 'clear', 'distinct', and 'evident'.
'Sight' is a metaphor for knowledge since both sight and knowledge
exemplify 'apprehension of what is clear, distinct, and evident'.
Moreover, each link in the latter chain plainly alludes to its counterpart in the former one. And 'the sun' serves as a metaphor for the
Form of the Good. Two chains of reference are of interest for our
purposes. One links the sun and the Form of the Good via their joint
exemplification (according to Plato's doctrine) of 'cause of the apprehension of what is clear, distinct, and evident'. Each element in
this chain also alludes to its counterpart in the chain just mentioned.
Furthermore, both the sun and the Form of the Good exemplify
'cause of things being clear, distinct, and evident'. So the links in the
chain allude to their counterparts in the first chain.[5]

---

5. Notice that if we refuse to admit The Form of the Good into our ontology, we
simply move the discussion of the last metaphor to a higher level. Our explication is
then in terms of the labels of labels that in Plato's work are jointly exemplified by
sun-descriptions and Form-of-the-Good-descriptions. And there is no difficulty in admitting Form-of-the-Good-descriptions into our ontology even if we are loath to grant
them a non-null extension.

This account of metaphorical likening comprehends exemplificational metaphors as well as denotational ones. Thus, e.g., a picture of
a deserted seashore painted in muted colors exemplifies sadness by
means of a chain like this:

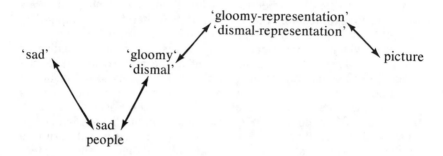

The labels 'gloomy' and 'dismal' are not, of course, exemplified by all
sad people. Some sad people present to the world such a cheerful
countenance that the extent of their unhappiness is never known. But
those labels are exemplified by *some* sad people, indeed by the very
ones who literally exemplify 'sad'.

Notice that even a simple metaphor like this one has room for aftershocks and reverberations. The people who literally exemplify 'sad'
may metaphorically exemplify 'blue'—a label that is literally exemplified by the picture. And other labels that apply literally to those
people—'cheerless', 'despondent', 'bereft'—may apply metaphorically to the picture. Yet other labels, such as 'leaden' may apply
metaphorically to both.

Likening of the metaphorical and literal referents of a symbol is not
always solely the result of joint exemplification. In some cases their
likening is effected by their denoting the same objects and/or
mention-selecting the same object-descriptions. Thus, for example,
musical works that metaphorically exemplify 'pastoral' may be
likened to literary and pictorial works that literally exemplify the label
because of their joint denotation or mention-selection of idealizations
of rural life. Needless to say, these works are likely to exemplify
some of the same labels as well. In that case there are two avenues of
metaphorical likening.

I have spoken of aftershocks and reverberations only in connection
with metaphor. Plainly, they occur in other forms of complex and
indirect reference as well. A caricature of Churchill as a bulldog may
forever alter not only the way we look at Churchill, but also the way
we look at bulldogs. And an allusion to Smith's incarceration in Sing
Sing effected by the phrase 'Smith's stay in Ossining' is reinforced as
we add 'as a guest of the people of New York'. Our various references, literal and metaphorical, direct and indirect, simple and complex, form intricate symbolic networks in which the application of a

particular term may shock, stultify, or simply serve; it may reinforce, undermine, or fail to influence the application of others.

The lore of our fathers, as Quine is wont to say, is a fabric of sentences—perhaps a more intricately woven one than he imagines. A term that denotes one thing alludes to something else. It has numerous metaphorical extensions depending on the contexts in which it is applied. Moreover, it mention-selects certain (accurate or inaccurate) descriptions and pictures. Perhaps the term or a phrase in which it is embedded exemplifies or expresses certain labels. In any case the objects in its various figurative extensions exemplify some of the same labels as the objects in its literal extension. (Just which ones these are varies from one figurative application to the next.) Such joint exemplification, as we saw, serves as a vehicle for metaphorical likening as well as for some non-metaphorical allusions. Finally, in mention-selecting descriptions and representations, the term brings it about that certain labels of labels are exemplified.

The complexity and interconnectedness of the term's various referential functions explains why, when a strand is broken, the fabric does not unravel. Typically a strand is tied down in several places. So, if it is broken in one place, it is still held fast in others. Moreover, to relieve the tension when the fabric becomes strained, we can sever a strand in any of a number of locations. And in different cases different types of alterations are recommended.

When ethologists discover that lions are cowardly and gorillas gentle, we safeguard our earlier metaphors and allusions by ending our chains of reference early; we take our figurative applications to recall or allude to lion-stories and gorilla-stories—false ones, as it turns out—rather than actual lions and gorillas.

When cognitive psychologists discover that their literal claims are at odds with the metaphorical claims taken from computer science, they may sacrifice their literal assertions in order to safeguard the metaphorical ones. In that case the metaphors can serve as a guide in the reinterpretation of the literal vocabulary.

And when it becomes implausible to continue to accept a sentence or a system of sentences as literally true, we may find that it can still be held true if interpreted metaphorically. Such metaphorical reconstruals are frequently attempted when, e.g., religious assertions are found to contravene the laws of science.

In the mature sciences, according to Putnam,[6] scientists often attempt to revise theories in a way that preserves the denotations of theoretical terms and that reproduces the old laws as limiting cases of the new. That is, they seek modifications that leave the literal extensions of selected terms intact as well as certain descriptions mention-selected by these terms—namely, the descriptions the science counts as its laws. To accomplish this goal, they are prepared to sever other referential connections. Interpretations of some terms are likely to be

6. Cf. *Meaning and the Moral Sciences*, p. 20 ff.

altered, even if those of the so-called theoretical terms remain fixed. And a given theoretical term may mention-select different 'accidental' descriptions in the context of successive theories, even if the 'lawlike' ones are preserved. Moreover, the metaphors that apply to the domain under the old theory need not apply under the new; allusions effected by the old theory may have no counterpart in the new; and the logical and mathematical relations exemplified by the laws of the old theory need not be the same as those exemplified by the new. Of course, should these alterations prove too costly, the attempt to preserve the favored referential connections can be given up and other connections retained instead.

A term's place in the language is likely to be secured by multiple referential bonds. As a result, a single failure of reference is not likely to be disastrous. Ordinarily, the realization that a term's denotational reference is null, or that its exemplificational reference is null, or that a metaphor or stereotype fails to apply, does not destroy our competence to use that term. For typically some of its other referential connections hold fast. And because they do, a good deal of the term's usage remains intact.

The multiplicity of referential connections results, moreover, in a certain latitude for choice. Our investigations may force us to conclude that some modification in a referential network is needed—that a given term does not refer in all the ways we thought. Still, empirical investigations do not pinpoint a unique source of difficulty or determine what form our modification is to take. Our choice among alternative revisions is grounded in an understanding of the various symbolic roles the term plays and in an evaluation of the relative importance and centrality of each of them and of the human enterprises in which they are embedded. If these choices are not uniquely determined by the evidence, neither are they *ad hoc*.

IX   ABOUT 'ABOUT'

1. PRELIMINARIES

Declarative sentences have a special feature that is not shared by other symbols. They are true or false. This feature is important not because truth matters so much more than other sorts of rightness (e.g., inductive, moral, or aesthetic rightness), but because it is symbols that have truth values that constitute the domain of logic. The virtues of logic do not need to be argued. What I am concerned to do here is show that certain logical relations among sentences give rise to perplexity and consider how such perplexity is to be alleviated.

The perplexity I have in mind arises when we attempt to determine what a sentence is about. It seems plain that, e.g.,

> 1.1   Smith is a scientist

is about Smith. If Smith is a member of the Wombat Society, it is also about a member of that group. Is it also about the Wombat Society? Certainly the society's prestige may be affected by the fact that one of its members is a scientist. So (1.1) is not entirely irrelevant to the society. But if (1.1) is taken to be about the Wombat Society, is it also about every other set to which Smith belongs? Exactly what are the limits on what this one small sentence is about?

Nor is this the only problem. If we conjoin (1.1) with another sentence, say,

> 1.2   Brown is a bandit

the resulting sentence,

> 1.3   Smith is a scientist and Brown is a bandit

is also about Smith. But not every sentence of which (1.1) is a conjunct is about Smith.

> 1.4   Smith is a scientist and Smith is not a scientist

concerns Smith no more intimately than it does any other entity. Under what circumstances are compound sentences about the things their constituents are about?

If Smith actually is a scientist, but Brown not a bandit, then although (1.3) is false and false about Brown, it is true about Smith.

Moreover, if (1.3) is unjustified because there is no evidence that
Brown is a bandit, it may nevertheless be justified about Smith. Indeed, (1.3) may be libelous about Brown. But even if it is false and
defamatory and about Smith, it is not false and defamatory about
Smith. It is then not libelous about Smith.

Problems in this area are easily generated. Solutions, unfortunately,
are harder to find. In this chapter I review two important papers that
go some way toward explicating the notion of *about*—Goodman's
"About", and Ullian and Goodman's "Truth About Jones." A good
deal of complicated technical work needs to be done to complete the
analysis begun in these papers. Instead of doing that here, I end the
chapter by identifying some difficulties in contemporary philosophy
that might be alleviated (or at least illuminated) if we take them to
concern what sentences of certain sorts are about or true about,
rather than just what their terms denote or the conditions under which
they are true.

First, however, it is worth reiterating a point about the relation of
an analysis to our preanalytical judgments. We are often prepared to
say, quite independently of any theory of aboutness, what a particular
sentence is about. Moreover, we have certain (tacit or explicit) convictions regarding the relations of sentences in general to the things
they are about. Difficulties arise when it becomes evident that our
various judgments about 'about' are jointly untenable. Then some of
them have to be revised so that a reasonable balance can be struck.
This is a tricky business, for what it is for a sentence to be about
something turns out to be a surprisingly subtle question. But even
though our initial judgments are defeasible, they play an important
role; for they serve as touchstones against which to measure the adequacy of any proposed analysis of 'about'.

'About' then is a semantic relation that links sentences and things.
Inasmuch as there is disagreement over what sorts of things there are,
there is bound to be disagreement over what sentences are about.
Nominalists restrict their ontologies to individuals; accordingly, they
maintain that sentences are about individuals exclusively. Platonists
are ontologically committed to classes as well as to individuals; they
thus consider sentences to be about both. Goodman seeks to give a
general definition of 'about'—one that will satisfy the platonist as
well as the nominalist. So he first formulates his definition in a way
that allows for reference to classes and then shows how that definition
can be modified to satisfy the strictures of nominalism. In explicating
his account, I do the same.

To facilitate reference to classes, let us introduce the notion of *designation*. A sigular term designates what it denotes; a general term
designates the class of things it denotes.[1] Thus 'Smith' designates

---

1. Cf. W. V. Quine, "Designation and Existence", *The Journal of Philosophy*
XXXVI (1939), 701–709. Like Quine, I identify a unit class with its sole member. Then
any term whose extension is a unit class of an individual designates what it denotes.

Smith; and 'scientist', the class of scientists. A sentence is said to *mention* whatever any of its terms designates [PP, 249]. It is in terms of designation rather than denotation that Goodman formulates his definition of 'about'.

A definition in terms of designation is preferable if classes are admitted into our ontology. The sentence

    1.5   Scientists are scrupulous

is evidently about scientists and about scrupulous individuals. But it does not seem to be about each (or any) particular scientist or about each (or any) particular scrupulous individual. It seems rather to be about scientists in general and about scrupulous individuals in general. So it is reasonable to take the sentence to be about the class of scientists and about the class of scrupulous individuals. (It may, of course, be about other things as well.) Designation rather than denotation then is central to the way the general terms of a sentence contribute to what the sentence is about. And since singular terms designate what they denote, designation also serves to explain the contribution of singular terms. Once we have introduced designation, we need not invoke denotation to explain how the reference of its terms contributes to what a sentence is about.

Should we say that (1.5) is also about the class of human beings? This is plausible inasmuch as the class of scientists is included in the class of human beings. But it leads to serious difficulties. The class of scientists is included not only in the class of human beings but in infinitely many other classes as well. So if we take (1.5) to be about the class of human beings, we should also take it to be about each of those other classes. Moreover,

    1.6   Bandits are crooks

is about the class of bandits, which, like the class of scientists, is included in the class of human beings. Ought we conclude that there is something (namely, the class of human beings) that both (1.5) and (1.6) are about? This conclusion is disconcerting enough. To make matters worse, it generalizes. By this reasoning, for any two sentences that are about anything, there is something that both are about.

Rather than accept this untoward result, Goodman distinguishes between what a sentence is *absolutely* about, and what it is about *relative* to some other sentence [PP, 248]. Just what the distinction amounts to will become evident as we proceed. All I want to do here is suggest that drawing such a distinction may be fruitful. There seems[2] to be nothing that both (1.5) and (1.6) are absolutely about.

---

2. I say 'seems' here because, until an acceptable definition is formulated we cannot say conclusively what any sentence is absolutely about.

But (1.5) is about the class of human beings relative to

   1.7   Scientists are human beings

and (1.6) is about the class of human beings relative to

   1.8   Bandits are human beings.

So relative to (1.7) and (1.8) respectively, there is some class that both (1.5) and (1.6) are about.
   The sentence

   1.9   Bandits break laws

may be taken to be about the class of bandits, the class of breakings, and the class of laws. This, of course, is open to dispute for the sentence can be parsed in a number of ways. One might, e.g., maintain that 'break laws' is a simple predicate that designates the class of law breakings. And what a sentence is about is likely to vary with differences in the expressions that are taken to be its terms. Still, we are not concerned here to discover criteria for the identification of terms and their designata. We seek rather criteria that determine what a sentence is about *given* what its terms designate [PP, 248].

2. ABSOLUTELY ABOUT

   It is tempting, perhaps, to hypothesize that a sentence is absolutely about[3] whatever it mentions. Then

   2.1   All bandits are disreputable

is about the class of bandits and the class of disreputable individuals. And

   2.2   All reputable individuals are nonbandits

is about the class of reputable individuals and the class of nonbandits. But (2.1) and (2.2) are logically equivalent. And it is reasonable to expect logically equivalent sentences to be about the same things. Otherwise, what a sentence is about is divorced from the conditions under which it is true.
   Should we conclude then that a sentence is about whatever is mentioned by it or by any of its logical equivalents? The difficulty is that every sentence has a logical equivalent that mentions any given thing.

   3. When I use the term 'about' without qualification, I use it in the sense of 'absolutely about'.

Our hypothesis is thus plainly unsatisfactory. For what is wanted is an account according to which 'about' is selective. To be about something, a sentence must be semantically related to that thing in a way that it is not related to everything else.

Two criteria for an adequate explication of 'absolutely about' emerge:

(i)   Logically equivalent sentences are about the same things.

(ii) 'About' is selective: A sentence is about k only if it stands to k in some relation in which it does not stand to everything else.

It follows from (i) that a sentence need not mention things it is about. (2.2) is about the class of bandits if (2.1) is; yet (2.2) does not mention that class. And it follows from (ii) that a sentence which mentions something may nevertheless fail to be about that thing. This is the case if what it asserts concerning that thing it also asserts concerning everything else. Thus

2.3   Brown is or is not a bandit

is not about Brown. For instantiating 'is or is not a bandit' does not differentiate Brown from any other entity. If a sentence is about Brown, it should have consequences that concern Brown specifically—consequences, that is, which do not generalize.

We thus need a way to compare the consequences a sentence has for particular individuals or classes with certain generalizations of these consequences. The *generalization of a sentence S with respect to an expression E* is the sentence obtained when every occurrence of E in S is replaced by a variable and a universal quantifier binding that variable is attached to the resulting formula [PP, 251]. To say that a sentence has a consequence for k that it does not have generally is to say that a consequence that mentions k follows from it, but that the generalization of that consequence with respect to the term designating k does not. An example may help to clarify this. It is a consequence of (1.2) that

2.4   Brown or the Brooklyn Bridge is a bandit.

The generalization of (2.4) with respect to 'Brown' is

2.5 (x) (x or the Brooklyn Bridge is a bandit)

which plainly does not follow from (1.2). Since (1.2) has a consequence for Brown that does not generalize, we might reasonably consider it to be absolutely about Brown. Now the generalization of (2.4) with respect to 'the Brooklyn Bridge' is

2.6 (x)(Brown or x is a bandit)

and this does follow from (1.2). So far forth then, we have no reason to think that (1.2) is about the Brooklyn Bridge.

In general then a sentence S is absolutely about k only if S has a logical consequence C that mentions k without also having as a consequence the generalization of C with respect to the expression designating k.

Were we in a position to say "if and only if" we would have the definition we seek. But we are not. It follows from (1.2) that

2.7   Every organization that is a club and admits Brown admits a bandit.

Now the only club that admits Brown is the Wombat Society. Does the fact that (2.7) follows from (1.2) give us reason to conclude that (1.2) is absolutely about the Wombat Society? If we consider the generalization of (2.7) with respect to 'club', it seems not.

2.8 (α)(Every organization that is an α and admits Brown admits a bandit.)

And this is a consequence of (1.2). But if we consider the generalization with respect to 'club and admits Brown', we get the opposite result. For that generalization is

2.9 (α)(Every organization that is an α admits a bandit)

which plainly does not follow from (1.2). The difficulty is this: If we conclude that (1.2) is about the Wombat Society because (2.7) follows from it but (2.9) does not, 'absolutely about' loses its selectivity. For parallel conclusions can be drawn regarding anything that stands in any relation to Brown. And everything is related to Brown in one way or another. E.g., it follows from (1.2) that

2.10   Whatever is a tree and shades Brown shades a bandit

but not

2.11 (α)(Whatever is an α shades a bandit.)

That the sentence 'Brown is a bandit' should turn out to be about a tree is implausible in the extreme.

Plainly, determining what a sentence is about requires a more sensitive criterion. Let us say that P is a *differential consequence* of S with respect to k just in case P is a consequence of S that mentions k but no generalization of P with respect to *any part of* the expression in P that designates k is also a consequence of S [PP, 253]. (2.7) is a consequence of (1.2) that mentions the Wombat Society, but it is not a differential consequence of (1.2) with respect to the Wombat Society. For although its generalization with respect to the expression that designates the Wombat Society—'club and admits Brown'—does not follow from (1.2), its generalization with respect to part of that expression—namely, 'club'—does follow from (1.2).

Goodman maintains that it is the differential consequences of a sentence that determine what the sentence is about. The definition that results is this:

> A sentence S is *absolutely about* k just in case it has a differential consequence with respect to k. That is, S is absolutely about k just in case there is some sentence P that follows from S differentially with respect to k [PP, 253].

The differential consequences of S with respect to k determine what S says about k. Moreover S and Q say the same about k just in case they have the same differential consequences with respect to k (except, perhaps, for the expressions in them designating k). And S says about k what Q says about j just in case the differential consequences of S with respect to k and those of Q with respect to j are the same except for the expressions in them designating k and j respectively [PP, 253].

As Goodman defines it, 'absolutely about' is strictly extensional. Since (1.2) is absolutely about Brown, and Brown is the most disreputable member of the Wombat Society, (1.2) is absolutely about the most disreputable member of the Wombat Society. And in general, "if S is absolutely about k and k is identical with j, S is absolutely about j" [PP, 256].

Goodman's definition satisfies our criteria of adequacy:

(i) If S and Q are logically equivalent, they have exactly the same consequences. So if P follows from S, P follows from Q. Moreover, if P mentions k and neither the generalization of P with respect to the expression designating k nor its generalization with respect to any part of that expression follows from S, then neither of the generalizations follows from Q. S and Q thus have exactly the same differential consequences and so are absolutely about the same things.

(ii) No sentence is absolutely about everything. For 'absolutely about' is defined in terms of differential consequences and the differential consequences of a sentence are precisely the ones that do not generalize.

Certain features of this definition should be noted. Inasmuch as what a sentence is absolutely about is determined by certain of its logical consequences, that determination depends on the choice of a logic. I follow the usual practice of using standard first-order logic with identity. But aside from convenience, nothing hangs on this choice. We have to invoke some logic to identify the consequences of our sentences, but the definition of 'absolutely about' does not favor any particular choice.

Whether a consequence C of a sentence S follows differentially with respect to some object k depends not only on the generalization of C with respect to the expression designating k, but also on its generalization with respect to each of the parts of that expression. Thus, the identification of those parts is crucial. But expressions can be variously parsed—their parts differently identified. E.g., the phrase 'club and admits Brown' can be taken to consist of two parts; viz., 'club' and 'admits Brown'. Or it can be construed as a single unbreakable term. (It can, of course, be construed in other ways as well. But for simplicity I limit my discussion to these two.) Under the former construal, it does not follow from a sentence's having (2.7) as a consequence that it is absolutely about the Wombat Society. Under the latter, a sentence that has (2.7) as a consequence is absolutely about the Wombat Society.[4] What a sentence is absolutely about then depends partly on the way the expressions that appear in its consequences are parsed.

Under different logics and different parsings then the same sentence can turn out to be about different things. But once we settle on a logic and a parsing, what a sentence is about is determinate.

There is one aspect of the logic I have chosen that deserves special mention—namely, that the theory of classes is not considered to be part of logic. As a result, even though logical constants are nondesignatory, 'v' and '∧' are taken to designate the universal class and the null class respectively.

Can sentences then be about the universal class? They can. Although we require that no sentence be about each particular thing, a sentence may be about the universal class, for it may have consequences with respect to that class that it does not have with respect to other things. E.g.,

2.12   The universal class is infinite

plainly has differential consequences with respect to the universal class. Sentences can be about the null class as well.

2.13   The null class is included in every class

has differential consequences with respect to, and so is about, the null class. Moreover, universally quantified sentences can be construed as

---

4. This construal does not, of course, make (1.2) absolutely about the Wombat Society. For if 'club and admits Brown' is construed as a single unbreakable term, (2.7) does not follow from (1.2).

sentences that mention the universal class and as sentences that mention the null class.

2.1 All bandits are disreputable

can be construed as

2.14 The universal class is identical with the union of the class of disreputable individuals and the class of non-bandits

and as

2.15 The null class is identical with the intersection of the class of bandits and the class of reputable individuals.

By familiar transformations existentially quantified sentences can likewise be construed so as to mention the universal class and so as to mention the null class. If such sentences are absolutely about anything, they are absolutely about the universal class and the null class. Indeed, any sentence that is absolutely about anything can be shown to have differential consequences for, and so to be absolutely about, both the universal class and the null class [PP, 258].

These results, as I said, follow directly from the decision to consider the theory of classes distinct from logic. Whether they reflect well or badly on that decision should probably be decided by someone whose intuitions concerning classes are clearer than my own.

3. RELATIVELY ABOUT

Even if a sentence isn't absolutely about k, it may be about k relative to some other sentence. E.g., (1.2) isn't absolutely about disreputable individuals,[5] but it is about disreputable individuals relative to (2.1). For together these sentences have a differential consequence with respect to Brown that neither has alone—namely,

3.1 Brown is disreputable.

As a rough approximation then, two sentences are about k relative to each other if and only if there follows from their conjunction a differential consequence that follows from neither conjunct alone [PP, 260].

---

5. When I say that a sentence is about disreputable individuals or has differential consequences with respect to disreputable individuals, I am to be understood as speaking of the class of disreputable individuals. And likewise when 'about' and 'differential consequence with respect to' preface other plural nouns.

Unfortunately, this approximation is too rough. For it follows from it that

1.1   Smith is a scientist

is about Brown relative to (1.2) since (1.1) and (1.2) together yield

1.3   Smith is a scientist and Brown is a bandit

a differential consequence with respect to Brown that follows from neither (1.1) nor (1.2) alone. Indeed, this criterion renders practically any sentence about anything about Brown relative to practically any sentence about Brown.

An adequate definition of 'relatively about' demands a tighter connection between sentences that are about something relative to each other. It is not enough that together the sentences have differential consequences with respect to that thing which neither has alone; these consequences must have certain additional logical features. Otherwise, the prospect of conjoining a sentence absolutely about Brown with one that has nothing to do with Brown is sufficient, so long as the latter is about something, to make it about Brown relative to the former. For the resulting conjunction will inherit the differential consequences of each of its conjuncts. But having nothing to do with Brown is hardly what makes a sentence an ideal candidate for being relatively about Brown.

We might seek to avoid this by simply stipulating that if S is absolutely about k then no sentence is to be counted about k relative to S. But this is too restrictive. Even though (1.2) is absolutely about Brown, it seems reasonable to take (2.1) to be about Brown relative to it. For together they yield (3.1), a differential consequence which follows from neither alone. Nor is (3.1) a loose composite of differential consequences that derive separately from the individual conjuncts. Indeed, (3.1) seems to be exactly the sort of differential consequence that indicates that relative to one another (1.2) and (2.1) are about Brown. What is needed then is a criterion that justifies taking (2.1) but not (1.1) to be about Brown relative to (1.2).

For two sentences to be about something relative to each other, their conjunction must have a consequence with certain logical properties. Goodman calls such a consequence a *unitary consequence*. A sentence is a unitary consequence if and only if it is logically equivalent to an *explicitly unitary consequence*—one in which the requisite logical properties are perspicuously displayed. Goodman defines 'explicitly unitary consequence' only for sentences in which no scope is governed by more than one quantifier.[6] Even so, the definition is fairly complicated.

---

6. In "Relatively About: Loose Composites and Loose Ends", Joseph Ullian carries the analysis further. I will not, however, discuss that paper here.

A sentence that follows from another is an explicitly unitary consequence if and only if:

(A)   It contains no descriptions or class abstracts, no sentence connectives except conjunction and disjunction, and no negation that applies to an expression already containing a negation, a conjunction, a disjunction or a quantifier;

(B)   Every disjunction sign is outside the scope of every existential quantifier; and

(C)   Every conjuction sign is within the scope of an existential quantifier [PP, 261].

Since every sentence has a logical equivalent that satisfies the first two conditions, it is the third that is decisive. "The requirement that all conjunction signs be captive guarantees that, so to speak, the consequence cannot be broken in two, that it does not consist of two statements lightly stuck together" [PP, 262].

Relative aboutness can now be defined.

Two sentences are *about* something, k, *relative to each other* if and only if there is a unitary consequence that follows differentially with respect to k from their conjunction, but from neither conjunct alone [PP, 263].

As defined, 'relatively about' is extensional. If (2.1) is about Brown relative to (1.2) and Brown is the most disreputable member of the Wombat Society, then relative to (1.2), (2.1) is about the most disreputable member of the Wombat Society. Moreover, if (2.1) is logically equivalent to

3.2   None but the disreputable are bandits

then, relative to (1.2), (3.2) is about Brown [PP, 264].

If two sentences are about k relative to each other, then their conjunction is absolutely about k. But a conjunction can be absolutely about k without its conjuncts being about k relative to each other. For a conjunction can have a differential consequence with respect to k without having a differential unitary consequence with respect to k. Such, as we saw, is the fate of (1.3) with respect to Brown.

4. RHETORICALLY ABOUT

It follows from the definition given above that (1.2) is about Brown, for it has consequences for Brown that it does not have for anything else. But in the case of

4.1   Robin Hood is a bandit

what are we to say? It has no differential consequences for Robin
Hood, there being no Robin Hood to have differential consequences
for. Should we just say that it is absolutely about the null set? It is.
But so is

4.2   The Artful Dodger is a bandit.

And so, for that matter, is every sentence that is absolutely about
anything. Still, it seems reasonable to contend that in some sense of
'about' (4.1) and (4.2) are not about exactly the same things and that
each of them is about something that (1.2) is not. What is wanted is an
account of what these sentences are rhetorically about.

To say what a sentence is rhetorically about, we need to distinguish
between the interpretation of 'about' as a two-place semantic predicate, and its interpretation as a one-place predicate that applies to
sentences directly. According to the former, (1.2) is about Brown, but
(4.1) is not about Robin Hood. According to the latter, (1.2) is about
Brown and and (4.1) is about Robin Hood. On the former interpretation, it follows from the fact that (1.2) is about Brown that there is
something that (1.2) is about. On the latter, no such conclusion follows. Since we want to maintain that (4.1) is about Robin Hood despite the failure of existential generalization, our definition of 'rhetorically about' should be based on the latter interpretation.

To avoid ambiguity, let us follow Goodman [PP, 266] in restricting
the schema 'about _____' to the former interpretation, and introduce
the schema ' _____-about' to capture the latter. Then we can define
'rhetorically about' in such a way that (4.1) is Robin-Hood-about even
though not about Robin Hood.

How are rhetorical'_____-about' predicates to be defined? The
definition, like that of 'absolutely about' requires selectivity. A
sentence that is Robin-Hood-about should have consequences concerning the expression 'Robin Hood' that it does not have generally.
The difficulty is delineating the appropriate set of such consequences.

Plainly, it is not enough to require that a replica of 'Robin Hood'
appear in the consequence. For there are a number of irrelevant ways
in which such a replica might appear—e.g., surrounded by quotation
marks or as part of a compound like Robin-Hood-about. It is clear
also that we cannot require the replica appearing in a consequence to
have a non-null designation. The intermediate position that is wanted
is this: For a sentence to be Robin-Hood-about, it must have a consequence in which 'Robin Hood' functions as a term, where to function
as a term in a sentence an expression must either occur as a predicate
or occupy an argument place of a predicate in that sentence [PP, 267].

For a sentence to be Robin-Hood-about, it is necessary, but not
sufficient, for 'Robin Hood' to occur as a term. For

4.3   Robin Hood is or is not a bandit

is no more Robin-Hood-about than it is about Robin Hood. To determine which of the sentences in which 'Robin Hood' appears as a term are Robin-Hood-about, we need some counterpart to the notion of a differential consequence. That counterpart is the notion of a *term-differential consequence.* A sentence T follows from S term-differentially with respect to an expression E if and only if E occurs as a term of T, T is a logical consequence of S, and no generalization of T with respect to any term of T that is part of E is also a logical consequence of S [PP, 267]. Then we can say that a sentence is Robin-Hood-about just in case it yields a consequence term-differentially with respect to 'Robin Hood'. And in general

> S is _____-about if and only if some statement T follows from S term-differentially with respect to '_____'

where in any single case the same expression fills both blanks [PP, 267]. A sentence that is _____-about then is rhetorically about whatever fills the blank. Instead of a single definition of 'rhetorically about', we have a general schema whose several applications define the family of '_____-about' predicates.

The schema does not apply exclusively to fictive sentences. (1.2) is Brown-about just as (4.1) is Robin-Hood-about. But (1.2) is also about Brown whereas (4.1) is not about Robin Hood. Still, even for sentences in which all terms designate, the distinction between rhetorical aboutness and absolute aboutness does not collapse.

> 4.4   The most disreputable member of the Wombat Society is a bandit

is about Brown, but not Brown-about; for it has no consequence that follows term-differentially with respect to 'Brown'.

Two general schemata capture the relation between being absolutely about _____ and being _____-about:

> I   If S is _____-about and '_____' designates k, then S is absolutely about k;

and

> II   If S is absolutely about k, then for some expression '_____' that designates k, S is _____-about [PP, 268].

Counterparts of the criteria of adequacy on a definition of 'absolutely about' are satisfied by this definitional schema for 'rhetorically about'.

> (i')   Logically equivalent sentences are rhetorically about the same things.

Since logical equivalents have the same consequences, any sentence that follows term-differentially from one, also does so from the other.

> (ii′)   'Rhetorically about' is selective: No sentence is rhetorically about each term.

For no sentence has consequences that follow term-differentially with respect to each individual term.

Although Brown is identical to the most disreputable member of the Wombat Society, a sentence may be Brown-about without being most-disreputable-member-of-the-Wombat-Society-about. Nevertheless, 'Brown-about' is extensional. For a sentence S is Brown-about just in case 'Brown' occurs term-differentially in a consequence of S. And if S is identical to R and S is Brown-about, then so is R. This is all that is required for extensionality. Since the classification of a sentence as Brown-about does not depend on the designation of the term 'Brown', that 'Brown' and 'the most disreputable member of the Wombat Society' are alike in designation is a matter of indifference [PP, 268].

5. NOMINALIST RECONSTRUAL

The foregoing definitions require certain revisions to satisfy the nominalist. The definitions of 'absolutely about' and 'relatively about' need to be formulated in terms of utterances and inscriptions rather than in terms of expressions. For utterances and inscriptions are individuals, while expressions, as we have understood them, are universals. Such a recasting of the definitions is straightforward.

Further, according to the nominalist, no sentence has differential consequences for classes, as there are no classes to have differential consequences for. The rhetorical '_____-about' predicates thus play a more central role for the nominalist than they do for the platonist. They are needed for a nominalist account of the way certain occurrences of predicate-inscriptions and general-term-inscriptions contribute selective focus. Although (1.2) is neither about the class of bandits nor about the class of bumblebees, part of its selectivity lies in its being bandit-about but not bumblebee-about.

To satisfy nominalist scruples, however, the schema that defines the '_____-about' predicates also requires reformulation. Inasmuch as the nominalist recognizes only individuals, his variables range over individuals exclusively. He has no variables capable of supplanting predicates or general terms. Accordingly, from no statement T that follows from S will the generalization of T with respect to a predicate or general term also follow from S. For, lacking variables of the appropriate type, the nominalist has no way to formulate the generalization of a sentence with respect to any such term.

The central idea of Goodman's suggested reformulation is this: Rather than comparing a sentence to its generalization with respect to a certain expression, we compare the sentence to one that results from substituting for that expression any other expression of the same syntactical category. The schema that defines the rhetorical '_____-about' predicates is reformulated as follows:

> S is _____-about if and only if S yields logically some statement T of which '_____' is a term, while for no term E that is part of '_____' does S yield logically every statement obtained from T by putting for E an expression of the same syntactical category [PP, 272].

Strictly, of course, the schema should be formulated in terms of inscriptions and utterances instead of statements and expressions. Recasting it in such terms presents no difficulties. Goodman's formulation is valuable because it so closely parallels the platonist schema. It is plain that, depending on how 'same syntactical category' is defined, the platonist schema and the nominalist schema will yield the same or nearly the same verdicts as to what particular sentences are rhetorically about.

The adequacy of the final formulation of the schema that defines the rhetorical '_____-about' predicates turns on whether we can explain what it is for utterances and inscriptions to be of the same syntactical category without going beyond the limits of nominalism. Actually, this should present no special problem. The notion of 'same syntactical category' that is wanted is one in which "two terms are of the same syntactical category if either may replace the other without disrupting the syntactical structure of any statement" [PP, 271]. Developing an adequate system of syntactical categories is obviously a difficult task. But once such a system is in hand, interpreting it nominalistically is not. The categories can be construed as a finite list of syntactic predicates whose arguments are utterances and inscriptions.[7] Then Goodman's talk of 'same syntactical category' can be construed in a way that requires no qualification over classes. E.g., inscriptions I_1 and I_2 are of the same syntactical category just in case I_1 is α and I_2 is α or I_1 is β and I_2 is β, or . . . , where the Greek letters are placeholders for the syntactical predicates defined by an adequate syntactical theory. It is unsatisfying but unavoidable that a full nominalist definition must await the formulation of such a theory.

6. TRUE ABOUT

When it comes to saying what a sentence is true about or false about, further complexities emerge. For even if a sentence is both true and about something, it need not be true about that thing.

---

7. In cases of homonymy, syntactic replicas fall under distinct syntactic categories. Thus formulating a syntactic theory directly in terms of utterances and inscriptions may be preferable from the point of view of linguistics itself. Cf., Noam Chomsky, "Systems of Syntactic Analysis", *Journal of Symbolic Logic* 18 (1953), pp. 242–256.

> 6.1   Smith is a scientist or Brown is a scientist

is true and about Brown, but it is surely not true about Brown.
Moreover, a sentence can be true about something without being true.

> 6.2   Smith is a scientist and Brown is a scientist

although false, is true about Smith. 'True about' then does not factor
into 'true' and 'about'. Some other account must be given.

Goodman and Ullian have made substantial progress toward constructing such an account. They have formulated definitions that
characterize the way singular terms contribute to what certain
sentences are true or false about. Their definitions apply only to
sentences without quantificational structure, and do not cover the
contributions of predicates. So the account needs to be expanded. At
the end of the paper they mention certain general features that they
expect such an expanded account to have. Except as noted they take
'about' in the sense of 'absolutely about'.

What criteria of adequacy can be set for a definition of 'true about'?
Goodman and Ullian suggest these:

   (a)   A sentence is true about (or false about) something only if it
         is about that thing;

   (b)   If a sentence is true about (or false about) something, its
         logical equivalents are likewise true about (or false about)
         that thing;

   (c)   A sentence and its negation cannot both be true about some-
         thing nor both be false about something;

   (d)   No sentence can be both true about and false about the
         same thing [TAJ, 320–321].

They resist requiring a law of excluded middle, for it is not obvious
that the negation of a sentence true about something is inevitably false
about that thing. Even though

> 6.3   Smith is no scientist and Brown is no scientist

is true about Brown, it is not clear that its negation, (6.1), should be
considered false about Brown. Since Smith is in fact a scientist, (6.1)
seems not to depend on Brown at all.

In formulating a definition of 'about', we demanded selectivity. A
sentence is not to be counted about something if it has exactly the
same consequences for that thing as it has for everything else. Selectivity is wanted in our definitions of 'true about' and 'false about' as
well. Here, however, we are not concerned with whether substituting
one term for another alters consequences, but whether it alters truth
value. We take

1.1   Smith is a scientist

to be true about Smith because when 'Smith' is replaced by 'Brown', a false sentence results. And the reason for doubting that (6.1) is false about Brown is that the truth of the first disjunct guarantees the truth of the whole no matter what we substitute for 'Brown'.

This suggests that a sentence about k is true about k or false about k just in case there is a term whose substitution for k yields a sentence with the opposite truth value. Unfortunately, this is too simple. No matter what expression we substitute for 'Smith' in

6.4   Smith is no scientist and Brown is a scientist

the resulting sentence is false. To obtain a truth, we need to replace both 'Smith' and 'Brown' at the same time. This difficulty arises in other cases as well.

6.5   Smith is a scientist or Brown is no scientist

remains true whenever only one name is replaced. Both 'Smith' and 'Brown' have to be replaced to obtain a falsehood. Still, it seems reasonable to take (6.4) to be false about Smith and false about Brown, and to take (6.5) to be true about them. Evidently a more refined criterion is needed.

In developing such a criterion, Goodman and Ullian introduce the notion of a *minimal set* of names for a sentence. A set of names is a minimal set for a sentence if and only if simultaneous replacement of all the names in the set can alter the sentence's truth value, but the replacement of only some of the names cannot do so [TAJ, 322]. Plainly, a sentence can have more than one minimal set.

It almost looks as though its minimal sets are sufficient to determine what a sentence is true (or false) about. A sentence, it seems, is true about Smith just in case it is true and a name of Smith belongs to one if its minimal sets. This criterion, however, fails for the case of a conjunction of a truth and a falsehood.

6.2   Smith is a scientist and Brown is a scientist

is false and has 'Brown' as the sole member of its only minimal set. Nevertheless, it seems plainly to be true about Smith.

Even though minimal sets do not immediately yield the desired definition, they are pretty clearly relevant to it. For it is by replacing the names that constitute a minimal set that we alter a sentence's truth value. Of course, not every replacement brings about a change in truth value. In particular, if the names in a minimal set are replaced by others with the same designation, no change in truth value occurs. E.g., the substitution of 'Tully' for 'Cicero' in

6.6   Cicero was an orator

does not affect truth value. The referents of the terms in its minimal
sets then appear to be crucial to what a sentence is true or false
about. Let us say that a sentence *strongly depends* on something if
and only if a term designating that thing belongs to one of the
sentence's minimal sets [TAJ, 323].
    (6.2) does not itself strongly depend on Smith, but one of its con-
juncts does—namely,

1.1   Smith is a scientist.

This provides a clue as to why (6.2) should be considered true about
Smith. To exploit that clue, we need to consider the conjunctive normal forms of sentences.[8] A conjunctive normal formula is redundant if
any of its disjuncts or conjuncts can be dropped without loss of
equivalence. Otherwise it is said to be *regular*. Every sentence whose
regimentation involves no quantification has a regular equivalent.
Now a sentence is said to *depend on* something if and only if all of its
regular equivalents contain one or more conjuncts whose conjunction
strongly depends on that thing.[9] (6.2) then depends on Smith because

8. A conjunctive normal formula is a conjunction of disjunctions where each disjunct
is an atomic sentence or the negation of an atomic sentence. An atomic sentence is one
that has neither truth functional nor quantificational structure. In speaking of the conjunctive normal form of an ordinary English sentence, I obviously take the sentence to
have a determinate parsing. In effect, I treat it as a (quantifier free) symbol in an interpreted formal system. Under alternative parsings a given sentence may turn out to be
true about or false about different things.

9. "The definition of dependence may seem to have three unwelcome complications:
it involves 'conjuncts whose conjunction' rather than just 'a conjunct'; it requires that
every regular equivalent have the trait, and not just one; it invokes the cumbersome
notion of nonredundance. The reasons for the three complications are worth taking
time to record.
    First consider the regular 'Qa v-Qk . Qb v -Qa', and suppose that the extension of 'Q'
contains a and k but not b. Then the first conjunct strongly depends on a and on a only,
the second on each of a and b. But the conjunction strongly depends on each of a, b,
and k, having $\{b\}$ and $\{a,k\}$ as its minimal sets. So no single conjunct of a regular
formula need strongly depend on k for the formula to have conjuncts whose conjunction
strongly depends on k. Next consider the equivalent pair of regular formulas

$$[(\delta) \sim Qk \vee Pk \cdot \sim Pk \vee Rk \cdot \sim Rk \vee Qk$$

and

$$(\epsilon) \ Qk \vee \sim Pk \cdot Pk \vee \sim Rk \cdot Rk \vee \sim Qk].$$

Suppose that everything is R, that nothing is P, and that 'Q' is true of some things but
not of all. The (ϵ) seems incapable of differentiating k from anything else, since each
conjunct of (ϵ) is permanently fixed in truth value no matter how we vary the reference
of 'k'. So any account that took (ϵ) to depend on k would be hoodwinking us. For all
that, (δ) has two conjuncts each of which strongly depends on k, its first and its third.

(1.1) strongly depends on Smith. Notice that a sentence strongly depends on k only if it is about k, but it may be about k without depending on k. ((6.1), for example, is about Brown but does not depend on him.)

We are now ready to present the definition of 'true about'.

(D1*) SS is *true about* k if and only if S depends on k and there is a regular equivalent of S in which every conjunct that is about k contains a true disjunct that is about k [TAJ, 326].

Since the criteria of adequacy set out above concern 'false about' as well as 'true about', it is best to define 'false about' prior to attempting an evaluation of (D1*). And before doing that, we should marshal our intuitions on the matter.

There are some sentences about k that do not depend on k. (6.1) is about Smith and about Brown, but it depends only on Smith. Since replacing 'Brown' with another term does not alter its truth value, we do best to say that its being about Brown is irrelevant to the issue of what (6.1) is true or false about. Thus, Goodman and Ullian conclude, only such sentences as depend on k are true about k or false about k.

The question then arises whether every sentence that depends on k and is not true about k is to be counted false about k. Plausible though this suggestion is, there are cases for which it seems to give the wrong verdict. Consider a sentence in conjunctive normal form:

6.7   (Smith is not a soldier or Brown is not a scientist) and (Smith is not a sailor or Brown is not a bandit)

It is a regular conjunctive normal formula that is unique up to the reordering of clauses. It depends on Brown, for one of its conjuncts is true about Brown. The other conjunct, however, although both true and about Brown, does not depend on Brown. It seems odd, though, to conclude that the latter conjunct renders (6.7) false about Brown.

Certain sentences that depend on k thus seem to be neither true about k nor false about k. Goodman and Ullian call sentences about k that are neither true about k nor false about k *twaddle about k*. Among these are true sentences and false ones, sentences that depend on k and sentences that do not depend on k [TAJ, 327].

What sentences that are not true about k are to be considered false about k? Such sentences, we have seen, are required to depend on k.

Hence consideration of just one of a formula's regular equivalents is not in general sufficient for our purpose, as the misleading (δ) shows. Now with 'R' and 'Q' still interpreted the same way, consider the formula '$\sim Ra$. Qk'. We presumably want to count it as depending on k (though of course not on a). If we demanded of *redundant* conjunctive normal equivalents of this formula that they pass the test required of non-redundant (i.e., regular) ones we would be thwarted by our old friend (β), '$\sim Ra$. Qk v Ra'. For (β)'s conjuncts could not care less what 'k' designates, since they remain false and true, respectively, no matter how 'k' is taken. Thus all three complications are well warranted" [TAJ, 324–325].

But this is not enough to decide the issue, for some twaddle about k also depends on k. Our difficulty is distinguishing between the false and the twaddle about k, and it must be admitted that intuitions on this point are not especially sharp. Still, if we consider our reason for denying that (6.7) is false about Brown, a plausible definition emerges. It seems wrong to consider (6.7) false about Brown because no occurrence of any name of Brown jeopardizes the truth of the sentence. That is, no occurrence of 'Brown' (or any other name of Brown) renders any conjunct false. This suggests that 'false about' be defined as follows:

> (D2*) S is *false about* k if and only if S depends on k and there is a regular equivalent of S in which some conjunct that is about k is false [TAJ, 329].

As defined, 'true about' and 'false about' satisfy our criteria of adequacy. Satisfaction of the first two is straightforward:

> (a)   Since a sentence is true about k or false about k only if it depends on k, and it depends on k only if it is about k, a sentence is true about k or false about k only if about k.

> (b)   Because logically equivalent sentences have the same conjunctive normal forms and so the same regular conjunctive normal forms, logically equivalent sentences are true about (or false about) the same things.

Satisfaction of the other two criteria requires appeal to a Useful Lemma and its Corollary—namely,

> Useful Lemma: Suppose that S is consistent and nonvalid and has a conjunctive normal equivalent with the trait that every conjunct that is about k contains a true disjunct that is about k. Then (i) every regular equivalent of S shares that trait; (ii) no regular equivalent of the negation of S has the trait unless vacuously (i.e., by having no conjuncts about k).

> Corollary to (ii): If a statement is true about k, then its negation cannot be [TAJ, 327].[10]

---

10. "Let a nonempty finite set of designated statement letters be given, and let U be a consistent, nonvalid conjunctive normal formula whose atoms are statement letters. We will show that if U has the property that every conjunct with an occurrence of a designated letter has a (plain, unnegated) designated letter as a disjunct, then (i') every regular equivalent of U does also but (ii') no regular equivalent of the negation of U does, unless it has no occurrences of designated letters at all. Both parts of the Lemma

Then

(c) That a sentence and its negation cannot both be true about something is the corollary to the Useful Lemma. That they cannot both be false about something is easily seen. To be false about k, a regular equivalent of a sentence has to have a conjunct about k that is false. Since the negation of a false sentence is true, the negation of any sentence that is false about k is a true sentence. A true sentence can have no false conjuncts, and so cannot be false about k.

(d) If a sentence is true about k, it has a regular equivalent in which every conjunct that is about k contains a true disjunct that is about k. It may, of course, have more

---

are then immediate: replace designated letters by atoms about k or their negations— whichever are true, other statement letters by other atoms, and drop any double negations thus formed. . . .

So let U have that property. Then U is a conjunction of (zero or more) conjuncts containing designated letters as disjuncts with (perhaps) some further conjuncts whose conjunction is Q. Q contains no designated letters. Let us suppose, *contra* (i'), that U' is a regular equivalent of U that lacks the property. U' must have a conjunct C which amounts to the disjunction of one or more *negations* of designated letters with (perhaps) further matter R, which—like Q—contains no designated letters. Now lest Q, and hence U, be inconsistent, there is an assignment of truth-values that assigns 'true' to all designated letters *and* verifies U. Such an assignment then also verifies U' and its conjunct C; but this requires that it verify R and that R not be null, since the assignment falsifies all *other* disjuncts of C—negations of designated letters. This means that R is implied by the conjunction of the designated letters with Q, or by the conjunction of the designated letters alone if Q happens to be null. So if Q is null then R, which contains no designated letters, is implied by the conjunction of those very letters; and if that is so then R is valid and U' is redundant, i.e., not regular after all. Therefore Q is not null. But then it follows that Q alone must imply R, since assignments to designated letters are irrelevant to the truth of R. So U', which is equivalent to U, which implies Q, must imply R. But this assures that the disjunction of negations of designated letters can be dropped from C without loss of equivalence, and that again belies the regularity of U'. This proves (i').

Now let us suppose that W is a regular equivalent of the negation of U that has the property. Then W is a conjunction of (zero or more) conjuncts containing designated letters as disjuncts with (perhaps) some further conjuncts whose conjunction is Q'. Q' contains no designated letters. Consider a truth assignment μ that assigns 'true' to all designated letters. If Q' is null then μ verifies W, so falsifies U, hence must falsify Q. But since Q has no designated letters this means that Q is inconsistent, contrary to consistency of U. Hence Q' is not null. Similarly, if Q is null then W is inconsistent, contrary to the nonvalidity of U. Hence Q is not null either. Now under μ, as under any truth assignment, exactly one of U and W is verified; hence under μ, exactly one of Q and Q' is verified. But how μ treats designated letters is entirely irrelevant to how it treats Q and Q'; hence Q' is equivalent to the negation of Q. Now W implies Q' and U implies Q, i.e., the negation of W implies the negation of Q'. So W is equivalent simply to Q', whence, being regular, it has no conjuncts beyond Q' and hence no occurrences of designated letters. This proves (ii'), completing the proof of the Lemma." [TAJ, 327–329].

> than one regular equivalent. But by the Useful Lemma,
> in each regular equivalent every conjunct that is about k
> contains a true disjunct that is about k. Since any con-
> junct that contains a true disjunct is true, no regular
> equivalent contains a conjunct about k that is false.
> Hence the sentence is not false about k. A sentence
> then cannot be true about and false about the same
> thing.

Certain additional features of the logic of 'true about' and 'false about' are worthy of mention. We saw that a sentence that is false about k must be false. One that is true about k may have either truth value. If a sentence is true about k, its regular equivalents contain true conjuncts. But they may contain false conjuncts as well so long as these do not depend on k. In that case, the sentence is false.

The negation of a sentence that is false about k is both true and about k.[11] But it need not be true about k. For only such sentences as depend on k are true about k.

The conjunction of sentences each true about k need not be true about k. It might not be about k at all, and even if about k, it might not depend on k. If, however, the conjunction of sentences each true about k does depend on k, it too will be true about k. This follows from the Useful Lemma.

No such conclusion can be drawn regarding the conjunction of sentences each false about k. For if the conjunction is redundant, certain component sentences have to be dropped to achieve regularity. And this can sometimes be done in such a way that no conjunct that is false about k remains. E.g.,

>   6.8   (Smith is not a scientist or Brown is not a scientist) and
>   (Smith is scrupulous) and (Brown is a sea otter)

and

>   6.9   (Smith is a sea lion or Brown is a sea otter) and (Brown
>   is a scientist)

both have first conjuncts that render them false about Smith. Their conjunction, though, amounts to

>   6.10 (Smith is scrupulous) and (Brown is a scientist) and
>   (Brown is a sea otter)

which is true about Smith, not false about him. This result is, perhaps, surprising. But Goodman and Ullian maintain that it is not

---

11. Cf. Hilary Putnam and Joseph Ullian, "More About 'About'", *The Journal of Philosophy* LXII (1965), pp. 305–310 for the proof that the negation of a sentence about k is likewise about k.

deeply disconcerting, for it simply reflects what is well known—that a conjunction does not reflect every logically interesting feature of its conjuncts.

The definitions of 'true about' and 'false about' formulated by Goodman and Ullian determine only how singular terms contribute to what a sentence is true or false about. Moreover, these definitions apply only to sentences that lack quantificational structure. Plainly, a good deal more needs to be done before we have a comprehensive general account of what sentences are true or false about.

Although they do not provide definitons applicable to predicates or general terms, they briefly discuss how the reasoning that led to the definitions applicable to singular terms might be relevant to developing such definitions. The platonist, at least, is in need of such definitions. Since he holds that certain sentences are about what their predicates or general terms designate, the platonist presumably also wants to hold that certain sentences are true or false about what their predicates or general terms designate.

According to the account developed above, differentiation of an object turns on the ability to alter the truth value of a sentence by replacing the name of that object with a name that has a different designation. Analogously, differentiation of a class should turn on the ability to alter truth value by replacing a term that designates that class with a term that designates a different class. A *minimal predicate set* for a sentence then is an irreducible collection of predicates all of which have to be replaced to alter the sentence's truth [TAJ, 336].

The parallels between the analyses of predicates and constants should not obscure a crucial difference between the two cases: "Some ascriptions of predicates to names fail to have strong dependence on the designata of those names—when the predicate applies to everything or nothing. But every such ascription will still strongly depend on the predicate's extension; for there is nothing that is uniformly in or out of the extension of every predicate" [TAJ, 336]. Still, strong dependence is not trivial, and does not follow automatically from the occurrence of a predicate in a sentence.

6.11 Smith is a scientist or Brown is a sea otter

strongly depends on the class of sea otters no more than it does on Brown.

One further point about predicates is worth mentioning. Predicates with different extensions have different complements. Accordingly, any sentence that depends on the extension of a predicate also depends on the extension of its complement. So a sentence that is true about or false about the class designated by a given predicate is likewise true about or false about the complement of that class [TAJ, 337].

This, to be sure, falls short of a system of definitions. But it does suggest certain features that the requisite definitions of 'minimal set', 'strong dependence', 'true about', etc. should have.

The nominalist, of course, denies that

1.2   Brown is a bandit

is true about the class of bandits, for he denies that there are classes for sentences to be true or false about. He is, however, prepared to admit that (1.2) is a bandit-true-about. The nominalist then may be more concerned than the platonist with the question of what sentences are rhetorically true (or false) about. Still, that question is not only the concern of the nominalist. For an account of rhetorical truth and falsity-about is needed by anyone who would explicate fictive sentences.

What a sentence is rhetorically true or false about depends on the identity of the terms that occur in it, not on their referents. Thus,

4.1   Robin Hood is a bandit

is Robin-Hood-true-about because substitution of, say, 'Romeo' for 'Robin Hood' yields a rhetorically false sentence. And it is bandit-true-about because replacing 'bandit' with 'baboon' yields a rhetorically false sentence. Schematic definitions of '_____-true-about' and '_____-false-about' that depend on terms rather than on their referents can be formulated to parallel the definitions of 'true about' and 'false about' given above. Thus

> (R1*)   S is k-*true-about* if and only if S depends on 'k' and there is a regular equivalent of S in which every conjunct that is k-about contains a true disjunct that is k-about;

and

> (R2*)   S is k-*false-about* if and only if S depends on 'k' and there is a regular equivalent of S in which some conjunct that is k-about is false.

A question that remains open at the end of Goodman and Ullian's investigation is how to define 'true about' and 'false about' for quantificational contexts.

It might seem that an enormous amount of effort and ingenuity has been expended to achieve a surprisingly limited result. Certainly a good deal more needs to be done before we have a comprehensive general theory that identifies what sentences are (absolutely, relatively, and rhetorically) about, and what they are (absolutely, relatively, and rhetorically) true or false about. Various combinations of these notions and those in terms of which they are defined will undoubtedly raise new sources of perplexity.

Still, this achievement is not negligible. The definitions formulated in "About" and "Truth About Jones" reveal that sentences have logical structures that mitigate the effects of holism. A closed sentence like

1.1   Smith is a scientist

is true of everything if true of anything. It is as true of lima beans and lipoproteins as it is of Smith and scientists. Moreover, despite the evidence in its favor, we might be warranted in giving it up to retain beliefs in other sentences. Even so, Smith seems germane to (1.1) in a way that lima beans, lipoproteins, and logical laws do not. Denotation, as we have seen, does not explain this. For sentences like

1.4   Smith is a scientist and Smith is not a scientist

and

6.12   Smith, like everything else, is physical

also contain terms that denote Smith. But these sentences seem to pertain to Smith no more than they pertain to anything else. By showing that (1.1) is about Smith and that it is true about Smith, our definitions show why (1.1) concerns Smith in ways that (1.4) and (6.12) do not, and in ways that (1.1) does not concern lima beans, liproproteins, and logical laws. And this is no mean accomplishment.

7. CONCLUSION

Without going into detail, I want to close this chapter by mentioning some philosophical issues that might be illuminated by consideration of what various passages are about and/or what they are true or false about, and by suggesting certain other concerns that might be clarified by the analysis of kindred notions.

Determining what a sentence is about and what it is true or false about are plainly germane to issues of relevance. Consider the inference from (1.1) and (1.2) to

7.1   If Smith is a scientist, then Brown is a bandit.

Admittedly, the fact that Smith is a scientist has nothing to do with Brown's being a bandit. Still, the inference is standardly considered valid, indeed sound, for both the antecedent and the consequent of (7.1) are true. Proponents of relevance logic maintain that the standard interpretation is incorrect precisely because it does not require the antecedent to be relevant to the consequent.[12]

Instead of tinkering with our logic, it seems better to recognize that there are cases in which in addition to validity (or soundness) some sort of relevance is required. Depending on the context, we might want, e.g., the antecedent to be about something the consequent is about, the antecedent to be true about something the consequent is true about, or the antecedent and consequent to be about something or true about something relative to each other. Although extra-logical considerations are required to decide which, if any, of these types of relevance is wanted, we need not go beyond logic to ascertain whether these criteria of relevance are satisfied.

Coherence is required of acceptable theories, explanations, narratives, etc. The difficulty lies in saying exactly what such a requirement comes to. Plainly, the sentences making up a coherent discourse should have some non-trivial connection with one another. Ullian suggests[13] that the requisite connection obtains when such sentences are about something relative to one another. Then their conjunction has differential consequences that do not follow from the separate conjuncts and are not 'loose composites' of consequences of the separate conjuncts. Relative aboutness can then explain how a discourse that coheres yields more information than is derivable from the individual sentences that comprise it.

I suggested earlier that defining additional 'about' notions might be philosophically fruitful. I have no intention of attempting to formulate such definitions here. I want only to mention a couple of topics that might merit such attention.

Epistemology has of late been plagued by a constellation of problems called 'Gettier paradoxes'. These are held to demonstrate that something more than, or other than, justified true belief is required for knowledge. Let me review one of them:

Suppose that on the basis of very good evidence Smith believes

7.2   Jones owns a Ford.

Since Smith is logically astute, he also believes

7.3   Jones owns a Ford or Brown is in Barcelona

even though he has no reason to think that Brown is in Barcelona. Smith then has a justified true belief—namely, (7.3)—that does not amount to knowledge, for Jones owns no Ford, but Brown is in Barcelona.[14]

12. Cf. Alan Ross Anderson and Nuel Belnap, *Entailment: The Logic of Relevance and Necessity* I (Princeton: Princeton University Press, 1975), pp. 17–23 and *passim*.

13. Joseph Ullian, "Relatively About: Loose Composites and Loose Ends", pp. 2–3.

14. Edmund Gettier, "Is Justified True Belief Knowledge?" *Analysis* 26 (1963), pp. 122–123.

The problem is that Smith's justification attaches to one disjunct, but (7.3) is true on account of the other. Smith has evidence that renders (7.3) justified about, e.g., Jones, the class of Fords, the class of Ford owners, etc. He has no evidence that renders it justified about e.g., Brown, Barcelona, the class of individuals in Barcelona, etc. (7.3), however, is true about Brown, Barcelona, etc., and not true about Jones, Fords, etc. It may be that the epistemic difficulty arises because (7.3) is not justified about what it is true about.

To evaluate this line of thought, a good deal needs to be done. We need definitions that determine what sentences are justified about,[15] and, perhaps, what they are believed about. We need to identify the requisite epistemic relation of what a sentence is justified about, what it is believed about, and what it is true about. And we need to determine the extent to which related epistemic difficulties are resolved, alleviated, or illuminated by the resulting analysis.

Another notion that might be fruitfully investigated is *evidence about*. There are cases in which evidence adduced to support or undermine a claim is not evidence about what is in dispute. A clear example is this: The Heisman Trophy is awarded annually on the basis of votes cast by American sportswriters. It is not unusual for a college athletic department to campaign for its candidate by publicizing the fact that he is, e.g., a model student, a Boy Scout leader, a practicing Christian. Admirable though these characteristics may be, they seem to have nothing to do with the issue at hand—namely, how well the guy plays football. Barring some accepted hypothesis connecting the aforementioned characteristics with the ability to play football, the evidence adduced is not evidence about the issue under dispute.

The question whether evidence is pertinent is a general one. It arises in law, science, and public policy as well as in the awarding of athletic prizes. And without a general account of what it is for evidence to be evidence about a particular issue, decisions as to when evidentiary statements are irrelevant and immaterial, beside the point, or question-begging, are liable to be made on more or less *ad hoc* grounds.

By no means do I think that the formulation of these and related definitions will be an easy matter. It is difficult enough to come up with adequate definitions of 'about', 'true about', etc., where only logical and truth theoretical intuitions and criteria need be satisfied. It is bound to be much more difficult when we have to satisfy epistemic, juridic, or moral criteria as well. Still, there is reason to think that such definitions could provide focus, yield standards of relevance, and enable us to resolve perplexities and paradoxes. If so, they would reward our efforts.

---

15. 'Justified about' may be closer in form to 'relatively about' than to 'absolutely about'. For it is likely that a sentence is justified about something relative to certain evidence statements.

X A DISCOURSE ON METHOD

Philosophy once aspired to set all knowledge on a firm foundation. Genuine knowledge claims were to be derived from indubitable truths by means of infallible rules. The terms that make up such truths were held to denote the individuals and kinds that constitute reality, and the rules for combining them into sentences and for deriving some sentences from others were thought to reflect the real order of things.

This philosophical enterprise has foundered. Indubitable truths and infallible rules are not to be had. Philosophy cannot expect to underwrite the assertions of other disciplines, for its own assertions are no more secure than the rest. Nor can it reasonably aspire to certainty. For without indubitable starting points, certainty is beyond our reach. This substantially undermines the conviction that some terms denote ontologically fundamental individuals and kinds, and that the formation and transformation rules of a language divide reality at its joints.

As a result, the nature, goals, and methods of philosophy have to be reconceived. If we look at the discussions in the foregoing chapters, we see something of the form such a reconception may take. With nothing given, with no absolute starting points or ultimately grounded assertions, we have to proceed tentatively, to subject our premises, conclusions, and procedures to critical scrutiny, to accept them provisionally, and to stand ready to reconsider, revise, or reject any of them as we go.

We begin philosophizing with our best presystematic judgments on the matter at hand. These are not thought to be certain or indubitable. They are not even thought to be definitely correct. They function, rather, as working hypotheses. We expect to discover that they are jointly untenable and insufficient to decide every case. So in the construction of a system they will have to be extended in scope, supplemented with additional hypotheses, and modified to accommodate one another. In the process, some are likely to be given up altogether.

The justification for beginning with such judgments is that they are our current best guesses as to how things stand in the field of inquiry. Even though they are defeasible, as our best guesses they have a measure of *prima facie* plausibility. In default of anything better, they are a good place to begin.

The judgments we start with are multifarious: they include not just statements of particular matters of fact, but also generalizations, methodological maxims, and theses about the ways the domain in question is to be related to other domains, and about the ways the system under construction is to be related to other systems.

In constructing a semantic system then we do not restrict our data base to assertions like

'Walrus' denotes walruses

and

Names denote their bearers.

Since the theory of truth belongs to semantics, any sentence that we believe true can serve as a provisionally fixed point in the construction of our system. If, e.g., we are convinced of the truth of the sentence

Torturing people is morally wrong

we can exclude from consideration not just accounts which label that sentence false, but also those which deny that ethical sentences have truth values. And if we are persuaded of the truth of

Fresh fruit is expensive in winter

we can disregard accounts which take truth to be the exclusive province of the exact sciences.

Such verdicts are, to be sure, provisional. Inasmuch as we have good reason to believe such sentences true, we are justified in expecting them to turn out true according to any acceptable semantics. But we also recognize that not every sentence we consider true actually is true. So we recognize that the foregoing generalization admits of exceptions. Some of the sentences we have good reason to believe can be expected to turn out false. So our acceptance of such sentences as fixed points in system building is tentative. We must be prepared to discover upon further investigation that our confidence in the truth of some sentences is misplaced.

Programmatic, methodological and logical judgments are provisionally accepted as well. We can, e.g., decide to restrict the logical apparatus of our system to the first-order predicate calculus. We can stipulate that every entity recognized by our system is to have determinate identity conditions. And we can build into our system the conviction that descriptions of beliefs, desires, preferences, and actions are interdependent. Such stipulations, restrictions, decisions, and decrees are not question-begging, for they are put forth tentatively, and are subject to withdrawal should they prove exceptionable.

Our starting points then are not presuppositionless, but neither are any others. No system is dictated by the evidence; each is imposed on it to achieve one or another kind of order. Moreover, with nothing given once and for all, it is our conception of the domain and of our goals in systematizing it that determines what is to count as evidence. And their reconception is always an option.

It is not just confirmed pessimism that leads us to expect our initial judgments to conflict. We coin and learn terms, set standards, and make rules on the basis of clear cases. We go on to form habits which guide their application to cases that are not so clear. But these do not amount to necessary and sufficient conditions for deciding every case. So if the context is sufficiently remote from the one in which a given term, standard, or rule originated, we may be uncertain whether it applies and equally uncertain how to decide the question.

Sometimes the difficulty manifests itself as a problem of vagueness. The way we are accustomed to use color terms, for example, may not suffice to determine whether the objects denoted by 'taupe' are in the extension of 'brown', in that of 'gray', in neither extension, or in both. Each alternative yields a different color system, and there may be nothing in our habitual employment of the terms that decides the case.

There are, to be sure, expressions whose denotations are more easily settled than color terms. But even these are likely to suffer from vagueness as to the limits of their mention-selective application. Even if our everyday usage determines exactly which animals belong to the denotation of 'cat', for example, we may have no basis for saying whether a portrayal of a cat-like creature standing taller than the Empire State Building is mention-selected by the term.[1]

Where vagueness is the sole source of indecision, we can generally decide the issue arbitrarily, settling the primary and secondary extensions of our terms by decree. Other cases, however, are not so easily settled. We saw that clear cases of what musicologists label 'quotation' do not satisfy the rigorous standards that apply to verbal quotation. In constructing a system that fixes the extension of 'quotation' then we face a choice: we can relax the standards on verbal quotation to accommodate the musical cases; we can deny that so-called musical quotations are genuine quotations; or we can abandon the attempt to construe 'quotation' unambiguously, and admit that verbal and musical quotations are semantically distinct phenomena that are subject to different standards. As we saw, the reasons favoring the different choices derive from the different system in which they are to be incorporated.

There are cases, such as biological taxonomy, in which even though "the facts" are neutral as between several systems of classification, our goals in systematizing mandate or strongly favor a particular choice. Seals, walruses, and whales are classed under 'mammal' rather than 'fish' because, given our taxonomic goals, their being warm-blooded, fur-bearing, and air-breathing is more important to their classification that is the aquatic habitat that they share with fish. Once we adopt such a basis for classification, there is no indetermi-

1. *Beyond the Letter*, p. 52.

nacy or indecision about how these animals are to be sorted. But the justification for the basis lies in its serving particular theoretical interests, not in its being more natural, more fundamental, or more faithful to its subject matter than the alternatives.

We could, to be sure, replace our system with one that takes e.g., habitat, diet, and degree of ferocity to be determinative of an animal's classification. But to do so would require serious revisions in our biology. For our current system is not merely justified by our biological interests, it is also integrated into our biological theories. It is not obvious that counterparts of, e.g., our ethological theories and of the evidence for them could be formulated in terms of the new categories. This is not to say that such replacement is impossible, or that it is inevitably ill advised. But we must recognize that giving it up involves more than a change in terminology. Substantive scientific theories and the interests that motivate them will require modification as well.

Even where our cognitive goals are clear, the choice of a system may not be automatic. For there is no guarantee that our goals are jointly satisfiable. Consider our difficulty in fixing the extensions of 'true' and 'false'. The conviction that every sentence is either true or false is in tension with the recognition that there are inevitably sentences whose truth value we cannot discover.[2] A number of resolutions have been proposed. We can adhere to bivalence while admitting that the truth values of some sentences cannot be ascertained. Such an interpretation allows for the construction of a logically elegant system. Or we can treat undecidable cases as neither true nor false. This renders truth and falsity epistemically accessible. It is in principle possible to discover the truth value of any sentence that has one. The logic of such a system is, however, somewhat messier. Or we can insist that only those locutions whose truth or falsity is decidable are genuine sentences. Then we obtain the benefits of both logical elegance and epistemic accessibility. The cost, however, is a severe restriction in the extension of the term 'sentence', and the loss of a grammatical criterion for its satisfaction. As a result, unless its truth value is known, we cannot tell whether a locution is a sentence. And that a truth value is epistemically accessible gives no guarantee that it is actually known. To achieve epistemic accessibility in the interpretation of 'true' and 'false' then, we have to sacrifice it in the interpretation of 'sentence'.

It is not unreasonable to hope to construct a system that combines logical elegance, epistemic accessibility, and an independent standard to demarcate the entities in its realm. In constructing a system for the interpretation of 'true' and 'false', however, such antecedently reasonable goals cannot all be satisfied. Each of the proposed interpretations has its virtues and its defects. None is entirely satisfactory. In choosing among the alternatives, we have to weigh them against one another to decide which gives rise to the best overall system.

2. W. V. Quine, "What Price Bivalence?" *Theories and Things* (Cambridge: Harvard University Press, 1981), pp. 31–37.

The conflicts we have identified result not from insufficient knowledge of a realm, but from the availability of alternative ways of organizing it. What is required to settle such conflicts is as much a decision as a discovery. Sometimes the decision can take the form of an arbitrary decree. In other cases we have to consider the interests and goals the system is to serve. If, as can happen, these also conflict, some have to be sacrificed that others might be served. We are required then to decide what combination of categories, interests, and goals is best on balance.

Even if system building begins with assertions whose initial claim to credibility derives largely from our (conceivably unfounded) conviction that they are correct, the result of our deliberations is a system of considered judgments in reflective equilibrium.[3] Accommodating our various assertions to one another is not an automatic matter. To strike an acceptable balance among competing claims we have to evaluate the strength and cogency of our reasons for believing each of them, and the strength and cogency of the systems that result from alternative attempts at adjudication. The justification for the systems we accept then derives from the method by which they are achieved—a method of rational adjudication of conflicts among assertions which are *prima facie* plausible.

The sentences of a system constitute a mutually supportive network of interdependent claims. Some are independently plausible. Others owe their plausibility to their place in an acceptable system. But the ultimate warrant for all of them drives from the system itself. For even independently plausible sentences may be given up in the process of adjudication. A system in reflective equilibrium then distributes warrant across its component claims.

The sentences that belong to a system in reflective equilibrium are not to be construed as certain. As we attempt to extend the system, articulate it, or incorporate additional information, we may discover new sources of tension. Then the process of adjudication begins anew. And previously accepted sentences may be given up. Even the sentences that belong to a system in reflective equilibrium are defeasible.

Of course, as Quine has emphasized, we can hold any sentence true come what may, so long as we are willing to make compensatory adjustments elsewhere in the system.[4] But it does not follow that every instance of such tenacity is reasonable. If the requisite adjustments turn out to be too cumbersome, if the plausibility of the entire system is diminished rather than enhanced by the modifications required to retain a particular sentence, the rational belief in that sentence will be undermined.

Nor is this method so subjective as it might appear. Although sys-

3. Cf. John Rawls, *A Theory of Justice* (Cambridge: Harvard University Press, 1971), p. 20, and [FFF, 64].

4. W. V. Quine, "Two Dogmas of Empiricism", *From a Logical Point of View* (New York: Harper Torchbooks, 1953), p. 43.

tem building involves choices, and there are often reasons favoring several alternatives, the choices we make are subject to public scrutiny. And if the approval or disapproval of our peers is not decisive, neither is it irrelevant. The evaluations of our peers are among the judgments we seek to accommodate as we construct our systems. They might be accommodated in a number of ways. We can construct a system that reflects the received view of things, or one that is powerful enough to persuade our adversaries, or one that incorporates an account of why otherwise intelligent people should be so benighted as to think differently. And here, as elsewhere, the selection of a strategy is a matter for critical reflection and is subject to peer review.

Even though the sentences that make up a system are defeasible, once we have accepted them we require reasons to give them up. The simple recognition that equally good systems might result from other choices does not of itself undermine any particular choice. Of course, reasons to give up a sentence are often not difficult to find. Still, incorporating a sentence into a system involves building in a bias in its favor. In subsequent revisions, the weight of precedent will be on its side. Thus the decision to do so should not be taken inadvisedly or lightly; but discretely, advisedly, and if not reverently and in the fear of God, at least carefully and in the recognition that enormous complications can be engendered by ill-considered choices.

Our initial judgments play another role as well. Although any of them is defeasible, and some are almost sure to be given up, collectively they serve as a touchstone against which to measure the adequacy of any proposed system. For the only way to tell whether a system is adquate to its subject matter is to compare it with our best understanding of that subject matter.

The integration of a sentence into a system of considered judgments in reflective equilibrium renders it rationally acceptable. But this plainly does not constitute a proof of that sentence. For the equilibrium may be unstable, and the acceptability of the sentence may yet be called into question.

This may appear an unwelcome weakness in our approach. But it seems less so when we realize that proof never provides an irrevocable guarantee. Proof is a matter of inference from true premises by means of valid rules. But neither the truth of our premises nor the validity of our rules is given *a priori*. Ordinarily an inference of an unsurprising conclusion from premises we take to be true by rules we take to be valid is considered to constitute a proof. But if by the same means we reach a conclusion that is particularly implausible, we need not accept it. For we can always argue that it demonstrates the falsity of some premise, or the invalidity of some rule. Nor is this cheating: for the best reason we could have for denying the soundness of an argument is that it yields a result which we are convinced is wrong. Perhaps the premises and rules of our inference are themselves susceptible of proof. Still it is open to us to deny the premises and rules upon which their proofs depend. This can go on indefinitely. For there are no self-justifying premises or rules to secure the chain of inference. The proof of any sentence then depends ultimately on premises and rules that are accepted without proof [FFF, 64]. "There can be no Archimedean point for the philosopher. Proof, he can offer only in the sense of so connecting his theses so as to exhibit their mutual support, and only through appeal to other minds to reflect upon their experience and their own attitudes and perceive that he correctly portrays them."[5]

Even though it does not prove its theses, our philosophical enterprise engenders no sceptical quandaries. The only ground for doubting a well supported claim is that it conflicts with other well supported claims. And such doubts can be resolved—either by the discovery of new evidence that shifts the balance, or by adjudication. Errors in adjudication can be discovered as well. For it is possible to ascertain whether a system is in equilibrium, and whether a wider equilibrium, or a better-integrated system results from different resolutions of our conflicts. Without an Archimedean point, there is no place for the sceptic to take his stand.

System building is, however, a fallibilist undertaking. It provides no guarantees that we are not actually in error. So the gap between truth and justification remains. Any of the claims we accept may yet be called into question. All that is excluded is the prospect of perennially undiscoverable error. We can rule out the sceptical worry that even though our convictions permanently satisfy the highest epistemic standards, they may nevertheless be wrong. What remains is the fallibilist worry that our systems contain discoverable but as yet undiscovered errors. And that, it seems, is worry enough.

But is it really? Is a philosophical program's inability to generate sceptical quandaries grounds for scepticism about that program? Ought we fear that despite our apparent epistemic successes we might still have things all wrong? If the growth of knowledge consists in the discovery of an independently existing order of things, sceptical worries have to be entertained. We need then to engage and defeat the sceptic, not just to avoid running into him. The problem is that once engaged, the sceptic proves surprisingly difficult to defeat. For once truth is admitted to be nonepistemic, it is hard to see how epistemic victories, however impressive, can be expected to secure truth.

But this entire conception of the relation between knowledge and reality is being given up. Instead of limning the true and ultimate order of an antecedently structured reality, the systems we construct determine the conditions on the identity and classification of the objects in their realms. They as much define as discern their objects. Reality then does not come already sorted. Rather, it is the sortings a system effects that determine what it counts as individuals and kinds. The sceptical proposal that even an epistemically ideal system might

5. C. I. Lewis, *Mind and the World Order* (New York: Dover Publications, 1929), p. 23.

get it all wrong is then undermined by the denial that independently of our systematizing, there is any *it* to get wrong (or, for that matter, right).

This may suggest another ground for scepticism. How can we be certain that there isn't a bigger, better, more balanced system to be constructed to cover the same domain? The answer is simple: We can't. This admission, however, gives rise to sceptical doubts about the adequacy of the systems we've got only if coupled with the claim that only the uniquely best system is at all adequate. But we make no such claim. The prospect of better systems prompts us to investigate further—to seek out errors and suggest improvements. It does not, however, impugn the adequacy of the systems that satisfy our standards.

Moreover, several systems—even concurrent ones that share a single domain—may be adequate. In some cases such systems realize distinct goals or answer to separate interests. In others, they result from different, more or less arbitrary choices. And where factors favoring different choices in system building are about equally balanced, it should be no surprise that the systems that result from different choices are—other things being equal—about equally adequate. Comparisons among such systems may reveal inadequacies in any of them. But the simple fact of there being several systems sharing a single realm discredits none of them.

Acknowledging a multiplicity of adequate systems commits us to ontological pluralism. A system determines the conditions on the individuation of the objects in its realm, and different, simultaneously acceptable systems, may decide such matters differently. In one system, for example, the term 'quarterback' denotes a position on a football team; in another, it denotes whoever plays that position. According to the former, there is one quarterback on each team, and several players who alternate in playing that position. According to the latter, each team has several quarterbacks, only one of whom plays at a time. Plainly, describing football in terms of either system involves no (implicit or explicit) denial of the adequacy of the other.

The relativity of ontology to a symbol system, and the availability of a plurality of independently adequate systems give rise to Goodman's controversial contention that there are many worlds if any [WOW, 96]. Without an Archimedean point we have no perspective from which to see that there is but one world which our several symbol systems order. Moreover, since individuation is relative to a system, only from within a system is it determinate what counts as being one thing. We have then no transcendental criterion of individuation to give content to the conviction that the world, apart from all our systematizing, is one.

Moreover, to the extent that symbol systems are constructs of our own, so are the facts that their symbols represent. This is plain if we consider a rudimentary system. Suppose that to illustrate a play a Monday-morning-quarterback takes a coffee mug to represent the quarterback. With which interpretation of the term 'quarterback' should the interpretation of the mug be identified?[6] One way to decide is to see what happens when a substitution is made. If the replacement of the quarterback is reflected in the replacement of the mug, the mug represents the player. If the mug continues in use no matter who plays quarterback, it represents the position. But suppose there just is no more to the symbol system than is contained in the illustration of the one play. Once the play is illustrated, the system dies. There is nothing in the illustration to decide between the rival interpretations. And there may be nothing in the user's intentions or dispositions regarding the symbol either. Since he constructed the system to illustrate a particular play, his intentions and dispositions regarding his symbols need not extend beyond what is required for that illustration. And under either of our suggested interpretations, the mug functions correctly in the context of interest. There is then no fact of the matter regarding which interpretation is correct.

There can be no fact of the matter as to the mug's interpretation until we develop a symbol system capable of distinguishing between the rival interpretations and incorporate the mug into that system. This seems clear enough. But its implications are striking. What facts there are is a function of the symbol systems we develop. That is, we participate in the creation of facts by creating symbol systems with the resources to represent those facts. Of course, we are not at liberty to create any facts we like. We can create no correct, factual representation according to which the quarterback was stopped at the line of scrimmage. For however we represent it, he made a touchdown.

We do not, of course, construct our symbol systems *ex nihilo*. The categories we start with are themselves symbols in a prior system. And if that system is not our creation, it is the creation of our forebears. Our "common sense" judgments and the vocabulary in which they are expressed are part of our cultural heritage. And if we find that we cannot live comfortably on our legacy, at least it provides the resources from which to build.

Such a philosophy plainly is not a "first philosophy"—a field of inquiry in which purely philosophical issues are identified and settled prior to and independently of the facts it seeks to systematize. For as our systems develop, even the identities of the objects in their realms may change. And our systems may develop in response to non-philosophical as well as to philosophical stimulation. Thus, e.g., when physics abandoned the sharp distinction between waves and particles, the domain of electromagnetism came to be seen to consist of quite different sorts of things.

Changes in the realm also prompt changes in our systems. If football originally allowed no substitutions, a system capable of describing the sport would not need to distinguish between the two interpre-

---

6. Plainly, there are other interpretations of the term. For simplicity, I restrict my discussion to the two mentioned above.

tations of 'quarterback' mentioned above. Once substitutions are permitted, the distinction is required. A previously adequate system needs to be modified to distinguish between a position on a team and the players who occupy that position. A change in the practice we seek to describe then necessitates a modification of the symbol system in terms of which our descriptions are to be formulated.

Our systems undergo another type of change that is worth noting. The uses to which the symbols in the system are put may shift its center of gravity. This can happen gradually through the cumulative influence of many works and many authors. Or it can happen abruptly, owing to the impact of a single major author or work. Such shifts are marked by sentences like these: "As the novel evolved, characterization came to be as important as plot" and "Beethoven's *Ninth* forever changed the nature of the symphony". Such shifts do not typically affect the extensions of our terms. The same works are considered symphonies and novels as before. What is altered is our estimation of the centrality and importance of the several criteria by which such works are classified. And this in turn may alter the way we employ the symbol systems in creating new works.

It is not only aesthetic systems that are subject to such shifts. A change in the center of gravity of an historiographical system is signalled by: "After Marx, social and political history could no longer ignore economic factors". And a change in a scientific sytem by: "The adoption of the uncertainty principle meant that determinism could no longer be taken for granted".

Changes in the center of gravity of a system are then changes in the importance we attribute to various features of that system. Although they typically do not affect the extensions of the terms in the current system, they may affect the sorts of modification we are prepared to make should the system become unstable. As Quine suggests,[7] in revising our systems we try to retain the statements that we regard as most central. So alterations in our estimations of the centrality of various claims bring with them modifications in our strategies for reestablishing equilibrium.

Philosophy then is viewed as an enterprise that seeks to achieve coherent, comprehensive systems in reflective equilibrium. Far from being aloof from and indifferent to changes in our scientific systems, our social institutions, and our aesthetic practices, philosophical revolutions are frequently intertwined with them. For correctly characterizing the methods, objects, and standards which are reflected in or necessitated by such changes often requires a revision of an entire field of inquiry. New rules, patterns, and categories need to be identified and brought into accord. A philosophy thus responsive to our theories, institutions, and practices can be expected to change as they change. It cannot be expected to consist in a *a priori* pronouncements whose truth is incontrovertible.

---

7. "Two Dogmas of Empiricism," p. 44.

Once we abandon the conviction that the order of things is out there waiting to be discovered, the quest for knowledge has to be reconceived. The categories in terms of which we describe, portray, and perceive things belong to systems of our own contriving. The growth of knowledge is not merely, and not mainly, a matter of accumulation of new truths. Often cognitive progress consists in the formulation of novel and illuminating categories. Of course, if the categories are verbal, their application results in new truths. But if they are, e.g., perceptual, pictorial, or musical, questions of truth and falsity do not arise. Then they contribute to the advancement of understanding by providing new ways of apprehending the perceptual, the pictorial, or the musical realm. Moreover, even for verbal systems truth is not the overriding concern. We seek systems, verbal and nonverbal, that organize things in ways that are interesting and informative, subtle and suggestive, powerful and perspicuous. These enable us to reconceive our domains in ways that reveal significant features which earlier systems had obscured.

Much of what I have done in this book can be seen in this light. Instead of arguing for specific theses from widely accepted premises, I suggest a scheme of semantic categories whose application to linguistic and nonlinguistic systems enhances our understanding of the ways our symbols function.

INDEX